FOXBOY

FOXBOY

INTIMACY AND AESTHETICS IN ANDEAN STORIES

CATHERINE J. ALLEN

WITH ILLUSTRATIONS BY JULIA MEYERSON

UNIVERSITY OF TEXAS PRESS / AUSTIN

Requests for permission to reproduce material
from this work should be sent to:
Permissions
University of Texas Press
P.O. Box 7819
Austin, TX 78713–7819
www.utexas.edu/utpress/about/bpermission.html

∞ The paper used in this book meets the minimum
requirements of ANSI/NISO Z39.48–1992 (R1997)
(Permanence of Paper).

Library of Congress Cataloging-in-Publication Data

Allen, Catherine J.
Foxboy : intimacy and aesthetics in Andean stories /
Catherine J. Allen ; with illustrations by Julia Meyerson.
   p. cm. —
Includes bibliographical references and index.
ISBN 978-0-292-72321-4 (cloth : alk. paper) —
ISBN 978-0-292-72667-3 (pbk. : alk. paper) —
ISBN 978-0-292-73484-5 (E-book)
1. Quechua Indians—Folklore. 2. Quechua language—
Texts. 3. Quechua textile fabrics. 4. Foxes—Folklore.
5. Tales—Andes Region. 6. Erotic stories—Social
aspects—Andes Region. I. Title.
F2230.2.K4A449   2011
398.2098—dc22   2011009122

(frontispiece) **Erasmo Hualla knits and talks.
Photo by the author.**

FOR TOM ZUIDEMA, TEACHER AND FRIEND

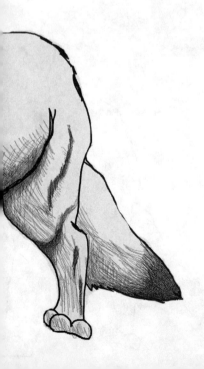

Let me tell you about my walk in the highlands.
I found Young Pascual (Foxboy). I was out there in Fox Time.

ALCIDES MAMANI

CONTENTS

APPENDICES

What we call the beginning is often the end.

And to make an end is to make a beginning.

The end is where we start from.

T. S. ELIOT

ACKNOWLEDGMENTS

"Thank you, I said." Because the end is where we start from, the last words of this book are also its first. Writing *Foxboy* has been an act of appreciation, an inadequate thank you to all the Andean storytellers and storylisteners who so graciously opened their homes and shared their lives with me. I recorded many stories in the community of Sonqo whose people have continued to welcome me over the past thirty-five years and to whom I owe a great debt of gratitude. Erasmo Hualla Gutiérrez, in particular, loved the idea of my publishing his stories and I regret that he did not live to see them in print.

Not quite at the end of the book — a few pages back — I mention taking an excursion, in 1980, to Q'ero, a remote cluster of communities in the same province as Sonqo. I think the first inklings of this book occurred on the long hike back from Q'ero, walking and talking with Peter Getzels about the Quechua stories we both loved. As years went by, the inkling slowly became an idea, and took shape in the back of my mind as I worked on other projects. Along the way a great many individuals, as well as several institutions, helped me develop this book and bring it to the light of day. I cannot even try to mention them all, as the list would be exceedingly long. Thanks go to my colleagues in the Department of Anthropology at George Washington University for providing me with a supportive environment, and to the University for several small but essential grants for travel and research in Peru, most recently in 2003. I am grateful to The Dumbarton Oaks Center for Precolumbian Studies (1993–1994), The National Gallery's Center for the Advanced Study of the Visual Arts (2000), and The John Simon Guggenheim Foundation (2001–2002), for fellowship support that opened up time to write, and provided logistical support and collegial stimulation. I am grateful, as well, to many Peruvian colleagues in Lima and Cuzco for their invaluable critical insights and practical assistance. *Foxboy* is dedicated to Tom Zuidema, my graduate school mentor, whose open-mindedness and willingness to take intellectual risks provide continuing inspiration.

I am beholden to Jaime Pantigoso, linguist, writer and native speaker of Quechua, who transcribed many of the stories and worked with me on the translations. Odi González, also a poet and native speaker, corrected my transcription of this book's master narrative. He enjoyed hearing Erasmo's recorded voice, which reminded him of his grandfather. I bear full responsibility, however, for any errors of transcription, translation or interpretation that may have crept into these pages.

Julia Meyerson's illustrations are informed by her deep knowledge of, and appreciation for, things Andean. While writing, I envisioned the book illuminated with little drawings, like a medieval manuscript. Julia was the perfect person to help me approximate this idea. Her meticulous yet lively drawings, many of which are framed with Andean textile motifs, give these pages an additional dimension. I thank Eugene Rizor, too, for his beautiful photographs.

I am truly grateful that the University of Texas Press has been willing to take on this unruly project. Especial thanks go to Theresa May, Victoria Davis, and everyone on the team of editors and designers who turned a complicated manuscript into the book you have before you. I am beholden to two anonymous readers for the Press, who provided insightful commentary and suggestions for improvement. After the manuscript was accepted, they revealed themselves as Bille Jean Isbell and Regina Harrison; I am grateful for their critical insights and I treasure our ongoing conversations.

In Cuzco, Lucila Cruz generously extended her friendship and opened her home to me. Madeleine Gutiérrez Cruz and her brother, Eldder, became my traveling companions and informal research assistants. I am still trying to absorb the heartbreaking news that Eldder died in a truck accident in October 2010 at age thirty. He was a lively, generous person and a dear friend.

Finally, I am grateful beyond words to my daughter, Andrea Sandor, for her steady moral support and intellectual curiosity. Many other friends and family members patiently sustained me through the years as well, in spite of their incredulity that any project could take so long. Thank you all for your love, support, and good food!

FOXBOY

FRINGE

Dear Reader—

There's a story they tell in the southern highlands of Peru about a tricky little Child Jesus who had a marvelous technique for spinning the finest thread imaginable.[1] What he'd do is shear the sheep and then feed them their own wool. Having disappeared down the sheepish front end, the wool presently emerged from the rear, all finely spun, ready to be pulled out and rolled into a ball—eventually to be woven into shimmering cloth.

I think words are like this wool. Language, too—that is, language digested, ruminated upon—is a miraculous excretion. We do in a sense "eat" our own words all the time, and they come back out in fine strands, ready to be joined with other strands. If the weaver—the wordsmith—is any good, the result is a shimmering composition.

Erasmo Hualla Gutiérrez, a Quechua-speaking potato farmer of the rural Andes, was a fine wordsmith. This book is built around a story he told me. It's a marvelous story, and I hope you'll enjoy it. What's more, I hope that by the end you'll understand (or at least have a feeling for) what goes into listening to it—listening to it, that is, as Erasmo's Andean listeners did in their world of cultural experiences and expectations.

Like any other cultural production, stories can be treated as having lives of their own, independent of the particular human beings who tell them and listen to them. But this loses the context in which stories actually exist, which is in the telling. Speaking and hearing actualize each other; a narrative exists through its listeners and becomes meaningful in terms of the relationships between speakers and listeners. Therefore this book is as

much about the listening as it is about the telling of stories, for to appreciate the storyteller's—the wordsmith's—art is to understand choices and
connections that listeners recognize and appreciate. Stories talk to each
other through associations the tellers raise in the minds of their listeners,
associations that may barely be conscious, that are felt rather than thought.

Thus Erasmo's story leads us into a whole world of stories and lived
experience that I, in turn, try to express in my written words. Rather than
produce a collection of folktales, I have tried to convey the nexus of mean-
ings that informed, always in different ways, the listening experience of
my Quechua-speaking companions; to recapture the process of storylisten-
ing—finding those connections on the edges of conscious awareness that
shape hearers' experience of stories. Of course, there's no single authentic
"hearer's experience," for every person—even the same person at different
times—makes different connections, consciously or not. Insofar as I was
a "participant-observer," I was one of the listeners, a watcher of listeners,
and a listener to listeners, but when all is said and done, the only listening
I can truly speak for is my own.

The main source for this foray into cross-cultural listening is my field-
work in a small Peruvian community called Sonqo, perched on the eastern
slopes of the Andes in the province of Paucartambo, about seventy kilometers by road northeast of the old Inca capital, Cuzco, now a city of 350,000.
I first went to Sonqo in 1975 to carry out doctoral research on ritual drinking practices. I spent almost a year there, accompanied by my then-
husband, Rick Wagner, living in the household of Luis Gutiérrez Churra, a
community leader. My research on drinking broadened into a study of coca
leaf as well, and I eventually wrote a book that used coca leaf as a window
into Andean culture.[2] But all along, as a side project, I recorded myths,
historical narratives, and folktales; these became my consuming interest
as I returned to Sonqo eight times between 1978 and 2008 for stays rang-
ing from a few days to two months.

Since 1975, Sonqo's population has increased slightly from about 300 to
about 320, with about ninety households spread over a roughly ten-square-
mile swath of rocky mountainside. In 1975, the houses were pretty evenly
dispersed across the landscape, but today they tend to line a road that was
constructed during the 1980s. This road runs from the town of P'isaq in
the Vilcanota Valley; crosses over a sharp divide; drops through Sonqo on
its way to Colquepata, district capital; and then passes to Paucartambo,

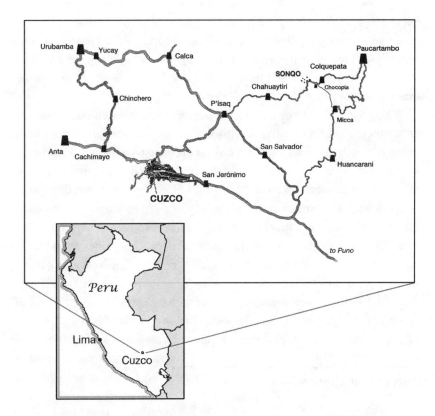

The Department of Cuzco, Peru, showing the road from Colquepata to Cuzco

provincial capital at the edge of the eastern rain forest. Sonqo's landscape is covered on its lower slopes with a patchwork of potato fields; its upper slopes are open pasture, broken by the occasional small field of high-growing potatoes. Traditional subsistence was based on potato farming and herding of sheep and llamas. The altitude, about 12,000 feet, is too high for maize cultivation, so Sonqo has traditionally depended on ties with lower-altitude communities to fill this gap. In the 1980s, oats and barley became popular cash crops, driving potatoes higher into the pastureland.

Highland–valley relationships figure strongly in the oral tradition, as does a history of complex ethnic tension between mestizo (*misti*) town dwellers of the district capital and the rural indigenous (*runa*) farmers of the outlying communities. Like the other indigenous communities, or *ayllus*, surrounding the district capital, Sonqo was never enclosed within an hacienda, a neofeudal type of estate in which laborers were bound to the land and the landlord. Nevertheless, economic and political power has historically resided with the Spanish-speaking townsfolk, creating a web of often abusive dependencies that persisted into the 1980s and even to some extent until today.

When I arrived in 1975, most Sonqueños were monolingual speakers of Southern Peruvian Quechua. This language, once spoken by the Incas, belongs to a family of closely related languages spoken from Ecuador to northern Argentina.[3] Today, though Quechua remains the first language of the home, most Sonqueños have some proficiency in Spanish as well. As in most Native American languages, Quechua words and phrases form through agglutination, that is, by piling suffixes onto a root. Agglutination also characterizes the other major Native Andean language, Aymara. Although Quechua and Aymara are not closely related, they have long existed in close proximity, trading vocabulary and some other linguistic features.[4]

Although I am a native English speaker, I have come to miss the person system of the Quechua language, which has two kinds of first person plural: the inclusive "we," which means "*you and I (and others)*," and the exclusive "we," which means "*myself and others—but not you*," excluding the addressee. In these pages, when I write "we," I usually intend the *inclusive* "we." That includes you, the reader, whom I hope to bring along with me as a fellow listener to these stories—listening, as it were, with your mind's ear. (If there's a mind's eye, why not a mind's ear?) Where I have to use an *exclusive* "we," I take pains to clarify the context.

AN EXAMPLE OF QUECHUA GRAMMATICAL STRUCTURE

ENGLISH: I'm arriving at the little house.
QUECHUA: Wasichata chaymushani.

WASI + CHA + TA
House + [diminutive] + [Direct Object]

CHAYA + MU + SHA + NI
Arrive + [Motion-to-Here] + [Present Progressive] + First Person Singular

---

The other source of material for this book comes from marvelous bilingual collections of Quechua and Aymara narratives compiled by my fellow travelers—other anthropologists, linguists, and folklorists who have dedicated themselves to Andean oral expression.[5] I draw on this rich body of work to put my master narrative, "The Fox and the Woman," in its creative context; to compare Erasmo's compositional strategies to those of other storytellers; and to bring out connections and themes that would not be apparent from his narrative in isolation.

Andean storytelling is interconnected in manifold ways with other expressive activities like weaving, music making, and dancing. In this book, I make broad comparisons with weaving. Weavers, I think, organize cloth in ways that parallel the organization of verbal compositions. The connection between cloth and language—wool and words—is very ancient. Fiber has provided a cultural focus in Andean societies for over three millennia, deeply affecting other mediums of expressive culture.[6] Prior to Spanish colonization (and even to some extent afterward), Andean people encoded information using fiber-based mediums.[7] Knotted cords (*khipu*) and patterned cloth supplemented and preserved the spoken word, producing a distinctive mode of communication and evaluation.

Andean textiles, melodies, and dances do not "tell stories." Rather, they share with narrative the same kinds of organizing strategies, the same ideas about how opposites should meet up with each other, about how strands in a braid disappear into its interior and then reappear on its surface. Artists in these different contexts produce striking effects by manipulating complex interactive relationships in parallel ways.

This is a work of literary nonfiction, not a theoretical treatise or a book about Sonqo. I use a powerful, erotic, and entertaining Quechua story as a master narrative, and employ Andean compositional strategies in order to write about them, adapting them to my "voice" in a written medium. I allude often to my own experiences in Sonqo, and to people I knew there—Erasmo, the storyteller; Luis, my teacher and host; Inucha, his adolescent daughter; and others. But this is not about me, or even about them. We are like the border or frame, a context whose purpose is to convey the *situatedness* of narratives. I begin and end with Inucha to contextualize the telling of narratives and give a sense of the interpenetration of stories and lived experience.

I had completed the manuscript for this book before I came across Mary Douglas's *Thinking in Circles* and discovered that what I had been writing all along was a type of "ring composition." Concentrating mainly on Western literature, Douglas describes ring composition as an "antique literary form" in which the ending meets up with the beginning, and meaning is packed in the middle. The middle is where two parallel halves meet up and reverse each other in a chiastic ABCBA sequence. This middle point evokes both beginning and ending; "the linking up of starting point and end creates an envelope" that contains the entire composition.[8] Erasmo's narrative, "About a Married Couple," is a beautiful example of ring composition, and I have built my own composition around and within his. "About a Married Couple" ends with a recapitulation, as the protagonist is obliged to reprise the sequence of events that led to her final predicament. As I work through this second telling of the story, I stop to explain contexts and connections that a native listener would take for granted.

And now, like the fringe edging a mantle or a poncho, I'll begin with a narrative of my own.

I'll tell you about my ride back to Cuzco in August of 1980. That was long before a bus started running between Cuzco and Colquepata, and we all traveled in creaky trucks that wound along the meandering dirt road that passed over the eastern cordillera and connected Cuzco with the tropical lowlands.

The road was one lane and one way, but not always the same one way. Traffic headed away from Cuzco on Monday, Wednesday, and Friday, and back toward Cuzco during the rest of the week. Sunday, market day in Colquepata, did double duty; trucks brought cargo from Cuzco in the morning and returned in the afternoon laden with sacks of local produce. On Tuesday, Thursday, and Saturday, trucks left Colquepata at the crack of dawn and about fifteen minutes later lumbered past Chocopia, the stop closest to Sonqo.

Now, Sonqo was almost a two-hour walk from Chocopia, which on weekdays meant getting up and on my way before daylight. Unfortunately, early starts have never been my strong point, especially in the freezing dark at 12,000 feet. So it was Sunday afternoon for me. This gave me a chance to sleep in until six thirty and to have a leisurely breakfast of mutton soup with the family, sitting near the fire in the crowded, comfortable one-room thatched house. Then I'd pack up my stuff and amble off to Colquepata after chewing coca for a while with Don Luis. I'd still have time to check out the Sunday market, visit the shopkeepers, and greet the local officials before climbing onto one of the two or three trucks that waited by the marketplace. If all went well, the truck would pull out

(above) Erasmo and his daughters enjoy a meal of potatoes at home. (below) Alcides, center, relaxes with his family on their patio. His father serves *chicha*. Photos by the author.

about one P.M., the trip would be uneventful and rapid (rapid being a relative term, of course), and we would arrive in Cuzco before dark.

This is why a clear, dry Sunday afternoon in July of 1980 found me sitting in the back of Martín Torres's[9] truck, waiting for us to get on our way. The word was that the trucks would leave early that day, so I climbed on about twelve thirty and seated myself comfortably on a sack of potatoes, with my backpack beside me. Trucks could get excruciatingly crowded, so I wanted to get on early and stake out my claim. A couple of the market ladies who trafficked between Cuzco and Colquepata had gotten there before me. They were also seated on potato sacks, their layers of full skirts tucked under them like extra cushions, and their white stovepipe hats perched jauntily on their heads. A few farmers from outlying ayllus like Sonqo clambered on and off, helping each other hoist up their heavy sacks and pile them toward the back of the truck. Then a Colquepata merchant arrived with a load of sacks filled with oats. More market ladies got on, a few with live chickens in bags and baskets, a few with babies on their backs wrapped up in carrying cloths. There was a commotion outside, and I saw a couple approaching with a desperately struggling piglet. I was relieved when they got onto another truck; few sounds are as unsettling to me as a pig in distress.

A proud driver poses with his truck on the way to Cuzco. Photo by the author.

Passengers in a relatively uncrowded truck. Photo by the author.

Looking over at the other truck, I noticed that Francisco, the eldest of Don Luis's four sons, was the driver. That was good. Francisco had finished his stint in the army a few years earlier and returned to Sonqo to help his widowed father. It was not where he wanted to be. Trained as a chauffeur in the army, he had "seen Paree," as it were, and down on the farm he hung around morosely, completely at loose ends. This opportunity to drive for Martín Torres was the perfect solution for him, so we thought.

I entrusted my backpack to an acquaintance from Sonqo, climbed down from the truck, and went over to him. He leaned out the window and greeted me with the happy swagger of a man who is twenty-two, handsome, and coming up in the world. I asked hopefully whether he had room for me in the cab, but unfortunately no, he'd promised that space already. I peeked in the back of his truck, thinking I might ride there instead, but it was already crowded, and anyway there was the pig, so I decided to stay where I was. When I got back to Martín's truck, it had filled up completely with more sacks of potatoes, oats, and freeze-dried potatoes called ch'uño. More passengers had arrived, and I anxiously asked after my backpack, which was nowhere in sight. My friend cheerfully pointed at one of its flaps sticking out from under a sack of oats, so there it stayed. By this time we were all sitting on piled-up sacks, several feet higher than when we started. The ayudante, Martín's assistant, was climbing around, picking his way through the passengers, who were by this time packed close together, each of us trying to stake out a small space that would be ours for the trip ahead. He bantered back and forth with the market ladies and joked around in a mixture of Quechua and Spanish with some of the other young men about his age. An arrogant-looking man in a bright red mestizo's poncho climbed on and got off again. He wanted a place in the cab and went off looking for Martín.

By this time it was well past two, the sun was beating down on us, and everyone was eager to leave. Everyone but the driver, that is, for Martín was nowhere to be seen. One of the trucks pulled out, and we watched regretfully as it rumbled off down the rutted dirt street. People started to grumble and complain to the ayudante, who perched uncomfortably on the sacks near the cab end of the truck and mumbled defensively. We could hear an equally impatient murmur from the other truck, and after a while, Francisco climbed out of the cab and walked away down the street. His swagger was fading, and though he tried not to show it, I could tell that he was bored and annoyed. He was a new employee, Martín was his boss, and he was expected to wait for him.

Francisco returned a few minutes later, brushed aside our shouted inquiries, and got back into his truck. By this time it was going on four o'clock. There was no way we could hope to arrive in Cuzco before nine at this rate, and my hopes for dinner and a hot bath were dwindling. The man in the red poncho reappeared and squeezed his way into a rear corner. He had found Martín, and, indeed, there was no room for him in the cab. That spot was already taken by a retired police officer, who even now was treating Martín to a few drinks.

This was not good news. Nobody likes to hear that the driver is off drinking, and this is doubly true when the road ahead is a narrow dirt track, cut in places into the side of the mountain with rock wall on one side and nothing on the other. We were already feeling cramped and tired, and conversation faded for a while to some subdued grumbling from the market ladies. A few people gave up and got off, and a few more clambered on and jostled and squeezed around to make themselves space. A young man about twenty years old, wearing blue jeans and a gray windbreaker, settled near a market lady who seemed to be some relation of his. His name, I was to learn, was Pedro. His companion, Sra. Ana, was surreptitiously carrying a sheep carcass destined for the black market in Cuzco. She was not happy at the thought of passing the Civil Guard's inspection posts at night, when guardsmen would have more time to search trucks for contraband like uninspected meat. Pedro yelled playfully at the ayudante to drive the truck himself.

About five o'clock, Martín's tall, heavyset figure appeared around the street corner. The drinking companion followed close at his heels, and the two men laughed loudly about something as they swaggered up to the cab and clambered noisily inside without acknowledging the sally of reproaches and protests issuing from their passengers.

"God help us," said a market lady, crossing herself. "Our driver is drunk."

And so we slowly set out, Francisco behind us, and lumbered up the long ridge from Colquepata to Chocopia, where only a few passengers still waited, and then on and up, stopping a few times to load up yet more sacks of potatoes and oats. ("No room!" we shouted, but somehow the sacks always piled on anyway.)

As we passed under the shadow of a steep, rocky hillside, we had a last view of a tall, pillarlike rock resembling a man in a robe. This was Pari Qaqa, Priest Rock. Pedro seemed not to know about this and listened with interest as Ana pointed it out to me. Long ago, that rock was a living priest. He finished celebrating a wedding mass in a fine city that existed then in the heights above

Lake Qesqay. Photo by the author.

Colquepata; night was falling, and he was hurrying home, when suddenly the city was inundated and everyone — including the priest — turned into stone. (Why? Well, I'll come back to that later.) Where the city once stood there now sits a frigid, rather bad-tempered mountain lake named Qesqay. Pedro leaned forward as he listened, hugging his shoulders to keep warm. "I'm used to Lima," he said to me in Spanish, shaking his head with a rueful smile.

"She speaks Quechua!" chimed in one of the market ladies reproachfully.

Pedro looked at me with new interest but continued to talk mostly in Spanish. "What kinds of crops do they work in the United States?" he asked me.

"Here we go," I thought. We launched into a familiar litany of questions and answers, not my questions to them, but theirs to me — and why not? "What plants grow there?" "What kinds of animals?" "Is there a lot of money?" (In years to come, the order of questions would change, and money would take pride of place. But this was still 1980.) "Are your parents alive? Aren't they sad that you've gone so far away?" "And why are you here?" — and I would explain, rather lamely, that I wanted people in my country to know about their way of life. Where are you going now? Are you leaving Peru? I commented that before leaving Peru I was going to visit a friend in Q'ero, a more distant region in the same province as Colquepata. "What?" "They speak funny Quechua there, and their music is awful." "And it's too far away, don't bother," said some of my companions. "They know a lot there! I'd like to go too!" said others.

The truck drove across a shallow stream running from Lake Qesqay, far out of sight above us. In the rainy season, its water would likely wash out the road for weeks at a time, but in dry July, it was but a friendly trickle, and we passed the ford with no problem. Below us, out of sight in the other direction, was the tinku, the place of encounter, where the stream joined with Q'enqomayu, a small river flowing onward toward the high jungle and the Amazon. I found it strange to think that the water splashing Martín's tires was starting a journey across the continent and into the Atlantic Ocean. I recalled the funeral custom of washing the dead person's clothing in a tinku of streams, sending the residue of lost life away into that inconceivable distance.

The truck lumbered along the dusty, unpaved road, following its own snake-like trajectory until it met up with the main Cuzco–Paucartambo road. On we crawled, up across the main divide and carefully downward, to arrive about nine o'clock at the Guardia post in the crossroads town of Huancarani. Huancarani had surely been bustling all day with Sunday traffic, but by this time there was but one lone soup vendor about ready to pack it up for the day, a few open shops, and—oh, welcome sight—a tough, rotund old lady (rotundity derived from her layers of skirts, shawls, and blankets) serving ponche de leche, a hot drink made from bean flour and milk. A Guardsman climbed into the truck, gave us all a cursory glance, and got off again. We breathed a sigh of relief. The man in the red poncho got off and disappeared into one of the shops. Nobody was sure how long we'd be there, but the hopeful opinion was that given the late start, Martín wouldn't want to stay long. About half the passengers, myself included, clambered down one by one to pee in the shadowy gutters (toilets not even being a consideration), to dine on the dregs of the soup pot and drink ponche de leche. Inside the truck, passengers stretched and unwrapped their little bundles (ququawas) of cold ch'uño and boiled lima beans. The night was turning very cold, and ponchos, shawls, and blankets began to appear from inside people's bundles. The red-poncho man reappeared and jostled with the rest of us to squeeze into a position that might remain . . . well, hardly comfortable, but perhaps bearable over the next several hours. Soon we were all settled and waiting expectantly for Martín to reappear.

What could be keeping him this time? Once again, Francisco climbed down from his cab and walked off—no swagger left at this point—to look for his employer. Briefly I wondered whether I should switch to his truck, but then I remembered my poor backpack completely inaccessible behind and under sacks of oats and crowded human bodies. Francisco came back, swung into his cab, and started his motor. There was a ripple of relief, and the last stragglers came rushing aboard, for surely this meant that Martín was about ready to depart. But Francisco abruptly pulled in front of us, and we watched, open-mouthed, as, after a brief hesitation, he disappeared down the road.

About ten P.M., a couple of singing drunks emerged from a side street and danced their way around the plaza and—oh, let it not be true—up to the truck. It was Martín and his retired policeman. They climbed unsteadily into the cab. What to do? I didn't know anyone in Huancarani, and there were no hotels. In the morning, the traffic would be heading away from Cuzco toward the jungle. So it was continue with Martín or—what? And then there was the problem of my backpack. So we all stayed on the truck and crossed ourselves in nervous camaraderie as the motor started up and the truck began crawling out of town. Coming up ahead of us was the steepest and narrowest stretch of road; I recalled how pictures taken along there looked like aerial photos. Unless Martín's truck had a secret capacity to go airborne à la James Bond, it was not a comforting prospect.

In all fairness, I should tell you that I traveled in Martín's truck many times over the years, and normally he was a steady, sober, hardworking driver. Hard-headed, unsentimental, and, of course, controlling, yes, he owned the truck and the trucks owned the roads. But this was the only time I saw him drunk.

We began to slowly, slowly thread our way along the cliff. Then we stopped. Martín had decided to take a nap. Just as well, though we were squished like sardines, waiting under the open sky while frost began to form on our heads. Under his poncho, Pedro was shivering in his thin shirt and windbreaker. Passengers elbowed each other and shifted around as they pulled out more blankets, ponchos, and shawls. My sleeping bag was buried too deep in my backpack, so, along with Pedro, I shared the edges of our companions' blankets. We huddled and dozed in the frost.

"Hey, this is too much!" yelled a young man about Pedro's age. "The sun is just too hot! I can't stand the way it's beating down on us!"

"That's stupid!" yelled Pedro. "I love it! I could lie on the beach forever!"

We laughed. "Oh, I'm so hot!" "It's like an oven!" "But we're moving too fast!" (This from the red-poncho man.) "Right, we should slow down and enjoy the sun!"

And so we leaned back and baked in the sun's rays as our truck raced head-long through the blazing sands—while frost fell from the winter stars, frozen droplets formed under our nostrils, and our truck sat as still as the boulders looming around us. Then we laughed some more and the spell was broken. We shifted as well as we could, blew on our hands, and settled into shawls and ponchos.

—And you, too, how about settling into your own shawl or poncho for a while? I'll come back to my yarn, but for now it's time to move on.

BEGINNING

Light with dark,
bright with dull,
merriment with mourning.

That's what Inucha was learning one cold, bright morning as she unrolled her narrow loom and sat down to weave herself a skirt border. The long threads of the warp stretched out in front of her, half again as long as a man is tall. One end was tied around her waist; the other, to a finger-sized twig stuck vertically into the ground, making what looked like a bridge for very tiny people. It was as a bridge, after all, that weaving came into the world, back in the story time. Two Little Mothers—Saint Inez and Saint Rosario—came upon a chasm in their path and had to invent a way to get across. They set to work spinning, plying, warping the yarn, and finally weaving until—there it was!—a bridge, and over they went. (Where to? I've no idea.)

Makiykiwan awayman! "I would weave with your hands!" Women whisper these words to the Little Mothers before they set to work at the loom. Every good weaver must find their hands in her own. *I'm going to tell you about that, too.*

Inucha was twelve or thirteen years old and beginning to think about her looks. The miniature bridge was destined to become a bright rim on the fullest and blackest of skirts—a skirt that would turn heads when she danced during Carnival or swished along the path to Sunday market. The edge of her skirt would shine and flicker; red against black, red—and all the colors red brings with it—against black. "We are *wayruros*," Gavina Mama told her, "red and black together." She spoke of the smooth round red-and-black seeds that belong in medicine bundles because they are so perfectly beautiful.[1] They come from the rain forest, far to the east and out of sight of the high alpine tundra where she and Inucha lived, yet not so far, no more than two long days of walking.

When Gavina dressed in her best, her skirt borders twinkled around her knees and wide red patterns flowed across her black mantle. But on this particular morning, her best skirts and mantles were stored away; she was dressed in two faded skirts and an old pink sweater turned inside out. Clay water jug in hand, Gavina was on her way to the stream, following one of the paths crisscrossing a dry grassy hillside. Emerging from the shadow of Ixchinu Hill into the bright morning sunshine, she glanced up at Luis Tayta's mud-brick house. Another path passed above the house; it cut across the hillside, dropped into the ravine, emerged on the other side, and wound out of sight over the crest of the next hill. Luis said one of the Incas had followed that path, but he didn't remember which one.

Twelve Inca leaders with their families fled into the jungle when the Pizarrokuna[2] arrived in Cuzco City. Right through Sonqo they went (some of them, anyway), for, like other communities in Colquepata District, Sonqo lies between the Cuzco Valley and the Upper Amazon forest. From the spot where Inucha sat weaving her skirt border, we could follow their route until it disappeared into a deep ravine where three streams meet between the *ayllus* of Sonqo and Sipaskancha. There an Inca girl was left behind, for she stopped to urinate and turned into stone. Nearby, the Incas left an enchanted place called Layqa Pampana (Sorcerer's Burial); anyone who tries to follow will fall asleep there forever. These traces are like promises etched into the landscape—past-as-potential-future—reminders that the Incas are still hiding and waiting in their hidden city of Siwiru Waititi. When the world reverses itself, so it's said, they will return over the same route. When the mood hit him, Luis talked about this eventual return. At night, his coca bag in his lap, his round facing shining with happy intensity, he talked about Incas appearing out of the jungle accompanied by pumas and carrying weighty ears of golden corn. In other moods, daytime moods, he thought it was looking pretty unlikely. Then he would turn his thoughts to the price of potatoes and his children's progress in school.

Gavina noticed Inucha weaving next to the stone wall of the corral and turned aside to check on her niece's work. Although no one taught children to weave—they just watched and eventually tried to do it themselves—somebody needed to look in on them from time to time. A few days earlier, Gavina had checked Inucha's warp threads and corrected a couple of the heddles (these are string loops that control which threads move up and down for each pass of the shuttle). If you got the heddles wrong, your fabric was a lost cause from the outset. Inucha had already learned to weave *hakima* ribbons while she pastured her family's flocks with other shepherd girls, way up in the high pastures. This skirt border was a new step for her, requiring a different technique. It was a technique that came over from Spain with the Pizarrokuna, but no matter, the Weaving Mothers had made it their own. Gavina watched the progress in her sister's child with hope and interest. She saw the fingers growing slender, hard, and capable, and looked forward to the day when she might help the girl prepare the warp for her first mantle. Inucha would be a young woman then, red and black, a *wayruro*.

Inucha's own mother, Rufina—a decade dead and for Inucha only the vaguest of memories—had not been a good weaver. She had depended on her sisters Gavina and Valentina to make her mantles and Luis's ponchos. Valentina Mama truly possessed those weaver saints in her hands; no one in Sonqo wove better than she did. But Inucha seldom saw her, for Valentina lived an hour's walk away and had quarreled with Luis. The *ayllu*'s eighty-five households were spread out over almost two thousand hectares of high treeless grassland called *puna*, and families easily distanced themselves from one another.

Inucha had a *comadre*—namely me (I was her younger brother's godmother)—but I was useless when it came to weaving. I was sitting beside her that bright July morning in 1984, hoping to learn from her learning. She was used to me, as this was my fourth visit to Sonqo in the span of a decade; the first visit, when Inucha was three, had lasted almost a year. By now she took it for granted that every few years I'd show up and hang around for a while.

She noticed my camera and asked me to take her picture. She sat proud and serious, looking straight into the camera, as I snapped the photos you see in these pages.

Skirt borders differ from much other weaving in the southern Peruvian highlands because in them, color is controlled in the weft. In most ribbons, mantles, ponchos, blankets, and carrying cloths, the weft disappears between tightly packed warp threads—not so in skirt borders! In them, the weft shines through and carries the pattern. You can see in the photos how Inucha was sliding colored acrylic yarns between the two layers of plain homespun threads (undyed except at the red edges). After each pass of the weft, she pulled on the string loops to lower and raise different threads and then slide more colored threads between them. Her pattern emerged as she repeated the process again and again. You can also see how she tucked some white yarn into her sleeve while she slipped in the blue threads of the emerging *ñawin puytu* design.

Inucha weaving her skirt border. Photos by the author.

Gavina arrived and paused to greet me before she leaned over Inucha's handiwork, a giantess inspecting a bridge. She approved of the eye rhomboids, *ñawin puytu*, in the pattern, then quickly turned her attention to the little bundle of colored yarns sitting open at Inucha's side. To weave a skirt border is to play with colors, to improvise with rhythmic alternations of dark and light. The bright border shines against the black skirt; it twinkles because it contains within itself yet other alternations of bright and dark.

Inucha set to work with no fixed color scheme in mind. This lack of plan was not due to inexperience, for adult weavers do the same. Borders give you room to play. The pattern is fixed in the warp threads, but when it comes to color, most anything goes as long as you keep bright and somber—*k'ancha* and *lutu*—separate and play them against each other. Each color change calls for a new decision: What bright color **X** should follow this somber dark blue ◆? Or shall we syncopate the rhythm, hold off with the *k'ancha* for perhaps half an **X**? Inucha looked at her bundle of colors and followed her mood. This is the trick, as with all improvisational art: to know some broad underlying rules, follow your mood, and get it right.[3]

She almost got it wrong. Gavina picked up a skein of vivid chartreuse yarn and put it aside. That didn't belong, she scolded; it was so bright it made *all* the others look dull. Inucha seemed suitably chastened, so Gavina picked up the water jug and continued on her way, disappearing into the ravine.

Beyond the ravine, a few pigs scavenged for potatoes in a harvested field. Corn does not grow on the high wind-swept slopes, so potatoes are the staple crop. About three hundred people depended on these fields and on their small herds of sheep and camelids. Each little cluster of houses among the knolls and dells in the hilly landscape was called, in the Quechua language, an *ayllu*, meaning a group of people with a bond to the land. *Ayllus* can exist at any scale—from a single household to a cluster of houses to a whole community, even to a cluster of communities. *Ayllus* nest within *ayllus*. Here, neighborhood *ayllus* on a great many-fingered ridge coalesced into a community called Sonqo Ayllu.

Six other *ayllus*, similar to Sonqo in extent and population, share the watershed of Q'enqomayu, a small river whose waters run into the Paucartambo River, which runs eventually into the Amazon. From where we sat, the narrow valley bottom was out of sight. Looking downhill, we could see the new road, snaking along like another kind of river. Just below the road,

Erasmo—Inucha's cousin (her father's sister's son but closer in age to her father)—was hard at work harvesting his potato crop in Waska Wayllar. A *wayllar* is a fertile bog, good for growing early potatoes called *maway* or *miska papa* (sweet early potatoes) that taste so good and sell so high in the Cuzco market. Waska Wayllar had sat idle for two generations because people were scared of it. Long ago, it was said, a white horse was sucked into the black mire, and on moonlit nights its skeleton rose up again to wander the soggy scene of its demise. Erasmo didn't really believe this, or maybe he found it more interesting than scary. "My grandfather worked this *wayllar*," he commented, "and nothing bad happened to him."

It had been a big job, draining that *wayllar* and turning it into a ridged field for early potatoes.[4] Chunks of sod had to be cut out using a foot plow and piled into long parallel rows. Then soil, dug from between the rows, had to be piled on top. By the time Erasmo was finished, the alleys between the ridges were deeper than he was tall. He walked through them happily, marveling at his own prowess. It was like living a story, he told me, and nobody in Sonqo knew stories better than Erasmo.

In the days before radio, storytelling was entertainment. At work parties, at night, and on rainy days, people told each other stories round-robin, one after the other. A good "speaker" would emerge from the give-and-take of conversation to hold the others' attention for a few minutes or many. As he or she spoke, the others responded with exclamations, laughter, questions.

Chaymantarí? And after that?

Hinaspas . . . ? And so . . . ?

Inucha and her brothers had learned stories this way—"by themselves, just by listening"—curled up in bed or cuddled next to their stepmother, Balvina, up in the high pastures.

On this particular morning, Inucha's mind was bent on her weaving; she turned back to the skirt border, asking how soon I'd have the photos ready. Down the hill, Erasmo's head was barely visible as he harvested potatoes in the ridged field where he felt as if "in a story." I wondered whether he was running through stories in his mind in preparation for our next recording session.

Storytelling is another improvisatory art, like weaving. Tradition supplies a stock of story events and characters, and the tellers put them together as they like. The narrative contracts or expands as time and inclination permit. Tellers leave out a detail here, an entire episode there, add new embellishments here, new episodes there. Listeners delight in new and unexpected ways of telling the well-known stories.

Erasmo could be a one-man round-robin when he set his mind to it. He was a maker of *karu kwintu*, "far-reaching stories," that stretched into the distance as one tale followed another, woven together with jokes, anecdotes, and rhetorical flourishes. The result was a new story, larger than the sum of its parts. Before he began, he would blow softly over his coca leaves, calling softly to mountains, hills, and lakes:

Allinta rimayman: "I would speak well!"

As far as I know, there are no Little Mothers or Little Fathers for speaking (although saints invented most other human skills—weaving, plowing, chewing coca leaves).[5] Speakers turn to the landscape's witnessing presence for support and inspiration.

Erasmo never let me record his long, lovely invocations to the places around us. The Record button's *click* had to wait while we shared coca leaves and little glasses of cheap rum; while we shared with the landscape by blowing over the leaves and flicking drops of liquor into the air.

Then he would ask:

Kwintuta willasaykichu?

Shall I tell you a story?

SHALL I TELL YOU A STORY?

Yes?
     Which one shall I tell you?
     mnnnnnnnnaa. . .
     There was a married couple . . .

        Yes,
           I'll

               tell

                   you

                      that

                          one.

Here I tell the story in my own words, following Erasmo's narration but freely translating and summarizing. The chapters that follow contain a transcription and line-by-line translation of Erasmo's own words. I use line breaks to indicate pauses in his speech.[6]

There

    once

        was

            a couple, wife-and-man, who lived together. One day the man loaded up his llamas and went off to market, to buy corn, I think. Well, it seems that the trip took time, and nightfall overtook him before he could get home. His wife was all by herself in the house as darkness fell, so she closed the door and lay down alone to sleep. Then came a little tapping at the door and a small voice calling: "Mama, please Mama, I'm lost! Please help me, Mama!" There was a little kid, just a boy, standing at the door shivering.

The woman took the child in right away, sat him down by the fireplace, and fed him some soup. Then she spread a nice sheepskin by the hearth and told him to get some sleep.

"Not on the floor! Not on the floor! I can't sleep on the floor!" he complained.

"Just sleep by the nice warm fireplace," she said, "you'll be fine there."

"Not by the fire! Not by the fire! They'll call me 'Cinder Boy,'" he retorted.

"Then sleep on the big grinding stone! Just go to sleep!" the woman exclaimed as she climbed into her bed. But the boy couldn't sleep.

"But I just can't sleep on the grinding stone, I just can't!" he whimpered. "They'll call me 'Mortar Boy' if I sleep there!"

"Oh, for goodness' sake, where can your mother be?" the woman mumbled. "This is just too much! Where DO you want to sleep, then?"

"At home I sleep cuddled up next to my mommy," he whimpered.

"All right!" she yelled. "Come here and get in bed with me, then, if you'll only be quiet!"

And so the boy climbed into bed with her. But it seems that he wasn't really a little boy at all. He was a fox, prowling after women. And once he was in her bed he started to feel her up. Groping, groping . . . He felt her breasts.

"Hey, Mom! What're these?"

"Those? Those are my breasts."

"Oh." He felt around some more, found her belly button.

"Hey, Mom! What's this?"

"That's my belly button."

"Oh." He kept feeling around. He reached between her legs.

"Hmm. And what's this?"

"That's where I keep your father's picnic lunch!"

"Oh, let me try a little!"

*And there they were, the two of them, in a compromising position when . . .
WHO should arrive but the man of the house, and his llamas laden with cargo!*

"Hey, the door's locked! Wake up, Woman! Open the door!"

"Get out, go away!" *whispered the terrified woman to the fox. But he just kept
going at it like crazy. She reached around with her hands, feeling for her knife . . .
found it and . . . cut off his prick!*

"ACK!" *yelled the fox. He jumped up and busted right through the door.*

"What's this? Did you have a dog in the house with you?" *grumbled her husband.* "Come out and help me!"

*So the woman went out and helped her husband unload the llamas and settle
them into the corral. Then they went inside the house and settled right down to
sleep.*

The next day her husband woke up grumpy. "Hey, I'm starving! Get up and
fix me some soup!"

*So the woman got up and went out to fetch water for the soup. She stopped to
pee on the way, and quietly let the fox's, y'know, his prick, slip out into the grass
near the spring. Then home she went and prepared her husband's soup.*

*Well, in a neighboring household there was a daughter, about thirteen years
old, who'd been away pasturing sheep. In the evening she rolled up the skirt
border she was weaving, rounded up the bleating animals, and came home. As
her mother was cooking, she went to the spring for water and what did she find
there but the fox's prick. She picked it up and brought it home. Yes, right into
the house.*

"Look, Mama, I found some neck meat! We can eat it for dinner!"

*Her mother took the "meat" and tried to cut it up in preparation for cook-
ing. Zing! It slipped right out of her hands onto her lap. She tried again. Zing!
It slipped right out of her hands onto her lap. Again she tried. Zing! It jumped
right inside her!*

And this time it stayed there.

*Well, the weeks passed and the woman found herself pregnant. Her husband
noticed, too, and began to wonder . . .*

"What's going on here? You didn't get pregnant by me, we're just a widow
and widower living together out of convenience." *He nagged her about it.* "You
must've been fooling around!"

"I have NOT been fooling around. Leave me alone!" *she retorted.*

Weeks passed, and then more weeks, and her belly kept swelling. And her husband kept nagging her for an explanation. "What's going on? I'm sure you've been fooling around!"

He got started nagging her daughters, too. (She actually had two daughters: the one who found the "meat" and another one a bit younger.)

"Whose daughters are you anyway? Anyone could be your father!"

"Leave them alone! Let them be!"

Everyone was miserable, quarreling, getting on each other's nerves. And the weeks passed, and her belly kept on growing . . .

Finally her time came, and she gave birth—out came three babies, little cubs, three gorgeous little foxes!

Well! Then the man was really upset!

"AchaKÁW! What kind of woman gives birth to foxes? How did this happen?"

"It must have been that neck meat the girl brought home," she explained. "When I tried to cut it up, it slipped right out of my hands and entered my body. It wasn't meat at all, but a fox's prick. That's how I got pregnant with foxes."

Well, what could they do but raise up those fox cubs? After all, they were her children. The little ones grew fast and lively, with shiny coats and sharp teeth. What an appetite for meat! They ate every last one of the guinea pigs; nothing was safe from them. And they never shared a morsel with their sisters. Not a bite.

The girls were furious. "This is just too much!" they complained. "These fox cubs are trashing the place, and we get nothing out of it but more work!"

One day the parents left the children—girls and foxes—alone in the house.

"Now's our chance! Let's kill 'em!" whispered the girls. And that's just what they did. They strangled those three little fox cubs, their own mother's children.

Then they felt frightened.

"Achakáw! Mother and Stepfather'll be home soon! What'll we do?" They thought about it. "We have to get out of here, run away where they won't catch us."

They quickly cooked up a meal and packed it to eat on the road. Off they went, leaving behind the little corpses—one on the grinding stone, another on the threshold, and the third in the very middle of the room. Off they ran, as fast as they could.

When their parents came home, the girls were gone, nowhere to be found. They had simply disappeared.

The girls ran as far and as fast as they could. I don't know exactly where, but at nightfall they found themselves on a high desolate plain. Finally they stopped to rest, huddled together next to a large boulder for shelter. As they sat there, lost and cold, they heard a dog barking, then a cow lowing. As they looked around, they espied a light coming from a neat little house. What a relief! They jumped to their feet and headed for the house. What a fine corral, full of healthy llamas, alpacas, and sheep! They peered into the courtyard.

"We're here, Mother! You have visitors," they called politely.

A pleasant old granny appeared at the door. "Ay! Won't you come in, poor little girls! Lost in the dark, poor things! Achakaláw! Come in and make yourselves at home!"

As they stepped inside, the girls admired the well-kept courtyard and storerooms bulging with corn and potatoes. "We're in luck!" they whispered to each other. "This is a prosperous household. Maybe we can stay if we make ourselves useful."

"Come in, come in, poor little dears! Sit down, wrap up in the blankets, I'll warm up your soup. Achakaláw! Nice young girls, poor things, poor sweet little things," the old granny was murmuring as she blew the embers of her fire and heated a hearty meat soup.

The girls accepted the soup gratefully and ate well. When they had finished, the old granny asked them if they had happened to see her son during their journey.

"He's a butcher and was out looking for work. Didn't you see him? He went off over that way."

"No, we came from the other direction," they replied.

"Oh well," the old granny responded. "You may as well curl up and sleep. I'm sure he'll be home eventually."

The girls settled down in the blankets and began to doze. Sure enough, there came a sound of heavy footsteps and then OOMPH! somebody kicked open the door. In came the old lady's son, clutching a woman's head in one hand and a bag of body parts in the other! But the girls were dozing and didn't notice.

"What a day, karahu, hell and damnation!" The son was in a nasty mood. "These humans led me a merry chase! All I got was this miserable stuff—bad as goddamn dog meat!"

You see, the son was a condenado, *a cannibal soul. The granny, too. It was a* condenado *household.*

The granny quietly hid the bag of human flesh. "I have some news. You've got some sisters here."

"Is that so?" the son looked more cheerful. "Sisters, eh? Let's have a look!"

"Girls!" the old woman called. "Wake up and say hello to your brother!" The girls opened their eyes and saw a nice-looking young man smiling down at them.

"Welcome, Sisters!" he exclaimed. "I'm glad you've come to help me. I have to keep watch tonight in the guard hut by the corral. Dear Elder Sister, you come with me so we can take turns watching. Tomorrow you can sleep and Younger Sister can help me pasture the animals."

The younger girl watched nervously as her sister left the house with this attractive new "brother." Something didn't seem right. She settled back in the blankets and tried to sleep. The old woman murmured soothingly to her, and the night was quiet. But she couldn't sleep. Couldn't sleep at all.

"Don't worry about anything, rest and sleep, little one," the granny called quietly. But the girl couldn't relax, couldn't sleep at all.

SHRIEK! A horrible scream came from the direction of the guard hut. She sat up in alarm.

"Oh, go back to sleep," murmured the old woman. "They're just yelling at some wild animal to scare it away from the flock. It's nothing. Nothing at all." The girl lay back down in her blankets and waited. There were no more shrieks, the night was dark and peaceful. Finally, she fell into a doze.

In the morning, her new brother entered the house, cheerful and wide awake. "Your sister was sleeping so nicely in the guard hut that I didn't want to wake her," he said. "Let's you and I pasture the flock today and let her rest."

The girl felt ill at ease, but she didn't know what else to do. So after breakfast, she and the handsome youth set out with the herd. It was a large flock, and the animals fanned out over great distances in the high desolate pastures. At one point the girl had to leave her companion to bring back some animals, and as she hurried along she saw a woman standing on the path in front of her.

She wasn't an Indian woman. Her clothes were more like those of a mestiza, but they were made of some wonderful shining material. Her long, thick hair flowed down her back, and her face was sorrowful and loving. She was a mamacha, *a little mother, a lady saint.*

"Oh, girl, silly girl!" she exclaimed. "What are you doing here? This isn't a human village, it's a village of demons. This youth is a condenado *who plans to eat you. Already he's eaten your sister."*

As the girl stood still in silent fear, the mamacha *pulled a cactus from the folds of her clothing.*

"Take this with you," she said, "but keep it carefully hidden. Persuade the youth to put his head in your lap, and as he does so you'll see a mouth on the nape of his neck. That's the mouth he uses for eating human flesh. Ram the cactus through that mouth with all your might."

She handed the girl the cactus and disappeared.

The girl did as she was told. Returning to her companion, she called out, "Brother, let me search your head for lice. Just come over here and put your head in my lap."

"I've got no lice!" he responded.

"Oh, come on, just let me check!"

He didn't want her to examine his head, but she nagged until he finally agreed. He lay down at her side and put his head in her lap . . . Achakáw! There it was! The cannibal mouth on the nape of his neck, still red with her sister's blood.

Quickly she pulled out the cactus and

CRRUNCH

rammed it down the bloody throat

CRRUNCH

as hard as she could

CRRAAK

again and again . . .

. . . until PPOWW!

the condenado *exploded,*

GROANING and HHHISSSSING *like a black cat screaming.*

That was the end of him. Leaving the flock, the girl ran back to the house and the old condenado *granny.*

"What are you doing here?" the old woman exclaimed. "You shouldn't have left the animals."

"A sheep is sick with bloat," replied the girl. "Your son sent me for a pot and a knife."

"Here, take them, and get going! He needs you!" insisted the old crone.

No argument there! The poor girl ran out of that condenado *house as fast as* she could. She rushed to the guard hut and gathered up the clothes and bones, all that was left of her poor sister. Then she ran back over the high desolate plains, ran and ran until she reached her parents' house.

The couple was sitting sadly by the fire. Just the two of them in the quiet house. They stared as the girl staggered through their door, pale, ragged, and totally exhausted. They didn't know her.

"Mama, I'm home!"

"This isn't your home. We had children once, but they disappeared."

You see, the ordeal had left the girl unrecognizable, even to her own mother. She had to recount the whole story before they recognized her.

SHE

SAID,

CHAPTER ONE

A MARRIED COUPLE

Warmiqhari tiyakusqa,
> There once lived a married couple.
chaymanta willasayki.
> I'll tell you about that.

Wait a minute. Let me tell you a little about how this story was told to me. Erasmo was looking curiously at the small metal machine that sat waiting to catch his words and store them away. "Is it ready?" he asked. *"Grabashanchu?"* He had been thinking about this story for a couple of days. "Yes," I replied and pushed the Record button.

That was thirty years ago. I have transcribed words from the tape we made that night, but there is more on the tape than words. Erasmo's wife, Cipriana, is blowing on the fire through a long metal tube; guinea pigs rustle and squeak under the family bed; the children giggle, cough, and whisper. Cipriana leaves off blowing and begins to grind something (I don't remember what) on the mortar stone. Sounds of an Andean family settling down for the evening, sounds of domesticity. "There once lived a married couple. I'll tell you about that." This is the story.

Strange way to tell about marriage! Isn't this grotesque little story *really* about Fox, daughters, *condenados*? Maybe so, but the marriage provides the frame. Fox may stand out because he behaves so memorably and outrageously near the beginning, but he is part of a bigger story. Marriage is the outward perimeter of the narrative and gives the interwoven story lines their overall coherence.

"About a Married Couple" is a two-part story, and both parts are old staples of the storytelling repertoire. Each episode—I'll call them "The Fox and the Woman" and "The *Condenado* Household"—stands on its own as a story in itself. In its minimal form, the first episode is just a familiar, off-color little story about Fox and his misadventures. I heard it, for example, in Q'ero, another region in the same province as Sonqo. The Q'ero version of "The Fox and the Woman" ends differently from this one: the woman simply throws the penis on the roof of her house (one does this with trash sometimes; it reinforces the thatch). There is poor Fox's penis, standing straight and tall "like a flag" (*bandera hina*), while its owner runs around searching pitifully on the ground. And that's the end.

Episode Two, "The *Condenado* Household," is another old chestnut —nothing new about it. *Condenados* are a fact of life for the people of Sonqo. The nighttime world is inhabited by these living corpses—green, rotten, and stinking—whose weight of *hucha* (sin) hampers their proper departure from this world. *Condenados* (also called *kukuchi*) roam glacial peaks and high pastureland; occasionally their all-consuming appetite for human flesh leads them to raid human settlements as well. For the listeners of such a story, the idea of stumbling into a *condenado*'s house is a distinct possibility. Strange, lonely households like this one may well harbor damned souls who beguile their travel-worn guests only to eat them. Don Aquilino Thupa Pacco of Usi recounted for César Itier the episode of the two girls in the *condenado* house.[1] In his account, they are "two gad-about girls" (*iskay chanchara p'asñakuna*) who foolishly get lost in the high pastures and venture upon the old *condenado* lady and her son.

So the episodes themselves are nothing new or surprising—the surprise lies in how the two stories are put together. Erasmo transforms the comic fox tale by juxtaposing it with the fearsome *condenado* narrative and framing the two together as a story of failed domesticity: the frame binds the two apparently unrelated tales together into a single whole; the story flows from the frame, and the frame is informed by the story. "There once lived a married couple. I'll tell you about that."

Warmis wasipi tiyasqa, huq,
> It seems this woman stayed home in the house,

qharitaqsi purisqa maytachá,
> and the man went off somewhere,

llamantin puriran rantikuq
> went off with his llamas to market

saramanchá no se maymanchá.
> for corn maybe, I don't know where.

Hinaspas, riran, chaymanta
> Well then, he went, and then

tardin tutatallan chayampusqa.
> he came home late, after dark.

Hinaspa tutatallan chayamun,
> Well, he came home after dark,

warmitaqsi wasipi puñukun.
> so the woman went to sleep in the house.

Not a desirable scenario! Families are used to sleeping together in one big bed with parents and children all snuggled together. Having to sleep alone in a house or even in a separate room feels unnatural and dangerous. People do sleep alone when they have to, but they don't like it.

This passage divides *warmiqhari*, the married couple (woman-and-man), of our opening sentence. Language itself emphasizes this separation with the suffix -*taq*, which indicates "and on the other hand . . ." The woman stayed home, while the man *on the other hand* went off somewhere. The man got home after dark, so the woman *on the other hand* went to bed alone. And therein lies our tale.

Warmi and *qhari* should not be divided, yet in practice they often are, a result of simple household economics, especially so if they live in a *puna* environment of high treeless grasslands. As Alejo Maque, from Arequipa, told Andrés Chirino:

In the inside of long ago, way high up in a lonely homestead, there lived a woman with her husband, that is, they were a married couple.[2]

Erasmo doesn't explicitly locate our couple in a *puna* homestead, but he does surmise that the man must have gone off with his llamas to buy corn, implying that (as in Sonqo) they couldn't grow their own. One lives in the *puna* by herding llamas, alpacas, and sheep and by growing potatoes and other high-altitude tubers. One of these tubers is the oca, which looks rather like a thick, bumpy parsnip. In Don Alejo's version, Fox masquerades as an oca harvester. Later he runs around begging for his "oca" penis, an amusing image that makes people laugh but also points to life in a *puna* environment and the lack of self-sufficiency that implies. For millennia, high *puna* dwellers have traveled to the warm valleys to exchange potatoes, meat, and wool for corn and other warm-weather crops. The interdependence of low valley and high *puna* is necessary, often difficult, and endlessly interesting, for it permeates the whole of one's life. It provides an omnipresent backdrop for Andean narratives.[3]

If only the husband hadn't had to travel, Fox would never have gotten into his house. If everything—corn, potatoes, peppers, fruit—grew together, there'd be no need for husbands to travel and wives to stay alone in their isolated homesteads. This is how stories describe heaven, Hanaq Pacha (The World on High). There, everything grows in great profusion; but in this world, this high mountain world, altitude determines environment, and no place is self-sufficient. These days the old trading relationships are changing, but men still spend much time (if anything, more time) away from home in search of cash income.[4] Their wives have to spend a lot of time making do on their own. It's a necessary and paradoxical theme in life: The sexes by their very nature depend on each other; and this interdependence requires them to separate. They have to separate because they belong together, and together they have to realize another kind of complementarity between valley and *puna*, between subsistence farming and the cash economy.

Erasmo's telling of the story assumes this ecological background but concentrates on the couple and their married relationship. Men of necessity have to travel, but trouble happens because the marriage is out of kilter in the first place. The husband in this story is surly and dictatorial, while his wife is lonely, long-suffering, and sneaky. The story grows out of their alienation.

Female and male elements ought to enfold each other to produce a single (but inherently dual) being. This lesson was implicit in many of the activities and conversations I shared with acquaintances in Sonqo, but I think Erasmo articulated it most clearly for me. It was in the same small adobe house—same setting, but years later—that he showed me how a complete human being is represented in offering bundles called *dispa-chu.*[5] Preparing these bundles is called *hampi akllay,* "choosing medicine." The Earth and Mountain Lords feed on the medicine as the bundle burns, and are moved to reciprocate for the meal according to the ingredients. Erasmo was preparing this bundle on behalf of a particular person who was to be embodied as a little stack of eight coca leaves composed of male and female elements, blended through a process of synecdoche so that the whole and the parts entailed each other mutually.[6]

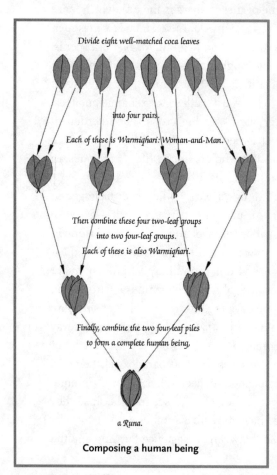

Divide eight well-matched coca leaves

into four pairs.

Each of these is *Warmiqhari:* Woman-and-Man.

Then combine these four two-leaf groups into two four-leaf groups. Each of these is also *Warmiqhari.*

Finally, combine the two four-leaf piles to form a complete human being,

a *Runa.*

Composing a human being

The offering bundle is itself conceived as a person, with a head and feet. When folded up, the feet become the head, and the head becomes the feet. In Sonqo, they say that "women know how to use their hands, while men know how to use their feet." Handiwork is the female aspect of oneself, and skills involving the feet employ the male aspect—for *any* person, male or female, possesses feet and hands and the capacity to use them. Each person, although endowed with a biologically given sex, is woman-and-man.[7] To express one's own gender, one must marry and become the "hands" or "feet" of another dual being, *warmiqhari.*[8]

This insistence reverberates through the Andes and comes up repeatedly in Andean ethnography. "Everything is man-and-woman" (*Tukuy ima qhariwarmi*),[9] say the Bolivian Macha, according to Tristan Platt.

Man-and-woman are *yanantin*, partners as the two hands are partners; they work together because each is the reverse, or mirror image, of the other.

> *Yanantin* expresses ". . . the binary logic which, in the linguistic sense, can . . . be said to 'generate' the system of representations by which Andean nature and society are ordered." (Tristan Platt)[10]

> The terms *yanantin* and *iskaynintin* represent what we could call imperative forces that "urge" the linkage of things considered to have a natural, complementary relationship to each other. (Gary Urton)[11]

In Sonqo, *iskaynintin*—literally, "doubled"—describes the state of being married: "*Ñan Cirilu iskaynintinña*" (Cirilo is married already).[12]

Erasmo's little stack of leaves "says" all this wordlessly, in a powerful and condensed form. His narrative, as it unfolds in time, implicitly contains the same design and, as we'll see in later chapters, it contains its own exegesis. Played out against the background of a dis-integrated marriage, the narrative leads us from the tale of Fox's penis into a gruesome looking-glass world of devouring *condenados*. The stories are mated; their images line up in a mutual reflection that is itself a new narrative.

Fundamentally, this composite story "works" because it evokes a visceral experience in a complex and interesting way. It exposes and distorts the nature of intimacy through graphic narrative imagery, moving listeners from laughter to horror. It reveals these experiences—laughter and horror—to be *iskaynintin*, two together, a pair. It leads us through a temporal experience of reflection and inversion, an aural path that leads back to its beginning.

Although narratives unfold over time, this story lends itself to a visual diagram. Laid out in two-dimensional space, it reveals an organization reminiscent of the ponchos and mantles created by mature Andean weavers like Gavina and Valentina.[13] These beautiful textiles are composed of parallel halves, each of which is woven separately. Each part consists of alternating bands that may contain complex designs; they are sewn together so that the stripes reflect each other. If the two halves are folded together, each band will meet up with its opposite from the other side.

Yet, as the photo shows, the two halves are never exactly symmetrical.

A man's poncho woven by Valentina Quispe of Sonqo. The two halves reflect each other with a slightly off-kilter symmetry. Photo by Eugene Rizer (property of the author).

Usually they are inverted as well. The top of one is like the bottom of the other, and vice versa.

Combining stories within stories is a common narrative strategy in Quechua and Aymara storytelling, perhaps a natural outgrowth of the old custom of round-robin storytelling.[14] As we'll see in the chapters that follow, each of these component stories can be combined with yet other staples of the Andean storyteller's repertoire. There isn't one "right" pairing of stories. Just as there are many potential marriage partners, there are many different ways of pairing up stories. And just as people express themselves differently in different partnerships—each partner drawing out different aspects of the other—so stories draw out different aspects of each other. Stories speak to each other, or better said, *listeners* hear echoes and traces of other stories layering over each other in a kind of aural palimpsest.

"*Kwintuta willasaykichu?*" (Shall I tell you a story?) Erasmo would ask when we started a recording session. I sometimes heard the phrase

PART A	X Transition	PART B	
A. A deceiver(foxboy) asks for charity.		A deceiver (condenada) gives charity.	**A'**
B. The foxboy appeals to mother-son relationship.	**i.** The Woman lies to her husband.	The condenado youth appeals to brother-sister relationship.	**B'**
C. The woman is seduced by her "son" the fox; their adultery is interrupted.	**ii.** She gives birth to fox babies. **iii.** Fox babies fail to share with their half sisters.	The elder girl is eaten instead of having sex with her "brother."	**C'**
D. The husband returns to his wife.	**iv.** The girls kill their fox brothers.	Mamacha appears to the younger girl.	**D'**
E. The fox's penis is cut off with a knife.	**v.** The girls flee.	The condenado's mouth is jammed with a cactus.	**E'**
F. The woman throws the penis away.		The girl escapes.	**F'**
G. A neighbor girl mistakes the penis for neck meat and brings it back to her mother.		The girl brings her sister's bones to her parents, who do not recognize her.	**G'**
H. The penis jumps between the mother's thighs; she is impregnated.		The girl recounts the whole story . . .	**H'**

THE OVERALL STRUCTURE OF THE NARRATIVE IS: [15]

Part A	X	Part B
a-b-c-d-e-f-g-h	i-ii-iii-iv-v	a'-b'-c'-d'-e'-f'-g'-h'

"*Kwintuta willasayki!*" (literally, "I'm going to tell you a story!") in conversations when people were bursting to talk about some unusual experience. The term seemed to be used almost metaphorically to frame an extended narrative containing elements of strangeness and suspense, and to claim the attention of the group.

But to tell the truth, I never heard Erasmo—or anyone else for that matter—ask anyone except myself, "*Kwintuta willasaykichu?*" before launching into a storytelling performance. It became the way they introduced their tape-recording sessions with me. I'm not even sure what the term *kwintu* meant before I showed up and started using it. I was there with folks who knew that I collected stories, and I was too much part of the context to know what they might have done had I not been there.

> This book is as much about storylistening as it is about storytelling. It is about learning to recognize and follow the aural/oral counterpart of weaving and braiding. The listening, of course, is my own, but I have tried to follow the lead of Andean acquaintances who listened with me. And I have tried to learn from and use Erasmo's creative compositional strategies in the process of writing about them. If I have carried it off, this book contains the strategies and is contained by them, just as it contains the story "About a Married Couple" and is contained by it.

I didn't realize back then how strange a situation I created when I arrived at the door of Erasmo's one-room adobe house, right at the appointed time and with my tape recorder in hand. This was a completely artificial setting (from the point of view of "natural" discourse, anyway), and Erasmo loved it. Here was storytelling as an occasion in itself—not a sideline embedded in other activities, or a diversion to while away the long periods of watching and waiting that characterize rural life in the Andes. I may have helped to create, or reshape, this speech genre in the process of studying it.

I was collecting stories as one might collect butterflies, and other researchers have done the same. We don't know much about "natural" storytelling events that were neither requested nor otherwise provoked by an investigator. Efraín Morote Best, a Cuzco folklorist, mentions reports of wandering storytellers who used to make a career of going from community to community, telling stories in exchange for coca, food, cigarettes, and a place to sleep.[16] Sonqueños, however, could tell me nothing of these wandering bards. What they did recall fondly was the old round-robin storytelling. Don Luis said that he used to be a *rimaq* (speaker), but he'd forgotten how for lack of practice. As a young man, he once walked to P'isaq in a rain storm and arrived soaking wet at the mayor's house. A group of older men were sheltering there as well, and they took to telling stories. After warming up and having a drink, Luis joined in and told such stories that the mayor himself jumped up and gave Luis his bed to sleep in. (*Ah*, sighed Luis, feeling his eighty years. *Those were the days* . . .)

I took to playing my tapes for anyone willing to listen. Erasmo's neighbors were eager to hear his recordings, and he was glad to have them do so. He was considered a particularly good storyteller; people commented that he had learned the stories by "going around" (*puriy*) a lot to other communities. Erasmo admitted to wandering in his younger days but rather testily denied that he learned his stories that way, insisting that he heard them from a *machula* (old grandfather) "right here in Sonqo." He prided himself as a master of the *karu kwintu* (long story) that weaves together episodes into a long, self-contained narrative. The word *karu* indicates spatial distance. People described me as coming from a *karu llaqta*, a "distant town." *Karu kwintu* conjures up a spatial vision of the story unfolding into the distance.

Basilia and Josefa prepare to weave a skirt border. Josefa (right) stretches the warp while Basilia (standing, center) prepares the colored weft yarns. Luisa (left), talks to her little son. Her coca cloth is spread on her lap. Photo by the author.

Not all Erasmo's *karu kwintus* met with his listeners' approval. The failures were stories that rambled on, whose episodes repeated each other and didn't join up in interesting ways. "About a Married Couple," on the other hand, met with great success, and continues to do so thirty years later. Listeners are held in rapt attention, their laughter turning to horror and finally to pity. There's surprise at the way one episode leads to another. "It turned into a *condenadu kwintu!*" commented Luis, obviously impressed.

Up in the high pastures, women are said to pass the long days telling their children stories. Doña Balvina insisted that this was the only setting she was comfortable telling stories in, so we took the tape recorder out to pasture with the sheep. Her children and I huddled in the rain under a big blue sheet of plastic as she told us some hair-raising stories—but when I played back the tape, we found the story drowned out by sounds of wind and rain.

I believe the closest I ever came to "natural" storytelling was a cold, slushy August afternoon when I helped out with Don Apolinar's llama festival. After duly standing around in the sleet attaching tassels to the animals' ears and dousing them with libations of alcohol, we retreated into the house for hot soup and a round of drinks. The weather worsened; we huddled around the low clay stove and—as Sonqueños usually do when they're cold and uncomfortable—started to joke around. Apolinar told a story about Bear. Julian followed with a supposedly "true" account of a young woman who tricked a rich old man into marrying her and then inherited his wealth when he died in her lap.

And yes, I also remember sitting up late one cold night with Basilia, Alcides, Josefa, and Crisologo. We drank a lot, laughed a lot, and traded short funny stories, most of which were about none other than Fox meeting up with other animals—Mouse, Duck, Guinea Pig, Condor—and getting tricked into all sorts of dire foolishness.

CHAPTER TWO

A FOX!

Hinaspas chayqa hamusqa huq maqt'a irqi chayasqa
> Then a little kid, a boy, came along
chay wasiman warmimanqa.
> to that house, to the woman.
Hinaspas chay maqt'a irqi chayaspa,
> Well, since the boy had come,
"Puñukuy machhucha," nispa, qarata mañun, qarata qon.
> "You can sleep here, sweetie," she says, and gives him a sheepskin
> and a blanket.
Hinaspas MAnan puñuyta munanchu.
> But he doesn't WANT to sleep.
"Manan puñuymanchu!" nispa nin.
> "I don't want to go to sleep!" he says.
"Napichá . . . q'uncha pampachapi puñukuy, chay q'uñichapi!" nispa nin.
> "Here then . . . sleep on the floor by the stove, nice and warm!" she says.
"Manan puñuymanchu!" ninsi.
> "I don't want to go to sleep!" he says.
" 'Q'unchapunku q'unchapunku' niwankumanchá!" nispa.
> "They'd call me 'Lazybones by the stove'!" he says.
Chaymantaqa warmiqa willantaq, "Intonces maran pampachapi puñukuy!"
nispa.
> And so then the woman tells him, "Well then, sleep on the grinding
> stone."
" 'Maran pampa maran pampa' niwankumanchá!" nillantaq.
> But he just says, "They'd call me, 'Lazybones on the grinding stone'!"

Manan puñuyta munanchu chay maqt'achaqa!
> He just doesn't want to sleep, that little boy!

Hinaspa—chay ATUQ kasqa.
> So—he was a FOX.

Manan maqt'achachu kasqa.
> He wasn't really a little boy.

ATUQ? "A FOX?" we exclaimed.
"Yes," answered Erasmo.

Arí! warmiman haykusqa.
> He came in after the woman.

Atuq kasqa.

This is not really a translatable sentence, simple though it may seem.

Atuq   ka- + -sqa.

(Fox) (to be) + (narrative past tense marker)

There's no good equivalent in English for Southern Peruvian Quechua *-sqa*.

> "He was a fox."
> "It seems he was a fox."
> "He must have been a fox."
> "He happened to be a fox."
> "He happened (once upon a time) to be a fox."
> "Now this you must understand, for it affects everything:
> He was a Fox."

None of these really captures *-sqa*, the tense for dreams, myths, inebriation, and sudden surprises. It indicates a particular state of consciousness in which things happened without the speaker's direct and willful participation. The suffix *-sqa* doesn't specify whether the events themselves were real or imagined; it tells us about the speaker's relationship to these events. Quechua stories tend to begin in *-sqa* and then shift to the simple present tense. They return to *-sqa* when something surprising happens or when our storyteller needs to remind us that we're no longer located in *kay pacha,* the world of normal consciousness.[1] Here is the same passage again, with *-sqa* highlighted and the present tense in upper case and marked with underlining (*-n* is the third person singular; *-spa* is a kind of gerund). You can see how it shifts between tenses.

Hinapas chayqa hamusqa huq maqt'a irqi chayasqa
    Then a little kid, a boy, came along
chay wasiman warmimanqa.
    to that house, to the woman.
Hinaspas chay maqt'a irqi chayaSPA,
    Well, since the boy had come,
"Puñukuy machhucha," niSPA, qarata mañuN, qatata qoN.
    "You can sleep here, sweetie," she says, and gives him a sheepskin
    and a blanket.
Hinaspas manan puñuyta munaNchu.
    But he doesn't WANT to sleep.
Manan puñuymanchu!" niSPA niN.
    "I don't want to go to sleep!" he says.
"Napichá . . . q'uncha pampachapi puñukuy, chay q'uñichapi!" niSPA niN.
    "Here then . . . sleep on the floor by the stove, nice and warm!" she says.
"Manan puñuymanchu!" niNsi.
    "I don't want to go to sleep!" he says.
"'Q'unchapunku q'unchapunku' niwankumanchá!" niSPA.
    "They'd call me 'Lazybones by the stove'!" he says.
Chaymantaqa warmiqa willantaq, "Intonces maran pampachapi puñukuy!" niSPA.
    And so then the woman tells him, "Well then, sleep on the grinding
    stone."
"'Maran pampa maran pampa' niwankumanchá!" nillaNtaq.
    But he just says, "They'd call me, 'Lazybones on the grinding stone'!"
Manan puñuyta munaNchu chay maqt'achaqa!
    He just doesn't want to sleep, that little boy!
Hinaspa—chay ATUQ kasqa.
    So—he was a FOX.
Manan maqt'achachu kasqa.
    He wasn't really a little boy.
"ATUQ?"
    "A FOX?" we exclaimed.
Arí! warmiman haykusqa.
    Yes, he came in after the woman.

There are words to describe events that happen in this world—under our own sun, in the light of the present:

> *chiqaq*   "true, straight"
> *sut'ipi*   "in clarity"
> **kunan**   "right now"

Tales of the true, straight, clear, and immediate are *located*; speakers testify to things that happened in specific places at specific moments in time—and they use a simple present or simple past tense. They bear witness not only to ordinary events but also to extraordinary events in the tellers' lives—like Erasmo draining a haunted marsh, which was "like a *kwintu*." In conversation, these memories surface as fragmentary anecdotes, not as dramatic performances.

Kwintus carry with them a particular quality of experience. Lack of context gives the narrator free rein to tell of marriages between humans and animals; of competitions among talking animals; of travelers encountering souls of the damned; of Star Woman marrying a human man. Events are decontextualized, located neither in our time nor in our landscape. *-Sqa* does not make a distinction between fact and fiction; it distinguishes among states of consciousness.

"Let me tell you about my walk in the *loma* (*loma purisqayta*)," Alcides told me. "I found *Wayna Pascual* (Young Pascual, meaning a fox). I was out there in the Fox Time (*Atuq Timpunpi*)."

Atuq kasqa . . .

Ah, we know about *Fox.*[2] He's a thief and a sneak, a show-off, a gullible trickster, and he always ends badly. Once he drank up a lake trying to catch Mrs. Duck, just drank and drank until he exploded. He can be pathetically stupid. Once he asked Mrs. Wallata (an Andean goose that lives around highland lakes) how her children got such nice little red feet. She said that she baked them in the earth like potatoes, so Fox baked his own children until they were cinders.

Once he persuaded Condor to carry him to the high glaciers. Don Crisólogo told that story:

> . . . and that condor asks him, after some time had passed, he asks,
> "Brother-in-law, are you cold?"
> "NOT AT ALL cold!
> Since when does a male get cold?" says Fox.
> So they're sitting there for a while. And after a while, he asks again,
> "Brother-in-law, are you cold?"
> "I-I-I'm n-n-not c-c-cold!," says Fox.
> And so, fine, Condor he sleeps for a while, and then he asks again,
> "Dear Brother-in-law, are you cold?"
> "I really am cold!" he replies (audience laughter) . . . he's sitting there
> all curled up like a dog.
> Condor's made himself comfortable and goes to sleep on the snow,
> covering himself with his wing.
> But then he yelled yet again, "Are you cold?"
> "I'm FREEEZing!"
> And finally at the last moment, damn it all, he asked again,
> "Brother-in-law, are you cold?"
> Silence!
> And there he was dead in the cold, he was, that dear brother-in-law!
> And the doctor (Condor) . . . mmm . . . it seems that he ate him up,
> he did![3]

But no matter—Fox always comes back for another try. Don Alcides told another one about Fox and Condor.

> Fox persuaded Condor to take him to a feast way up in the sky. It
> was quite a spread! That slob just lit right into the food; he guzzled and
> snarfed until his disgusted host flew away without him. There he was,
> marooned in the sky. Finally, he made himself a rope so that he could
> climb down to earth. And on the way down he insulted some parrots.
> *"Hey, beak-face, big old tongue!"*[4]
> The parrots bit right through the rope, and down fell Fox. He cried for
> Diego the Mouse to spread out a blanket to catch him, but the mouse put
> out pointed rocks instead.
> *. . . down he fell right on the pointed rocks and—POW!*
> *splattered in little pieces all over the mountains. (audience laughter)*
> *That's why he's multiplied and there are so many of Pascual Fox.*[5]

But in other versions of this widespread story, Fox turns into a kind of inadvertent Prometheus. In a version recorded by Efraín Morote Best,

> [when he fell], from his entrails scattered all the products that he'd eaten raw in heaven and that only existed up there: potatoes, corn, *ullucus* [an Andean tuber], barley[,] and everything else that now exists here to feed men on earth.[6]

According to Ricardo Valderrama and Carmen Escalante, it's said in the Colca Valley that Fox once lived in heaven as the youngest and favorite son of *taytacha* (God).[7] The other sons were the Condor, Puma, Falcon (*alqamari*), and Parrot. One day when God was busy creating the world, He gave Fox a handful of quinoa and instructed him to prepare quinoa puree for lunch:

> Little Fox is left behind complaining: "What a stingy old guy! He wants me to cook a little handful of quinoa in that tiny pot!" And he pulls out the very biggest pot and fills it with plenty of water and an arroba of quinoa! And Little Fox waits for it to boil: "Now I'll have a real quinoa puree." But as the pot's beginning to boil, its contents start to grow. Buuuuu! It starts to overflow, and the little fox can't do anything about it. The pot keeps growing and overflowing until it fills the whole cook house. From the cook house it overflows into the patio, and from the patio into all the corrals, and from the corrals into all the streets, until God's whole village is buried under a lake of quinoa puree. The little fox is ashamed that he hasn't followed God's orders, and he tries to eat it all up, but he just can't. And when God comes home, there's Fox sound asleep with a bulging belly.[8]

Well, God forgives his naughty son, but the little guy just can't keep out of trouble. God warns him not to peek in the big chest where He's keeping the sun, for God created the whole world by candlelight and only hung out the sun later, but of course Little Fox can't control himself and peeks inside—and that peek is enough to scorch him all over and burn his tail black!

At that, even God loses patience. Spoiled little Fox is banished to the newly created earth, along with his four brothers. Down they go, descending by a rope in order from youngest to oldest: Fox, followed by Parrot, then Alqamari, then Puma, and finally Condor. And the rest isn't hard to guess. Fox just can't resist insulting Parrot—"Hey, Nosey Face! Hey, Trumpet Nose!"—so Parrot bites through the rope, and down goes Fox!

When he landed, he burst into little pieces. From those pieces originated all the foxes in the world, unhappily for those of us who raise animals, for shepherds.

Fox's shit stuck to the p'isqi p'isqi cactus and that's why it's all hairy. Fox shit is like that, all hairy.[9]

A Bolivian storyteller comments that fox droppings prognosticate the coming year. If he defecates corn, a good corn harvest will follow; if potatoes, a good potato harvest; and if his turds are wooly, there's a good year in store for the herds.[10]

Here is a glimpse of a different side of Fox—as Trickster-Creator, like Coyote and Raven in North America. This must be the fox whom Quechua speakers see in the dark spot in the Milky Way (that which English speakers call the "Coal Sack").

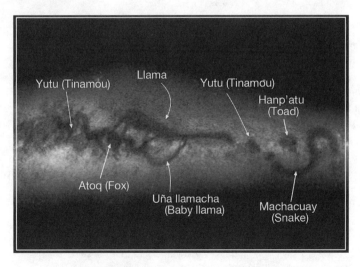

Andean "black cloud" constellations in the Milky Way

It also may be the fox who appears in *The Huarochirí Manuscript,* a central Andean mythology from about 1600: Fox-from-Above meets up with Fox-from-Below, and the two stop to exchange the news. A poor homeless man overhears the gossip:

A lord . . . who claims to know a whole lot, to be a god himself, is terribly ill . . . No one can identify his illness. But his disease is this: while his wife was toasting maize, a grain of *muro* (spotted) maize popped from the griddle and got into her private parts. She picked it out and served it to a man to eat. Because of having served it, she became a sinner in relation to the man who ate it . . . "As a result of this fault," he told the fox who'd come from down below, "a snake has made its dwelling on top of that magnificent house and is eating them up. What's more, a toad, a two-headed one, lives under their grinding stone. And nobody is aware of these devouring animals."[11]

Foxes understand these things—hidden, indecent things.[12]

"A FOX?" we exclaimed.

"Yes," answered Erasmo. "He came in after the woman."

So a fox got in. A fox in little boy's clothing, begging for help from a solitary woman. How could she deny a lost child, and why should she fear for her safety? The trick played on her loneliness, for here was a little kid to keep her company during the night.

Hinanspa, nin, na . . . "Kay purun pampachapi puñukuy!" nispa nin.
>So then she says, "Go sleep on the floor by the door!"

"Manan kay pampapi, punkupiqa puñuymanchu: 'Hawapunku, hawapunku' niwankumanchá!" nillantaqsi.
>But he responds, "Not on the floor! Not by the door! They'd call me, 'Lazybones, lazybones by the door'!"

Chayñas, al ultimo, manataq maypipas puñuyta munanchu maqt'acha!
>And so it goes on, the boy just won't go to sleep anywhere!

Chaysi warmiqa nin, "Mamaykiri mayllapitaq puñuchisunki, chaytaq manari maypipas puñuyta munankichu?" nispa nin.
>So the woman says, "And where do you sleep in your mother's house— or don't you sleep anywhere?" she said.

Chaysi nin chay maqt'a irqa—atuqyá chay kasqa—chaysi atuqqa niran,
>And so the kid says—well, he was really a fox, so that fox said,

"Mamaypa pupunpatachallapi puñukuni!" nispa.
>"I sleep right next to my mother's belly button!" he said.

Chaysi warmiqa wahan, "Hamuyyá chhaynaqa, pupuy patapin puñukunki!" nispa.
>So the woman yells, "Then come sleep next to my belly button!"

Hinaspas wahahtin, maqt'a irqiqa rin puñuq pupunpataman,
>And so when she yells to him, that kid goes over to sleep next to her belly button,

chay atuqqa.
        that fox.

Things may not be what they seem when you're alone at night. They have a way of starting out as one thing and finishing up as something else (like this story).

CHAPTER THREE

INNER THREADS

"Q'uncha pampachapi puñukuy, chay q'uñichapi!" (Sleep right here in front of the fireplace, all nice and warm!) These were familiar words for me. They still bring to mind snug one-room adobe houses, the door closed for the night, the fire guttering down to a few hot coals, a single candle burning in a niche. Children are snuggled up in heavy blankets on a platform slightly smaller than one of our double beds. Their parents check the livestock one last time before they, too, climb onto the waist-high platform. There they are, all three—five—eight—of them, cuddled together in their nest of blankets, taking comfort in one another's warmth.

"Allinchu kanki, Kumadri Katalina?" (Are you okay, Comadre Catalina?)

"Arí, allinmi." (Yes, fine.)

I'm in my sleeping bag stretched out on a sheepskin in front of the fireplace.

"Allinmi chaynaqa. Bwinus nuchis!" (Well, that's fine then. Good night!)

"Good night!"   "Good night!"

            "Good night!"   "Good night!"

            "Good night!"   "Good night!"

Somebody blows out the candle and we talk for a little while in the dark before dropping off to sleep. Then, with a curious burbling murmur, the *qowis* (guinea pigs) venture from their hutch under the bed platform to scavenge the detritus of the day. After a while, I wake up with a start to feel them running across my sleeping bag or poking their little noses in my face.

One night the *qowis'* murmur was mingled with a sound of quiet love-making. There were four children in this family, the youngest a baby and the eldest a boy in his late teens who had recently brought home a wife. The parents went off with the baby to sleep in a storeroom, leaving the bed to their son, his wife, and his two younger sisters. I awoke to the rustle of *qowis* and the newlyweds' urgent whispering, the girl apparently instructing the boy, who followed her lead. I retreated to the depths of my sleeping bag. The two little sisters slept quietly (if indeed they were asleep) there in the bed with their brother and sister-in-law.

Hinaspas . . . atoq makin aknata llankukachaykuyta qallarin, atoqpaqa, lluyta!
> Well then, Fox's hand starts groping around everywhere!

Hinaspas, ñuñuntan tardirun, warmiq ñuñunta.
> He finds her breasts, the woman's breasts.

"Mamáy, imaykitaq kaychari?" nispa nin.
> "What's this you've got, Mommy?" he asks.

"Ñuñuyyá chayqa," nispa nin.
> "Those are my breasts," she answers.

"Annn!" nispas nin.
> "Ah!" says he.

We all giggled.

Chaymantaqa, llamipakun, llamipakun, aknata!
> And then he keeps groping, groping, groping, unhuh!

pupunta tardirun.
> He finds her belly button.

Chaysi pupunta tardiruspaqa, nillantaq,
> When he finds it, he speaks up again,

"Mamáy, imaykitaq kayri?" nispa.
> "What's this you've got, Mommy?" he asks.

"Pupuymi chayqa," nispa nin warmiqa.
> "That's my belly button," she answers.

Chhayas, yapamantaqa llamipakun llamipakun
> So he keeps on groping around

phakanta haywayrapusqa.
> until it seems he reached her inner thigh.

"Imaykitaq, Mamay, kayri?" nispa nin.
> "Mommy, what's this you've got?" he asks.

"Taytaykiq qoqawunmi chayqa," nispa nin.
> "That's your dad's picnic lunch!" she answers.

"Patallanta, Mamay, malliychiway!" nispas atuqqa nipun.
"Oh, let me taste it, Mommy, just a little bit!" Fox entreats her.
Hinaspas, nispa niqtinqa
And talking like that
warmiyá chay atuqwan kunprumitikapun!
Fox and Woman started going at it!

How deftly our trickster changes from waif to lover. How easily he misdirects the warm intimacy of the family bed! *"What's this you've got, Mommy?"*

"It's all a joke!" he's telling her. "I'm not really a little kid!" By the time he reaches between her thighs, she's in on his game. *"That's your dad's picnic lunch!"* Playfully they blur relationships, conflating woman-man with mother-child, and the act of sex with that of eating.

"Hey, Mom, what's this?"

The routine is familiar to Quechua listeners as a prelude to lovemaking,[1] a sex-talk version of stylized repartee called *chansanakuy* (reciprocal joking). One hears *chansanakuy* shouted back and forth across market plazas; called out laughingly between passengers on long, cold truck rides; acted out dramatically during all-night funeral wakes.[2] Somebody calls to his would-be partner:

"Yaw, P'asña!   "Hey, Girl!"

And if the other cares to duel, she answers:

"Yaw, Maqt'a!"   "Hey, Boy!"

Or they may banter back and forth:

"Yaw, Kuraq!"   "Hey, Elder!"
"Yaw, Sullka!"   "Hey, Junior!"
"Yaw, Machu!"   "Hey, Old Man"
"Yaw, Wayna!"   "Hey, Young Man!"

These need not correspond to real-life roles; occasionally two men vie as *maqt'a* and *p'asna*, two *runakuna* as *runa* and *misti*. The roles may transform in the process, *maqt'a* and *p'asna* metamorphosing into *runa* and *misti* or into *machu* and *wayna*. Woven into our story as an extra colorful thread, *chansanakuy* reveals to us the exact moment when the woman both recognizes and succumbs to Fox's trickery.

"That's your dad's picnic lunch!"
"Oh, let me taste it, Mommy, just a little bit!"

We need no cross-cultural translation to perceive the shadowy implications of incest hovering behind the foolery. *"What's this you've got, Mommy?"* But a foreign listener won't recognize other connotations that compound and sharpen that implication. In Andean narrative and ritual, Fox is invariably cast—not in the role of "Son" or "Husband"—but of "Wife's Brother." Fox is often addressed in southern Peru and Bolivia as *lari*, or "wife's kinsman." When he's not called *lari*, Fox may be addressed as "Tiyu." It was as Tiyu—Condor's wife's brother—that we met him freezing to death on a glacier. In the Quispikanchis version of that tale, he's *Lari*. In some Bolivian Aymara marriage celebrations, the groom dresses as a condor and playfully carries his wife's brother, called *larita* (fox), around on his shoulders.[3] Son or brother, Fox is the insider who comes too close, or who comes close in the wrong way.

Hinaspas, hinallaman qosan chayanpun
    And so, at that very moment her husband arrives
tuta, llamapi kargantin.
    in the dark, with his llamas laden with cargo.
Hinaspa, wasipi chapakusqa.
    Well, the door's locked.
Hinaspas rinigasqa chayamuspa wahakamun hawamanta:
    And the man's in a bad mood anyway, so he really yells from outside:
"Kay kargata paskaysiway!" nispachá, imanispachá riki.
    "Come unload this cargo for me!"—or something like that.
Hinaspas, rinigasqa chayamun,
    So there he comes home fuming,
mana lluqsiyta atinchu warmi riki.
    and the woman can't come out.
Atuqqa mana warmimanta, riki, hatarinchu.
    Fox just won't get out of her.
Hinaspas, kuchilluta tariruspa, kuchilluwan atuq pichikunta mut'urparipusqa warmi!
    So she found a knife and with that knife she chopped off his prick, she did!

Chaysi qhariqa: "Imata ruwanki kunankama?" nispa nimun hawamanta.

There's her husband, yelling from outside the house, "What's taking you so long?"

Chaysi, "Llawita mana tarinichu, chapakuspan puñurani," nispa nin warmiqa.

And she's saying, "I can't find the key, I was sleeping with the door locked!"

Hinaspas, atuqqa p'itarun, "WARAQ!" nispalla punkuta phawarapun.

But then Fox jumps up yelling "WARAQ!" and bursts right through the door.

Chaysi, "Alquntinchu puñunki imanankitaqri, karaho?" nispa qhariqa phiñarikun.

Then, "What the hell, are you sleeping with a dog?" The man's furious.

"Ima alqucha haykumun riki wasita," nispas nin.

"Some little dog must've gotten into the house somehow," she answers.

Dogs are ubiquitous in the Andean countryside, but you'll never find them in the house. They live at the margin, guarding the homestead and its livestock from predators (like foxes who sneak in after lambs and chickens). People name their dogs and are mildly fond of them—they're insiders to the household whose business is to keep their distance, to whine and growl on the other side of the door. So the husband in our story is horrified to see what he thinks is a dog rush out of his house.

This dog/fox confusion seems like a stray thread; it surfaces only for a moment in Erasmo's telling of the story. Yet other tellers of the tale include it as well. It surfaces momentarily in an Aymara telling when the woman, pinned down by Fox's penis, cries out in dismay, "Stuck together like dogs!"[4] Alejo Maque's version picks up the "dog thread" and weaves the narrative around it.

> *In the inside of long ago, way up in a lonely homestead, there lived a woman and her husband, that is, a married couple. And their dog was a fox. Whenever the man was away on a trip, Fox would talk with the woman.*[5]

Fox-dog whines and whines to be let into the house. Finally the woman lets him come in and—well, he won't sleep anywhere—and things develop from there:

> *Fox says, "I'm used to sleeping right on my mama's belly." So the woman replies: "Then just come here and sleep on this belly!" So Fox happily climbed onto her belly and started screwing her every night.*[6]

We know what happens . . .

> One night the husband comes home and Fox was paralyzed with fear. But his penis was stuck between the woman's legs, stiff as a sling handle, and he couldn't get it out. The man was already in the patio with his llamas yelling at the woman . . . So the terrified woman couldn't do anything else but grab a knife and cut off Fox's penis.[7]

This version puts a different twist on the insider who comes too close. Fox hangs around outside the house crying and crying.

> "Mommy, give me back my oca!"[8]
> Mystified, the man asked him nicely,
>   "What oca did this woman take away from you?"
> And Fox, unable to stand the pain, cried
>   "She's got it between her legs, she's got it between her legs, she's got it between her legs!"[9]

So the man searched, pulled out the penis from his wife's vagina, and —tossed it back to Fox!

> Fox licked it all over until he could stick it right back in place. And for that the man beat his wife until she was dead. After that Fox disappeared; never again was he a dog for mankind. And what's more, dogs have hated foxes up to this very day.[10]

Don Alejo's "Fox-as-Dog" emphasizes the precariousness of domestication: tame insiders have ways of turning predator; savagery is never far below the surface. The Fox-as-Dog version brings out the subhuman, bestial quality of an adulterous, implicitly incestuous coupling. The woman pays for the mistake with her life—seduced by an animal, she's then violated by her husband, who yanks the penis from between her legs and beats her to death. With humans, too, it seems, savagery is close to the surface. When Fox goes back to the wild at the end, we understand that wildness has moral dimensions.

And there Alejo Maque ends his tale of failed domestication. The household dissolves: woman dies, man is a lonely murderer, and their "dog" continues his rapacious career as a wild animal. In this version, the incest theme is submerged, running beneath the surface, only hinted at by Fox's whining subterfuge, "I'm used to sleeping on my mommy's belly!"—and, of course, by Fox as *Tiyu/Lari*, the wife's brother, an insider who should keep his distance.

And while we're looking at inner threads, we just saw another one in Don Alejo's version: *"Give me back my oca!"* We don't hear about ocas in Erasmo's version. Is this "penis as oca" just a one-off joke of Alejo's, like Erasmo's embroidery with the *chansanakuy* sex talk? It seems not, because other tellers play with this thread as well. In the Aymara version, Fox goes running around asking passersby if they've found an oca. Our teller from Quispicanchis, Agustín, brings the "oca thread" to the fore.[11] For him, Fox is a little boy hired to harvest ocas. Later, as in Alejo's version, Fox runs around the house calling, *"Give me back my oca!"*

But this woman is smarter (or luckier), for she manages to fool her perplexed husband.

 "Yesterday he helped me harvest ocas, but I didn't pay him. That must be why he's yelling at me now," she tells him.[12]

Then in the morning she hides the penis in a load of ocas until she has a chance to throw it away near a stream. An old lady then mistakes it, not for neck meat, but for an oca, and when she finally throws it away, it's with the exclamation,

"What a swinish oca!"[13]

Another high-altitude tuber works its way into Don Agustín's version as well. When her husband returns unexpectedly, the woman yells at Fox,

"Hey, suyt'u *(long snout)! What* suyt'u *got inside? Suyt'u, damn it all!"*[14]

Suyt'u (oblong-shaped thing) gets used as an epithet for long-faced people and animals, particularly dogs, and here the woman is trying to cover her debauchery by pretending to discover a dog in the house.

But long before I learned that particular usage, I knew *suyt'u* as a kind of potato, *papa suyt'u,* "oblong potato," good for baking in an earth oven. And like the oca, people joke about *papa suyt'u,* comparing it to another oblong object—a penis.

Inucha understood this comparison by the time she was four years old. I well remember how, as we rested dusty and tired after a morning of potato harvesting in 1975, we ate our baked *papa suyt'u*. I was talking to Luis Tayta about potatoes. Were they male and female? "Potatoes are female," Luis replied flatly. Seven-year-old Esteban picked up a *papa suyt'u* and exclaimed, "This one isn't!" Inucha giggled appreciatively.

I followed this up with Basilia, who explained that *papa suyt'u* is a *qhari papa* (male potato). "Don't peel them with a knife!" she cautioned, "or they'll cry!" A man should eat them to get strong, yet, she added, a woman should eat some *suyt'us*, too, or at least split some with her husband. He can't bully her if she has some male strength herself.

"*What* suyt'u *got inside?*" exclaims the woman in Agustín's story. *Suyt'u* is a dog, a penis, and a male tuber. Because for Andean people tubers are quintessentially female plants, a *qhari papa*, "male potato," is male in a female domain. And that makes it a potential troublemaker—like a wife's male kinsman, or a marginally domesticated animal.

In Erasmo's narrative, what happens to this "oblong thing"?

Chaysi, hinalla lloqsirun warmiqa, chaysi . . . mmm . . . hinalla pasan,
> Well, the woman comes on out, mmm, comes out,

hinaspas chay warmiqa lluqsin,
> well, she comes out,

hinaspa lluqsispa paskaysin.
> comes out and unloads the cargo.

Hinallamantas paskaysispa, karga lluyta allichanku ima, haykupunku
> When every last bit of the cargo is unloaded, they go inside

Chaysi . . . na . . . chaymantaqa hina puñupunku riki.
> and then, um, go right to sleep!

Chaysi qusanqa tutaymantaqa: "Wayk'uy!" ninchá, imaninchá riki.
> Well, first thing in the morning the husband's yelling, "Start cooking, won't you?"

Hinaspas pasan warmiqa chay, unuman pasan, unu aysaq.
> So the woman goes out, goes out to bring water.

Hinaspa chay atuqpa . . . nantaqa . . . pichikuchantaqa hisp'arparinpusqa maypichá, unupatakunapi.
> And she pisses out Fox's—y'know—his penis next to the water source.

The fate of Fox's penis varies among the versions of our story. In a short, simple version from Coaza, the girl simply tosses the penis away, and Fox is left running around outside her door crying for his "*vela*" (candle).[15] In Don Alejo's version, the man returns the penis to Fox, who licks it back in place and takes off for parts unknown.[16]

In four other versions, another character enters the story. In three of the four (Aymara, Quispicanchis, and Q'ero), she's an old lady who takes the penis home for dinner, thinking it's a piece of meat or an oca. But—surprise!—this meal has a life of its own and behaves so outrageously that the old lady throws it away.

In the Quispicanchis version, Fox finds it and segues into another familiar Andean story: Condor helps Fox reattach the severed member and then carries him to a banquet in Heaven.[17]

Our Don Erasmo, however, is heading to meet up with another story—a Condenado Kwintu—and for this he needs a *p'asña*, an adolescent girl.

Hinaspas, chaymanqa huqñataq p'asña risqa.
  Well then, later on a girl passed that very spot.
Hinaspas, p'asña irqiqa tarikusqa.
  And that girl child found it.
"Aychata, Mamay, alqu aparamusqa, chayta kunkan aychata tarirakamuni!" nispa pasachin.
  She brought it back, saying, "Mommy, I found some meat, some neck meat that a dog must have stolen!"
Hinaspas, pasayuqtin apaykun mamitanman.
  And so she brought it home to her mother.
Chaysi, mamitanqa huqkaqpiña, huqpiña chayqa; huq wasipiña karapusqa.
  By the way, her mother wasn't the same woman; this happened in a different household.
Hinaspas, TAkan
  So anyway, [the girl's mother] WHACKS it,
hachawan k'ullupatapi
  with a hatchet on a stump of wood,
kunka aychataqa, atuq pichikullantataqsi takaykun!
  whacks that neck meat, that fox's prick!
Hinaspas,
  And then,
takan! Yapaqa chay warmiq takasqan phakallanmantaqsi pasaykun!
  she whacks it again! And it jumps into her lap!

Takan! Yapaqa phakallanmantaqsi pasallantaq.
Whacks it! Again it jumps into her lap!
MAnan wit'uchikunchu riki, wit'uchikunchu chay kunkan aychaqa!
NO WAY will it break, it won't break, that neck meat!
Hinaspas, huqta TAkan, chay takaq mamitanpa phakanman pasayrapusqa.
Then, with another WHACK, it jumps right up between her thighs!
Mana aycha kapunchu!
It isn't meat at all!
Chay atuqpa pichikullantaqsi kasqa chay.
It seems it was really Fox's penis.

So here is Fox in the house again under false pretenses. Well, a piece of Fox—but what's the difference? With Fox, it's a *part-for-whole* relationship.

> . . . *down he fell right on the pointed rocks and — POW! — splattered in little pieces all over the mountains. That's why he's multiplied and there are so many of Pascual Fox.*[18]

Every piece of Fox is yet another Fox. That's what makes him a trickster—you can never really get rid of him.

And when it comes to *this* particular piece of Fox—his penis—it's a *whole-for-part* relationship. What other part of Fox matters? In the beginning of our story, he behaves like an ambulatory penis, and in certain respects this episode is a reprise of the beginning. Fox/penis enters the house under false pretenses and tricks his way into the woman's lap. The penis is all that's needed to produce those baby foxes and propel our narrative into a Condenado Kwintu.

Andean expressive culture delights in this kind of exuberant synecdoche—*part-for-whole/whole-for-part*—as in the textile design on the next page. In narrative, Fox contains a similar synecdoche. Wild and tricky, he outruns himself. The alternative ending of the "Fox in Heaven" story reveals a bountiful potential in his craziness:

> . . . *[when he fell], from his entrails scattered all the products . . . that now [exist] here to feed men on earth.*[19]

Either way, his appetites produce both destruction and multiplication.

Fox's lost penis brings to mind another figure who loses his penis in flagrante. In the 1920s, the great Peruvian anthropologist Julio C. Tello

described the principal deity of the Casta region in the province of Huarochirí in the highlands east of Lima:

Once, it was said, the now barren lands of Huarochirí were exuberantly fertile, filled with fruit and flowers, thanks to the rapacious sexual appetite of Wallallo, son of the Lightning and master of the forces of nature, who engendered twins in all living things. But all this was lost when a jealous deity named Wampu tried to overthrow him. Wampu persuaded a female deity to let Wallallo seduce her, and then, in the act, she would grab his testicles and yell for help. And so it happened. The struggle caused such a lot of rain, hail, and lightning that Wallallo escaped—but without even noticing that he'd lost
> . . . the endowment that enabled him to provide for the people of the region abundant harvests of maize, potatoes, quinoa and ocas and all the other crops that the earth offers up. It was this power that enriched Wallallo's region.
When Wallallo recognized his loss, he went off searching for his lost member.
> (His) disappearance was the ruin of his subjects; the land became sterile; the forests that provide wood for firewood and the construction of houses and temples, the extensive pastures that served to feed the herds—all disappeared due to the rapacity of Wampu, who carried it off to his own territory.[20]
Wampu hid the severed penis in a cave where a traveling medicine man from Lake Titicaca found it and, recognizing it for what it was, took it home with him. Wallallo finally learned of its whereabouts and wandered south in search of the medicine man. He did recover his penis eventually, and along the way acquired a wife who kept him occupied in the southlands while Huarochirí suffered through years of drought and famine. After a while, Wallallo came back, bringing rains with him. He tried to restore the region, but it never again achieved its former richness. Finally, he returned to his new wife in the south. Every year he comes only for a short time to bring the rains and fertilize the fields. He makes his entrance, Tello and Miranda tell us, in September or October, accompanied by rain, hail, and lightning, with eyes sprouting fire and roaring like a lion.[21]

Fox is far from being a fire-breathing deity, but he resembles Wallallo in his libidinous, excessive cravings and, of course, in the loss of his penis in flagrante delicto. At the heavenly banquet, Fox can't stop eating; on the way down he can't refrain from insulting the parrots. Finally he explodes, scattering all the fruits of the earth. Here, too, fire deity and foolish fox converge, for volcanic Wallallo is the source of the cultivated crops "maize, potatoes, quinoa, and ocas."

Wallallo has been around for centuries. He shows up around 1600 in *The Huarochirí Manuscript* in the form of a terrifying *huaca* (powerful place-deity), "a burning fire" (probably a volcano).[22] In the beginning, his lands were all jungle, even up to what today is barren highlands, "huge snakes, toucans, and all sorts of animals filled the land." Like the twentieth-century Wallallo, the *huaca* had a connection with twins: "[He] ordered the people to bear two children and no more. He would eat one of them himself."[23] Finally, he met his match in battle with the great mountain Paria-caca, who snuffed out Wallallo's fire by taking the form of red and yellow rain. Victorious Pariacaca stopped the people from sacrificing their children. Wallallo turned into a high mountain lake, and the jungle receded to the lower valleys. As in twentieth-century Casta, his defeat resulted in the sterility of the highlands.

As for Wallallo's detached penis, I imagine the medicine man's face lit up when he saw it, much as Doña Basilia's did when we came across stone penises in the Cuzco archaeological museum. There they were among the Inca *qunupas*, most of which are beautiful little stone alpacas and llamas. Basilia was quite familiar with these stone miniatures.[24] They encapsulate the well-being of herds and crops, and almost every family in Sonqo keeps a bundle of them hidden carefully in their storeroom.

Children exclaim,

> "*MuNAYcha!*" (How PRETTY they are!)

on the few occasions every year when the bundles are opened.

> "*Khuyaqkuna!*" (Loving protectors!)
> "*Kawsaqkuna!*" (Living ones!)

In the museum, Basilia pointed at a stone penis in delight:

> "*Kawsaq kikin!*" (The living one itself!)

I imagine that she, too, would have liked to take it home.

But our story isn't about a talisman penis; no, it's Fox's "swinish oca" that gets taken home by mistake. Tricky and utterly self-serving, this jumpy "neck meat" can only reproduce more creatures like itself. This is the Fox who falls from heaven only to splatter bits of himself all over the place. "*It's because of him that there are so many foxes.*"

CHAPTER FOUR

STRANGE SPOUSES

Fox isn't the only animal said to pursue human girls. Listeners in firelit houses; in rainy pastures; and on long, crowded truck rides are reminded of other story spouses, nonhumans who complicate human lives.

"Condor was like that, too; he came after a girl out pasturing her sheep."

"And Bear, he tricked the girl, and then she was caught."

"But Star-Woman, she was something else!"

This chapter takes us on an excursion through these other stories because they interpenetrate and speak to each other.

 ## *Kundur qatay kasqa . . .*
Condor happened to be a son-in-law . . .

Condor and Fox run in and out of stories, sometimes together, sometimes apart. Theirs is a cooperative yet sinister relationship: They are brothers-in-law. Crisólogo's joke about Fox and Condor on the glacier pivots around the refrain "*Tiyu, alalachu?*" (Tiyu, are you cold?). Condor calls Fox "*tiyu,*" a term that (although derived from Spanish *tío,* "uncle") refers in Quechua to the wife's brother. By implication, then, Condor stands in the relationship of sister's husband—*qatay*—to Fox. Indeed, if you're an Andean listener, this doesn't have to be spelled out, for you know that **Condor happened to be a son-in-law . . .**

Here's how:

There was once a pretty young girl who used to tend her parents' flocks way up in the high pastures. Well, one day a young man, a mestizo, came and started following that shepherdess, the man's daughter. *Aña-ñáw*, he was gorgeous, with a white necktie and a fine black jacket—and playing the flute!

But—you know something? He wasn't really a young man. He was a condor who wanted that human girl.

He just started following her, talking and playing the flute, until she got used to him. Then they started playing games, you know, piggyback, hide-and-seek, that kind of game. *Achakaláy!* All of a sudden he just carried her off, to be his wife in the barren rocky Village of Condors.

Oh, she was miserable in Condor's nest, cold and almost starving! She gave birth to a baby, half-human and half-bird, who died as soon as it saw the light of day. This was too much for her. She decided to deceive her husband and his family. María the Frog helped distract her husband while she ran away, home to her parents' house.

But it's not so easy to leave a condor! A hummingbird told him where she had gone and showed him the way to follow her home. That condor son-in-law came to their door, and knocked.

"*Ñachu? Ñachu?*" (Ready yet? Are you ready yet?)

"*Manaraq!*" (Not yet!) said the young woman. "I'm getting dressed."

So Condor waited for a while. But you know what they were *really* doing inside? They were boiling water in a big, big cauldron—and they covered the cauldron with a poncho to make it look like a seat. Finally they let that son-in-law into the house and asked him to sit down. Into the pot he went! Pshhhhh! And then he was eaten. He was devoured by his wife's parents.[1]

Erasmo told me the story twice, in 1975 and 1980. The version in 1975 was longer and dwelt on the courtship of Condor and the girl and the distress of the girl's parents on learning of it. All their anger and scolding was to no avail—she insisted on playing with the handsome stranger until he carried her off.

Sad to say, the tape was ruined. Five years later, Erasmo recorded it again as a gift for my husband, Rick, who had been with me in 1975 but never returned to Sonqo after that (eventually we split up). Erasmo worried about Rick and wanted to maintain a connection with him.

I'm going to send a story about Condor to Mr. Richard.
So he'll remember.

> So he'll remember,
> I'll tell you a little story about Condor.
> It seems there just might have been a condor.
> He went wandering, and he changed his form to that of a human youth.

With Rick's permission, I've included the whole transcription as an appendix (A). This new version moves quickly to the girl's escape and the hummingbird's mischievous taunting:

> Well, "Hummingbird, karahu, I'm swallowing you!"
> He swoops in, catches the hummingbird, and swallows him up.
> Well, he doesn't even chew him,
> swallows him whole! And so it seems hummingbird gets shat right out
> again, whole . . .

"Oh no!" I exclaimed, laughing.

> . . . alive!

Listeners were gasping in laughter, shouting,

> "This is bad!"
> —alive and well!

That left us giggling, the children falling over each other on the floor. But Erasmo moved on to Condor's sorrowful discovery of his wife's desertion, his pursuit, and arrival at the house of her parents, who, alerted by Hummingbird, have laid their trap . . .

> He arRIVES as a young man, playing his flute so fine, ah—
> with his white neck scarf!
> "To his mother-in-law's house!" explained Cipriana, excitedly.
> To his mother-in-law's house!
> To the girl's parents' house, and so
> "DO come IN," they say, greeting him so nicely.
> "Ay!" I exclaimed in alarm.
> "Are you my son-in-law?" she says.
> "Yes, here I am, dear Mother!" he replies.
> So they get him to sit down, no?
> "Do be seated," they say oh so politely, "right on this sheepskin."
> "Ay!" again.
> And so Condor sits down and . . .

And so KERSPLASH! down he goes — that Condor — into the boiling water!

"Oh!" I exclaimed. "The poor Condor!"

Condor dies — Fff-LOPP! Fff-LOPP! Fff-LOPPP! — he dies in the boiling water.
They peel off everything.
And then, his mother-in-law eats him up!

"Ay!" I blurted out. "Swegruchu? And the father-in-law?"

Yes, his father-in-law eats up Condor, his SON-IN-LAW!
"He eats up his son-in-law!" added Erasmo's son Eusevio. "Qatayninta mihurapun!"
WELL THEN!
That's how the girl was saved by escaping to her parents' house.
He never returned from there.
And that's that . . .

Eaten by his in-laws! The tale of "Condor Son-in-law" expresses the disquiet family members feel when a man attaches himself to their daughter and sister. In-laws are ever problematic. They're outsiders who've gotten inside, part and yet not part of the family.[2] *Qatay* intrudes himself into the intimacy of the family group, stealing their kinswoman's loyalty. *"Suwakuna!* The thieves!" exclaim desconsolate parents, describing their daughter's in-laws. Yet bride-capture (*suwakuy*) in itself is not abnormal; it may even be arranged ahead of time, or played out as a game in the wedding festivities.

Condor Qatay's crime is not so much that he abducts the girl as that he does it under false pretenses of being human. Only after he abducts her does the girl discover her husband's true animal nature. When she runs away to her parents, Condor tries to put the best possible face on the situation and present himself as a good human son-in-law. Erasmo's whole family was caught up in the tension of this final encounter when Condor ARRIVES at his mother-in-law's house, playing his flute all very fine, a gorgeous young man in a white silk neck scarf. Suddenly the tables turn and Condor is the victim: "DO come in!" say his in-laws. They attend him oh so well! . . . "Do be seated," they say oh so politely, "right on this sheepskin," until KERSPLASH! down he goes flopping and dying in the boiling water.

And yes, that old couple eats him right up. Nothing is simple; both sides are cruel.

Newlyweds usually move in with the husband's parents, but live there only until they can set up their own household with the inheritance of animals and use rights to land each receives from their parents.[3] To stay is to live in subservience. A woman who lives with her mother-in-law has to get up first in the morning to light the fire, carry the water, and do most of the cooking. A man who lives with his wife's parents takes orders from them until they become feeble or die. They swallow up his time and energy: Condor Qatay gets boiled alive and eaten.

Nevertheless, if you're a young man, it may be worth your while to marry a youngest daughter and live with her parents because you can look forward to becoming a householder when your in-laws die. This is a time-honored method for outsiders to work their way into a new community. Erasmo described himself as descending from such an arrangement. In fact, he described his father's family, the Huallas, as doubly *qatays*, in-marrying sons-in-law of an in-marrying son-in-law:[4]

He came from way off as a son-in-law, he did, our ancient grandfather.
And so then came his sons-in-law, the Huallas,
from Kallatiya, or who knows where the three of them came from! . . .
They had plenty—as that man's sons-in-law they had lots and lots of land,
got hold of a big extensive section, plenty,
and it was plenty for lots of people and their children all the way up
    'til now; there's a whole lot of land there.
It's ours, the Huallas.

The in-married son-in-law bides his time, waiting for his wife's parents to die: Condor Qatay circles around them, waiting.

Condor is powerfully ambiguous: huge, impressive, beautiful, ugly, even revolting, even a bit comical. Venerated and feared, admired and loathed, representative of the Mountain Lords: how well our paradoxical Condor expresses life's contradictions!

Mountain Lords are community guardians, the *uywaq* (nurturers), the source of health and prosperity.[5] The *ayllu* coheres around them; ancestral

Indian (Runa) and Mestizo (Misti):
· a racial idiom referring to cultural differences;
· a linguistic distinction that misleadingly implies the existence of two groups of people.

One might expect to be able to classify an individual as belonging to one group or the other, as either *runa* or *misti*. But the terminology is deceptive. The distinction is not racial but a difference of cultural styles. A single individual may be *runa* or *misti* in different contexts and at different times by changing language, clothing, and behavior.

Ethnicity is to a large extent situationally defined. A truck driver who is bilingual in Spanish and Quechua, participates in the money economy, and wears factory-made Western-style clothing may—if he goes broke—return to his *ayllu*, raise most of the food he eats, wear traditional handwoven clothing, and offer coca leaves to Mother Earth and the sacred landscape. He may eventually even forget much of his Spanish. Or he may choose to traffic on a small scale as a local middleman, speaking Spanish and wearing his *misti* clothing when he is in town and changing back to his *runa* ways in the *ayllu*.

This kind of code-switching is situationally convenient; the problem is that the values associated with the two styles are often in opposition. This really is the crux of the dilemma—the *misti-runa* distinction is rigid in concept but tends to be fluid in practice, thereby setting up a state of inner tension and ambivalence well expressed by the "Condor Qatay" story.

force resides within them. Yet they are moody and arbitrary; they can cause crop failure, landslides, and all-around bad luck. Like mestizo landlords and shopkeepers, Mountain Lords are wealthy, powerful, and not to be trusted. Here is the paradox: Mountain Lords are like *misti* (mestizo) landowners, yet they provide a basic grounding for *runa* identity.[6]

The Condor Qatay figure contains a similar inner tension. He appears to the girl and her family as an elegantly dressed mestizo. In other tales, he's addressed as "Doctor," like a lawyer or a priest. His *misti* identity emphasizes disagreeable outsiderness, but also implies sources of power unavailable to his in-laws. Yet, at the story's end, Condor is stripped of his fancy accoutrements, boiled clean even of his feathers. *Qala!* Naked! like a mestizo.

To a Quechua listener, Condor's nakedness at the end is doubly poignant. It brings to mind an image of the (falsely) beautiful young man revealed as an ugly featherless biped, exposed and at the mercy of his parents-in-law. Yet, the word simultaneously underscores Condor's mestizo identity, for mestizos are called *qalakuna*, "the naked ones."

Is *qala* a metaphor for cultural loss, a "naked" state shed of values, language, and behavior associated with an Andean way of life? I think not. The

Not a dove, but a condor, hovers over the Christ Child in Andean folk representations of the nativity. Photo by Eugene Rizer (property of the author).

"In the Andes, to wrap a body in textiles is to humanize it" (Arnold and Yapita 1998). Luisa Illa and her husband, Alcides Mamani, pose for a photo in front of their house. Except for Luisa's vest and their hats, all their clothes are homespun and handwoven. Photo by the author.

grounding for this image is more concrete: To eyes and bodies accustomed to *runa p'acha* (indigenous clothing), mestizos really do look "naked." Mestizos wear factory-made cloth, cut and tailored so as to fit the body and reveal its contours. In contrast, *runa* women's shawls and men's ponchos are not tailored, but rather folded and wrapped so as to envelop the body. Handwoven cloth is an integral and signifying part of *runa* identity.[7]

> *Ñachu? Ñachu?*
> Ready yet? Are you ready yet?
> *Manaraq! Manaraq! P'achakushanin!*
> Not yet! Not yet! I'm getting dressed!

My acquaintances in Sonqo often asked me to photograph them with their families. Making these portraits was a time-consuming process. When I arrived, camera in hand, my friends would disappear into the house "to get dressed." I had to wait an hour or more until they finally emerged looking (to me) like carefully arranged mountains of cloth. When I wore *runa p'acha* myself, I discovered a different experience of my own body. My center of gravity had to shift, and I felt an unaccustomed sense of weightiness and substantiality. Mestizo "nakedness" is a metonym for cultural difference and culture loss. For Condor's wife, getting dressed is not only a delaying tactic, but a return to her former way of life.[8]

Is Condor Son-in-law villain or protagonist? The answer is both and neither. *Qatay* is a relative category; a man is simultaneously *qatay* to one set of people and *tiyu* to another. To have in-laws is to be one. Part of the listener, especially the male listener, has to identify with the condor as *qatay* while at the same time being set dead against him.

Men also identify with BEAR, another ambiguous figure.[9] But while condors and foxes are part of the highland environment, bears are not. A common metaphor, *"Ukuku kani!" (I'm a bear!)*, does not arise from an intimate routine experience of bears and, in fact, does not correspond very well with the only bear native to South America — *Tremarctus ornatus*, the spectacled bear, denizen of the forested eastern slopes of the Andes. This small and rather peaceful creature seldom wanders as high as Sonqo's open, rocky pastures, so  few people in Sonqo have ever seen a bear. In 1975, the eyewitness descriptions in Sonqo came from two generations back: "No, I never saw an *ukuku*, but Domingo Quispe's grandfather saw one once." It was light brown and furry, about as long as a man but running on all fours like a dog, with marks around the eyes — a pretty good description of a spectacled bear.

Back in the 1970s and early 1980s, a little boy named Cirilo often sat by my side while I listened to *ukuku* stories and questioned the older generation about them. The boy grew into a man, and in the year 2000, I sat with Cirilo in the sun outside his house, talking about the *ukuku* again as his own children played around us. To my surprise, he was of the opinion that the *oso* (Spanish for "bear") and the *ukuku* were different animals. The *ukuku* is "like a little person with a tail" (*runacha hina chupayuq*). Then there's the *cusillo*, which is a *mono* (Spanish for "monkey"). He couldn't explain how the *cusillo* and *ukuku* are different. Then there is the *oso*, which is "separate, not an *ukuku*" (*sapaq, manan ukukuqa*). His wife, Ernestina, chimed in at this point. She comes from Challabamba, closer to

"Ukuku kani!"
"I am Bear!"

Bears look a lot more like **human** beings than condors do. Bears can stand upright on two feet (though not for long) and often sit upright, propped against trees or rocks, using their forefeet like hands. Like humans, they are omnivorous, a diet that produces a rather humanlike dentition. Bears' lips are not attached to the gums, rendering them protrusive and mobile, like those of humans. A. Irving Hallowell, who wrote his dissertation on the diffusion of bear symbolism from Siberia through the Americas, tells us that Native North Americans were known to comment on "the skinned bear's pitifully human-like appearance." He remarks on the bear's facial and bodily expressiveness, commenting that bears may shed tears and whine pleadingly when cornered. He also notes that the bear's traces—footprint and excrement—resemble those of humans. In the Andes, bears are believed to resemble humans in their sexual habits and preference for sexual intercourse in a face-to-face position. Girls are warned about bear-rape. In the *"Ukuku"* story, the half-human sons of Bear grow up abnormally fast, in a parallel with the bear's actual life cycle. The gestation period of the spectacled bear is eight to eight-and-one-half months, approximating the human gestation period, but the cubs are self-sufficient in approximately six months. Now of course the bear has many *non*anthropomorphic characteristics, the most striking of which is its annual "hibernation," or period of winter sleep. Possibly these alternating periods of dormancy and activity gave rise to the widespread Andean belief in the bear's immortality.

The tale of "The Bear's Wife and Her Children" is as widespread and familiar to Native Americans as "Cinderella" is to Europeans. One can trace versions of this story all the way from the southern Andes through Mesoamerica into the North American southwest. In California, it meets up with Native North American bear tales belonging to a complex of bear ceremonialism that originally diffused into America from Siberia. In the Andes, this very ancient pre-Columbian tradition is thoroughly interwoven with a Spanish story, "Juanito el Oso" (Johnny the Bear). Far from being a "pure" survival of pre-Columbian times, "Ukuku" is a story woven out of the colonial experience.

---

the forests. The *ukuku* is separate from the bear (*oso*) she said definitely. It's very strong: "It can carry a cow on its shoulders. They talk like humans. We have them in Challabamba. It's got a little bit of a tail." (*Wakata apan muchunpin. Runa hina parlankupas. Challabambapin kanmi. Uñaña chupan.*)

Whatever they are, it is through playful conversations, stories, and dances that highlanders learn about these awkward, sometimes fierce, rather humanlike creatures. If a woman describes her husband as an *ukuku,* you know she's feeling fed up with some kind of disruptive, overbearing, or aggressively sexual behavior. Even men occasionally describe themselves this way: "*Ukuku kani!*" Sometimes family men pull out the old *ukuku* mask they wore in their youth and use it to frighten unruly children, who cry and run away seeming to be genuinely terrified. Until recently, almost every young man at some point danced the *ukuku* role in the ritual cycle leading up to Corpus Christi. These *ukuku* dancers—hundreds of them—actually scale the glacial snows above the Qoyllur Rit'i sanctuary and spend the night on the ice. As *ukukus,* young men have the courage to face cannibal souls on the nocturnal ice; as *ukukus,* fathers terrify their children; and as *ukukus,* men are taunted and criticized by their wives. *Ukukus* paradoxically combine awkwardness with power. They are dangerously comical and comically dangerous.

Several people, including Don Luis, told me the *Ukuku'*s story, but as usual, Erasmo's was the longest and best. This, too, I've included as an appendix (B).

> Now I'll tell you a story, I will
> about the *ukuku,* Compadre.
> They say that the *ukuku*
> prowled after a girl who was herding sheep.
> And so, as she herded the sheep
> he turned into a playmate, into a boy, and went after her.
> He followed and followed her.
> And then he carried her off!
> Off to a cave!

No wonder women don't use *ukuku* as a complimentary term! About ten seconds into the story we learn that Ukuku was a kidnapping trickster—hardly the ideal husband! Nor is a cave what a girl hopes for in the way of a home:

> And there in the cave
> there he cared for her, cared for her;
> they lived there a long time:
> soon they had a child.
> And so that child, it's getting bigger and bigger!
> And the girl is still living shut up in the cave
> closed off with a rock.

What an image of family life! The mother's held captive by her brute of a husband, and as if that weren't bad enough, the kids are shut up in there with her.

> And so, then
> Bear goes off, goes after a cow, where to? Far away!
> He carries the cow on his back,
> lots of corn on his back: LIKE THIS!
> Sheep too . . .
> He gets a lot of stuff.
> He carries the whole corn crib on his back
> and loads the cow on top!
> That's how he carries them.
> And so then
> well he gets that stuff
> and well the baby is getting bigger and bigger: like this.
> There's one child; there're two children. And they say the woman just
> stays there, shut up in the cave.
> Caring for them.

Listeners chuckle knowingly, recognizing a caricature of rural Andean married life in all its worst aspects. There is the female, "all hands and no feet," sitting immobilized in the cave. There is the tough male, all feet, always on the move, an outsider in his own home. Ukuku is trying to be a good husband, ravaging the countryside to support his prisoner-family, running himself ragged while his wife sits captive behind the great rock door. Meanwhile, the children grow into his strength, but their sympathies all lie with their mother. She sends the old *ukuku* off on a fool's errand, and while he's gone, his sons **KICK** aside the rock closing up the cave:

> So they're opening the door, the one their father put there!
> Cipriana giggled.
> Their father's an old *ukuku*!
> And it seems the little *ukuku* children are kicking it!

—and they go out to **FIGHT** with their father. Their mother watches anxiously, for they've told her that red smoke will rise up if the old *ukuku* wins, and blue smoke if he loses.

And so the blue smoke rises up to their mother's watchful eyes.
And their mother DANCES, damn it all!
"I'll bet they've killed the old dog!" Haha!
We all laughed.

And so the girl—no longer a girl, but mother of two big sons—is free at last, and returns to her parents' house.

Well, this is a long story, definitely a *karu kwintu*. As it continues from here, the mother quietly fades out of the picture. Her awkward, rambunctious sons accidentally kill off her parents' livestock, and finally her father turns them over to their godfather, a priest. The rest of the story revolves around the priest's attempts to keep them under his control. It ceases to be an exaggerated portrait of family life and becomes the story of these half-human sons of *ukuku* struggling with social institutions. I'll return to them in another chapter.

Like Condor, Ukuku is an impossible husband. In a version of the story I recorded with Cirilo's father, Luis, Ukuku emerges, like Condor, as a mestizo:

They say there was once a *misti*
who went around after a shepherdess,
bringing her cloth.
And so that's how it is, but he keeps coming, just keeps on coming,
comes every single time she goes out herding.
And so finally—he succeeded in leading her away.
"Let's go away together!" he says,
and leaving her sheep behind, leaving her mother behind,
she went with him.[10]

As Luis's story continues, the *misti* imprisons the girl in a cave and she gives birth to two sons. So far, Luis hasn't even identified this figure as an *ukuku*. This comes almost as an afterthought:

Luis: So he—that *misti*—goes off after closing up (the cave) with a big rock.
Me: Ah yes, the *misti*.
Luis: Um hmm, I mean him.
Me: And then?
Luis: Guess what? That *misti* was an *ukuku*!

> **Me:** An *ukuku?*
> **Luis:** He was an *ukuku.*

Luis's story moves ahead along the familiar route. The boys free their mother and kill their father. She takes them home to her parents.

> "Wherever have you been all this time, my child?" (her mother) says.
> Then they go out to the places she'd herded the sheep
> and had hidden the cloth, hidden the soap,
> and look for all those things.
> But she'd been gone a really long time,
> and it seems the stuff had all rotted away into compost."[11]

So the woman gets nothing at all out of her liaison except a couple of uncontrollable bear-sons. As in other versions, she fades out of the picture as her sons take over the story.

Back in 1904, the German anthropologist Max Uhle recorded a version of the "Ukuku" story.[12] The beginning exactly parallels Erasmo's rendition, but the story ends like "Condor Qatay." Instructed by that same irritating hummingbird, Ukuku pursues his "wife" and sons all the way to her parents' house—where he gets tricked into the cooking pot and eaten.

This points up how "Ukuku" and "Condor Qatay" are versions of the same story, emphasizing different aspects of marriage and its intrinsic difficulties. Ukuku's story foregrounds gender struggles inherent in the structure of the household as authority passes from one generation to the next. Ukuku is never called *qatay*, nor are the woman's parents described as his *swigrus*. While Condor is a predatory son-in-law, Ukuku is a tyrannical husband and father. When women call their husbands *ukukus*, they refer to this part of the story; they liken their husbands to *machu ukuku*, the overcontrolling, aggressively sexual father bear. His story exaggerates the way men and women—even when properly paired up as stay-at-home "hands" and outgoing "feet"—exploit and tyrannize each other. Father Ukuku keeps the woman prisoner, while she bosses him around and sends him on fool's errands. The struggle between father and sons emerges as an inevitable extension of this parental conflict.

While Ukuku and Condor Qatay emphasize different aspects of married relations, their stories share an undercurrent of ethnic tension. Both stories play with a semantic ambiguity that surrounds the word *runa*, a term that refers in a generic way to human beings, but in a more restricted sense refers to a particular kind of human being, to *runa* as opposed to *misti*. Animals have to disguise themselves because they're not *runa*, not human beings. Animals are not-*runa,* and mestizos are not-*runa.* There-fore, aren't animals mestizos? And by implication, aren't mestizos animals with the same predatory, deceitful qualities as Condor and Ukuku? And don't animal-mestizos give out an illusion, a false promise of riches, luxu-ry, and power?

This sad yearning for the wealth and beauty of a different social stratum expresses itself poignantly in the story of the

✦✦✦ **"Star-wife,"** a story properly told by women (the only one of this kind I encountered). Erasmo gently refused to record it, deferring to his wife (though eventually he did record it under her supervision). Like the Condor and Bear stories, "Star-wife" plays on the impossibility of pair-ing up with a creature too different from oneself. But here the perspective is inverted: this time the woman is a divinity and it's not an animal but a human youth who captures—and then loses—this other-worldly wife. Star-Woman is an impossible daughter-in-law; she comes from a different sphere, inaccessible to poor *runa* farmers.[13]

"Star-wife" was the first story I heard in Sonqo and the first I recorded from the lips of my friend Basilia (a complete transcription is included as Appendix C). Normally garrulous and wonderfully expressive, Basilia was intimidated by the unfamiliar tape recorder and irritated by her son Al-cides, who—apparently because he couldn't imagine storytelling outside a social context—tried to create the background illusion that we were hold-ing some kind of celebration. About halfway through the story, he started serving imaginary drinks.

✦✦
> Well, it seems there was a star living with a young man.
> Why did the star live with a human youth?
> But it seems that indeed she did live with him—
> in this world.
> She was a young woman.
> And so she, it seems, bore sons for that human youth,
> three of them!
> And she wore this human clothing
> that (star-)woman did.

But she doesn't like it:
"It's ITCHING me! It's ITCHING me!" she says.
"It's awful!" It seems she didn't like human clothing;
her own clothes never itch her.
. . .

All the SEED potatoes the youth raises, she COOks
that (star-)girl does!
She puts the pot on the fire—and it breaks—
puts the pot on the fire—and it just breaks again—
puts the pot on the fire again—and it just breaks again.
She completely finishes off the seed potatoes.
And then she takes off, when the seeds are all gone
and the pots are all broken, takes off for heaven.
"Where's your mother?" asks the youth, home from the fields.
And (the child) answers: "My mother took off like this llikwww.
She just went away up there!"

The young man runs around in despair, searching everywhere for his wife. While he's away, the Star-Woman returns "with a sound of '*chikkk-chikkk-chikkk*'" and takes away one of the children, and then another.

And that's why in the mornings and evenings there's a star,
Y'know a star
who has two littler stars.
She comes out with one of her star-children in the evening.
Alcides was getting restless and pretended to pour a glass of *trago*:
        Drink up, Compadre! Drink up!
Rattled, Basilia continued:
    And the other, she comes out with the other
    as the morning is dawning, y'know.
    Just two little children, the other child—
    it seems she left the other one with his father.
    And therefore
    that's where the youth goes to look for her—
Alcides: Drink up, Comadre!
Basilia: So then
    he goes to heaven.
    And the moment he arrives, she comes out of Mass,
    gorgeous, going LLIP-LLIP-LLIP.
    "Is that my wife! AY! What am I going to do?
    I can't possibly support her,
    I can't possibly afford her clothes!"

Alcides: "Service! Let's have some service!"
Basilia: "CHHIW! her clothes are shining all the way to the street!
Those two—(hesitating) the two little children—
Okay, that's it! I'm finished!"
Alcides: "Let's drink up! There's plenty of beer left, about three whole
cases!"
Basilia: "You all made me nervous and made me make mistakes, really
make mistakes!"
Alcides: "We'll remember (the story) later, won't we? When we're drunk!"

Weeks later, Basilia finished the story for me: The star-wife recognizes
her husband and—while explaining that she will never return to earth and
human clothing—she takes him to her house in heaven.

> With the youth weeping,
> she fed him boiled potato seeds and pork
> and sent him away (back to earth)!

Basilia said little more about the young man, but another version of the
story, told to Jorge Lira by Carmen Taripha in Calca, captures his anguish:[14]

> And so he lived, sick at heart. "That woman is my heart's only desire. How
> can I go on suffering like this? I'll give myself up to weeping," he said.

But Basilia's thoughts had turned away from the man back to Star-
Woman, devourer of seed potatoes:

> And when Venus comes out bright in the evening
> or the morning, a mother with her child,
> a young woman with her child,
> then there's really hard frost, y'know.
> "Frost!" they're saying
> (when) she comes out splendid in the evening.
> "There's the Star-Girl!" they say, watching her.
> And that's all I know.
> (laughing) I've never been in the Star-Time.

Star-Woman: ineffably distant yet inextricably connected to human life
in the highlands. It's not just that she lived for a while on earth and that her
little star-children had a human father. It's because frost is dangerous yet

indispensable in the potato-raising economy. Potatoes have to be stored in a freeze-dried state called *ch'uño*, produced through a process of alternate freezing at night and thawing during the day. Basilia and I spent some of our pleasantest days and had our best conversations sitting around a pile of thawing potatoes, squeezing out the water and spreading them out to (hopefully!) freeze again that night.

But freeze-drying is exactly what one *doesn't* want to happen to one's *seed* potatoes — either in the storeroom or later in the ground. Late frost can destroy a newly planted crop in one fell swoop. Star-Woman's greedy (pot-breaking!) appetite for seed potatoes well expresses the way frost can undermine a family's livelihood. It also expresses Star-Woman's incompatibility with human (that is, *runa*) existence, for she rejects two hallmarks of *runa* lifeways — their clothes and their food. This is a vision of mestizos, not as *q'alakuna* (naked ones) but as gorgeously dressed in superior clothing that *runakuna* could never afford or produce.

One hardly has to scrape the surface to find the current of ethnic tension in this story. Country Boy follows his glamorous alien wife to a heavenly city where he finds himself overwhelmed and out of place. His connection with the alien world destroys his livelihood, for without seed potatoes he has no crops to plant.

The threads of ethnicity and affinity (in-law relations) run together through Star-Woman's story, as they do in the stories of Condor and Bear. This comes through especially clearly in Carmen Taripha's version from Calca.[15]

In Doña Carmen's version, Star-Woman is a celestial princess who comes down at night with her sisters to steal potatoes. The young man manages to capture her and takes her to his watch hut. Here is my translation of Carmen's Quechua:

> . . . the youth was trying to deceive the girl, saying, "Now come on, let's go to my house."
>
> But the princess replied, "Your parents absolutely must not see me or meet me."
>
> "I've got my own house," said the youth, and took her away when it got dark. And so he took her to his parents by means of this trick. He made her go in against her will, all shining as she was, inexpressibly beautiful.
>
> And so they took her in and cared for her, looked after her very well.

But they wouldn't let her go anywhere, nor would they let anyone see her. And so the girl lived that way for a long time with the youth and his parents. She got pregnant, and after a while she gave birth. But the baby died; for some reason it didn't live. They took the shining clothes away from the girl and locked them up. They dressed her in common clothing. And so they cared for her. One day the youth went off to work in the fields. Meanwhile, the girl went outside, just outside the house, and little by little she stole away. Off she went up to heaven.

A Condor hears the youth weeping on a hilltop and agrees to carry him to heaven in exchange for two llamas (a hefty price). One llama he picked clean on the spot; the other they butchered and loaded up for the journey.

"You must shut your eyes tight. You mustn't open them for any reason. Only, when I say 'Meat!' you must put some meat in my mouth," said Condor.

And so he carried him, and the man didn't open his eyes. He kept them tight shut. When Condor said "Meat!" he stuck some meat in his mouth.

But as they flew along, the meat ran out. Condor had warned the youth before they left, saying: "If, when I say 'Meat!' you don't put any in my mouth, I'll just throw you off anywhere!" So that young man, he cut some meat from his own calf. After that, every time Condor said "Meat!" he put it, bit by bit, in Condor's mouth. With that meat, they made it to heaven. It's said that it took them three years to get there.

He not only loses his potato seed, but gives up his own flesh to follow her to heaven—to no avail, for though he does eventually find his wife, she hides him from her parents, Sun and Moon.

And when they get to her house, the man is shivering from hunger. Seeing this, the girl speaks to him: "Go cook this quinoa," she says. And she gives him a little spoonful of quinoa. But the youth sees where she got the quinoa from. He looks at the bit of quinoa in his hand, and says in his heart, "Is this all she gives me! And this skimpy serving is supposed to satisfy me after going hungry for years on end?"

The girl says, "I have to go see my parents. You mustn't be seen by them. While I'm away, just go ahead and cook what I gave you."

As soon as she's gone, the youth gets up and adds more quinoa. He adds lots of quinoa, and then he cooks it in a big pot. No sooner is it cooked but it fills up the pot and boils over. He's already filled up all the plates. Skimpy it isn't—it's boiling over! All the pots are overflowing. Skimpy it's not—it's running out all over the place! And he's eating as much as he can. Just a little bit fills him up, and there's no way he can finish it—it keeps on coming and coming. And so he goes and buries it underground. And even underground it just keeps pouring out, and it starts to sprout.

With all this going on, the princess came back.

"Whatever are you doing?"

"That bit of food I was cooking boiled over. I can't finish it, so I'm burying it," he replied.

"That isn't how you eat our quinoa! We only cook a little tiny bit at a time. Why did you add more? You've cooked ten times too much!" she said.

And so the girl set to helping him bury the leftover quinoa because she didn't want her parents to see it.

And so the youth is hidden away; and she brings food to him in hiding. He lived with her there for a year. After a year, the woman didn't remember to bring the youth food anymore. She gave him nothing more and didn't return to the house. "Get out! It's time you left!" she said one day.

So the youth went away weeping . . .

Returning home on Condor's back (at a price of two more llamas), he vows never to remarry, and remains dependent on his parents for the rest of his life. In other words, he's destroyed as a social being: he forms no new household and contributes nothing to the perpetuation of society.

This story of an impossible marriage conveys a sense of despair deeply rooted in the ethnic tensions of rural Andean life. Condor and Bear are comic figures, unlike the *runa* youth who expresses a ruinous longing for inaccessible splendor. In Don Agustín's version from Usi, the *runa*'s voyage to heaven is even more disastrous: *Taytacha* (Christ) the Sun emerges from the church and burns him to a crisp.

This begins to sound familiar. Isn't that the sort of thing that happens to Fox? And what about Fox? We began with him, after all. Both Star-Woman and Fox can be found in the sky: Star-Woman is Venus; Fox bumps along as a black spot in the Milky Way. And like our young man, Fox takes an ill-fated journey to Hanaq Pacha on the back of a condor. Both of them eat their fill in heaven and then are sent back to earth. Doña Carmen's version even includes the Fox-like episode when the quinoa boils over and the young man buries it. The episode is Fox-like because the youth is foolish and funny; and Fox-like because, by implication, it recounts the origin of quinoa, a cultivated plant. But quinoa episode aside, the Young Man is a tragic counterpart to comic Fox. He can't keep coming back to trick and get tricked another day. When he's burned, he's burned; when he's rejected, he's done for. Not like Fox, who splatters all over the world and keeps coming back for more.

Fox is the seducer with a difference. He doesn't find his girl on the high pastures; he comes right into the house. And only Fox sinks so low as to bring a strong whiff of incest with him (*"Hey Mom! What's this?"*). Condor and Bear prey on shepherd girls, not married women, and afterward both do their clumsy best to behave as husbands. Only Fox is simply beyond the pale. Alejo Maque warns us:

> If you ever sleep in a herder's hut, some of them don't have doors, not like the ones here with doors that close . . . If you sleep in such a place and the moonlight awakens you, look at the doorway: There'll be a fox watching you, saying, "hah, hah, hah" and licking its chops . . . It likes that . . . If it's male and it sniffs out a sleeping woman, then it really wants to screw her. But if anything else is there . . . a dog, for example, the dog chases it off. The fox runs away, rushing around like a blind thing.[16]

CHAPTER FIVE

LISTENING TO NUMBERS

Hinaspas, hinallamanta—
> Well, after that—

biyuda puraña chaykuna kasqaku.
> oh, by the way, it seems [the girl's mother] was a widow who'd joined households with a widower.

Chay, chay warmiq qusanqa, kallantaq chayqa, chaysi phiñakun,
> And see, he, that woman's husband, is bad-tempered,

k'amin, imananchá iy?
> insults her, does any old thing, y'know?

Unquq rikhuripun señora,
> Well, the lady turns out to be pregnant,

chay aycha takaq warmisyá chay unquq rikhuripun.
> that's the woman who whacked the meat, she gets pregnant.

Chaysi, unquq rikhuripuqtin phiñakun . . . naqa . . . qusanqa.
> And when she turns up pregnant her, mmm, husband gets furious.

"Imaynapin unquq rikhurinki, manataq nuqawan imapipas kanchischu; wenu, huqwanchá qanqa—pantanki!" nispa.
> "How on earth did you get pregnant?" he says. "It wasn't by me, we never do anything; it's obvious you've been with somebody else—fooling around!"

Hinaspas nin: "Manan piwanpis pantanichu" nispa.
> "I haven't fooled around with anyone!" she retorts.

"Chay kunkan aychata tarikamusqa irqikuna.
> "It was that meat the kid found.

Chaytan takarani, chaymi pasayruwan korpuyman,
> When I tried to tenderize it, it passed inside my body,

chayllamanta khayna kashani" nispa willakun
    and that's why I'm like this!" she explains
... mm ... qusanman.
    to her ... mmm ... husband.
Hinaspas, unquq rikhurin unayña, unayña, unayña.
    And so, the pregnancy drags on and on and on.
Hinaspas, iskay kasqa chay warmiq ususinkunaqa riki:
    Oh, and it seems that woman had two daughters:
huq chay tarikamuq kaq,
    the one who found the meat,
huqtaqsi wasipi kaq, sullk'akaq.
    and another, younger one, who stayed home.
Chaysi phiñakun, waputachá riki qusan, chay runata, biyuda purataq tiyaranku.
    Well, the husband was furious, really furious about it because they'd
    been living together as widow and widower.
Chay wawankunatapis kaqllataq k'amin riki, ususinkunata:
    He even insulted the daughters:
*"Mamaykichis chhayna unquq rikhurin chayqa, huqchá taytaykichis!" imanispachá
nin riki ...*
    "If your mother gets pregnant like this, who knows who your father is!"
    he said, who knows what awful things he said ...

The tape ran out.

"Suyay ... " (Wait ...), I said.
    Erasmo paused.

Erasmo's phrase *"Biyuda puraña chaykuna kasqaku"* is difficult to translate. "It seems they were widow/widower together." This means that each had lost a spouse through death and their two truncated households had merged as a matter of expedience.[1] This isn't unusual in a highland village where life is harsh and health precarious, but expedience doesn't guarantee compatibility in a household patched together from the remnants of previous marriages. This marriage, like the first one in this story, is at risk. Erasmo's very hesitations express its fragility—should he call this man her "husband"? Hmm ... And when trouble comes along, as it does here in the hands of an unsuspecting daughter, the center doesn't hold.

I fumbled "Side B" into place, and Erasmo continued:

> *Chay unquq rikhuriruspaqa, yastá wiqsayakun, wiqsayakun, wiqsayakun,*
> So there she is pregnant with her belly growing and growing and growing,
> *yastá wachakapun,*
> until finally she gives birth,
> *chay warmiqa:*
> that woman does:
> *KINSATA atuq uñachakunata!*
> to THREE little baby foxes!

"Atakáw!" I exclaimed.

> *Atuq uñachakuna munay surrukunasyá!*
> Little baby foxes, gorgeous chestnut-colored foxes!

We all laughed in a subdued sort of way.

> *Fox babies!*
> *Not one, not two, but three.*
> *Why? Why are there <u>two</u> daughters and <u>three</u> fox babies?*
> *Why not <u>two</u> fox babies?*
> *(Bear and his human captive produced two rambunctious bear babies.)*
> *Or why not <u>one</u>?*
> *(Condor and his human wife produced that single ill-fated condor*
> *baby with the dirty diapers.)*

Numbers are structuring features of any culture's stories and scriptures, but cultural traditions relate to numbers differently, and it can take many words to convey that difference. To appreciate the experience of numbers Quechua listeners bring to a narrative requires an excursion into moral arithmetic. This is a culture that expresses moral significance through the ways different numbers meet up, form groups, and enclose each other. According to Gary Urton,

> numbers are not conceived of in Quechua ideology as abstractions whose nature and relations to each other rely on the predications of pure logic . . . Rather, numbers are conceptualized in terms of social—especially family and kinship—roles and relations.[2]

Myth and story put flesh on the numerical bone to offer a visceral, emotionally affecting experience of morality. To approximate this experience requires a roundabout route, a pathway through social and moral connotations of numbers that a native listener takes for granted and feels only on the margins of consciousness.

HUQ/ONE
There are two kinds of "one":

One as matrix contains within itself a set, a collection of interrelated things. One is *mama*, the "mother" of numbers, just as darkness is the mother of colors. It possesses a containing, unifying, and productive force.

One thing by itself—*chullaña*—is intrinsically lonely and incomplete, like one hand without the other. Condor Baby is *chullaña*. He has no identity separate from his parents, who are irreconcilably of different species. His dirty diapers provide a pretext for his mother's escape, and that's the last we hear of him. I asked Basilia what happened to him, and she replied nonchalantly, "Oh, he died."

Our solitary Fox, on the other hand, is single in a different (but no less problematic) way. Fox is full of himself. Every bit of him is potentially another whole Fox. With his ravenous appetite, he is solitude run amok, proliferating endlessly.

Listen, for example, to this episode late in the "Ukuku" story (the complete transcription is included as Appendix B).

And then, really, the damned one breaks in, through the ceiling, up there!
First, hmm, one hand appears.
"Hey! What's this?" He's watching. Hahaha!
Well, and so he's watching.
Well, *karawchu*!!" he says. "ONE!" he says, as one hand reaches in.
And then another one tears through, the whole hand up to the wrist.
"TWO!" he says casually. So then, so then again, gnashing his teeth,
(the bear) bolts down the roast—see?—the roast beef.
And then, once again, more of the body appears—this much of it.
"THREE!" he exclaims.
And then more—the HEAD appears.
There it is! "FOUR!"

> And then more: the feet. "FIVE!"
> There it is, its whole body! "SIX!"
> The Bear's counting.
> Somebody's definitely coming in. More of it appears, there it is,
> the head's all the way inside now, there it is!
> "SEVEN!" he says.
> There it is, waist and all! "EIGHT!" he says.
> There it is. Then the rest appears, all of it, *karahu*, there it is!
> "TEN!" It drops onto the floor.
> (soft) *Kukuchi.*

In Quechua, counting is inherently divisive. "Numbers are considered, by their nature, to *separate* things. . . . The practical implication . . . is the . . . prohibition on the counting of things considered to be inseparable."[3] For Quechua listeners, *counting* parts of the body runs deeply counter to a normal order of things. And so do *kukuchi*s (aka *condenados*), for they are damned souls unable to die and leave their rotting bodies. Counting the body parts dropping from the ceiling stresses the *kukuchi*'s dis-integrated condition.

TWO:
And there are two kinds of "two":

A *complementary pair* (*yanantin*) is composed of two things whose differences complete each other in order to form a single unit like *warmiqhari*, the married couple. Erasmo makes a point in his narration that neither married couple functions well as a unit. This failure of *yanantin* relationships provides the fulcrum on which the story turns.

Two similar things, *doubles* of each other like same-sex siblings (especially twins), are *masintin*, comrades who reinforce each other.

The two daughters in our story are *masintin*. Let's take a closer look at another sibling duo, the two sons of Bear in the "Ukuku" story we left unfinished in Chapter Four. These beast babies are *masintin*, yet they run amok very much like the fox cubs. We left them accompanying their

mother to her parental home after opening the cave and killing their father.
After a happy homecoming, they stayed on in their grandfather's house.

> Well, there are some other kids there
> and the Boys play and play with them, play at marbles.
> And it seems they kill them all off, shooting marbles.
> And then, they just keep playing (like this!), they do in the chickens,
> [they just kill off] everything everywhere.

Their grandfather gives up on controlling the pair and takes them to
their godfather, the village priest.

> So, they're taken to the godfather.
> And well, it's just the same at the godfather's.
> There are servant boys, and they play with them.
> And they [kill] them off,
> kill them off.
> Again they keep on playing—they order around everything
> and they kill off whatever there is.
> . . .
> And the Priest is getting mad.
> "What kind of troublesome kids have they brought me?"

Cipriana laughed.

> Alright, how to punish them, then?
> What shall I do?" he says, furious.

What shall he do? The *karu kwintu* unrolls with episode after episode as
the Godfather-Priest tries to "kill off his sons." First, he sends them off to
school—"The teachers'll take care of them!" he says. But those two Bear
Boys just keep fooling around with their marbles and kill off the whole
school, teachers and all. So, the Priest sends them off to the army with an
iron club, but the same thing happens: they kill the officers.

> (*fast*) CRACK! *Karahu!*
> CRACK bam boom smash
> They ice off every last one of (the officers)!
> And when they've killed the lot of 'em,
> they go right back to their godfather, to the priest!
> . . .

We started to giggle.

> The Priest is just dying! Jumping up and down!

We were doubled over laughing.

> "What will come of this?
> Whatever can I do?" he's saying.
> "And there's the other one, the younger one, too!"

(long pause)

> And then he says, "How will I kill them, hang them? How can I get rid of these children of mine?"

He looks closer to home, and sends the Bear Boys to the bell tower of the church.

> ". . . and the *ayllu runa* (townspeople), *karahu*, the *ayllu runa* will push them off!" he says.
> "They'll dig a hole at the bottom of the tower!
> The *ayllu runa* will push them into it," he says.
> "They'll be buried in the hole," he says.
> So he sends them, both of 'em, y'know?

Cipriana leaned toward us and added in an undertone,
  "It seems the other one was about this big . . ."
Erasmo paused and added,

> "It seems the other one was about as big as Cirilucha."

As big as Cirilucha! That's not very big. Little Cirilo was about two feet tall when Erasmo told us this story. What's this miniature sidekick doing here? The story line doesn't seem to need him.

For this listening ethnographer, the tiny brother brings to mind an Inca practice. Early chronicles tell us that each Inca ruler had as *wawqe* (a variant of *wayqi*, "brother") a small effigy of himself, carved from stone or precious metals.[4] This *wawqe* was assigned lands, flocks, and servants; visiting lords would greet him before they greeted the Inca himself. He accompanied the ruler into battle, or even went in his stead, dressed in a miniature version of the imperial garb and shaded by a royal parasol. These days a similar idea seems to be at work in the *ukuku* dolls, tiny replicas of themselves that *ukuku* dancers carry onto the perilous Qolqepunku glacier during the great Corpus Christi pilgrimage to Qoyllur Ri'ti.

While Erasmo's listeners don't know about the Inca's *wawqe*, the idea of a tiny double makes perfectly good sense to them. All their domestic animals and food crops have tiny prototypes called *enqaychu*, sources of vitality and well-being.[5]

But our story bear is about to lose his little brother. While the cubs are shoving the townspeople into the hole at the bottom of the tower:

> Well, the younger one got pushed in, too.
> Now there's only the older one left.
> And so, he goes right back . . . um . . . to the priest.
> (*fast*) "Papa, people came after me bothering me for no reason at all, and so I got mad and pushed them all out," he says.

Cipriana laughed.

> He keeps on coming back, doesn't he . . . to the priest.

The Bear Boy manages well enough for a while without his little sidekick. The Priest sends him off to get wood in the jungle (expecting that he'll be devoured by wild beasts), but he harnesses the animals and loads the firewood on their backs. In his final and most difficult ordeal, however, Bear Boy faces a formidable adversary. The desperate priest sends him to a rich hacienda, haunted by the horrible damned soul (*kukuchi*) of its landlord. "The damned one'll get him for sure!" he says. So the *ukuku* makes himself not one but two companions — a wooden baby (*qullu wawa*) and an iron baby (*hiru wawa*).[6] Unafraid, the *three* of them (one Bear and two dolls) hunker down for dinner in the old manor house . . . and this is when the *kukuchi* starts dropping through the ceiling. The three together vanquish the *kukuchi*:

> When the bear man gets tired, then the iron one jumps up for another round, see?
> And when he gets tired, then the wooden one jumps to its feet again, *karahu*!
> SLAAAMS him, *karahu*! makes him sing!

And when the wooden one gets tired, the Bear Man jumps up and
SLAAMS 'im, see, the damned soul.
And so there we are, it's day already, it's getting light,
karahu, and so he saves the damned soul, y'see, makes him yell, makes
him talk.

. . .

"I'll leave you my manor.
Thank you, you just saved me," and saying this [the damned one] turns
into a white dove and flies off at daybreak.

Three not only vanquishes the disarticulated *kukuchi*; three "saves" him
and sends him off to heaven.

Moving from two to three involves a new order of complexity, with
potential permutations and combinations impossible for two. Braiding,
for example, requires a minimum of three strands. A traditional woman
spends her life with her hair braided. Only in the privacy of her own courtyard does she very occasionally undo her braids to wash her hair. Her only
public appearance without braids is in death, for she is put to rest with her
hair unbound. In Chumbivilcas, this unbraiding is a poignant event in the
burial ritual, ideally performed by the deceased's daughter-in-law.[7]

THREE carries a mixed message: If two is good, then *three* is excessive—and yet three is the perfect number, the prototypical union of odd (1)
plus even (2). As Urton comments:

> It is important to note that, with only one consistent exception, [in
> Quechua] even numbers are considered to be a good sign, odd num-
> bers are a bad sign. The exception is with the number, and collection
> of, three. . . . Three is reckoned to be the—or at least a—number
> signifying wholeness and completion.[8]

Three consistently shows up in connection with social order and the organization of society. A three-pronged whip signifying the *ayllu* sits on the
ceremonial table at Sonqo's important ritual celebrations. It is accompanied by three drinking vessels: two wooden drinking cups called *qero* and a
low clay bowl called *puchuela*, which means the "too-much thing."

Wordless this symbolism may be, but it is not abstract: Anyone who
has scarfed down these consecutive three drinks can attest that it is, indeed, *puchu* (more than enough) and that everyone gets drunk pretty fast.
However, this drunkenness has a purpose. Ritualized intoxication opens

channels of communication with the Earth and sacred places. The third, apparently extra, drink is the one that does the job, that transgresses existential boundaries and makes the ritual effective.

In Andean representations of society, tripartition teaches us about the *ayllu*, the basic social unit.[9] Listen to all the threes—and the interplay of one with three—in another narrative (this, too, I include in its entirety as Appendix D). This is Erasmo's reply when I asked him how Sonqo Ayllu came into being. He describes it as rescued and dominated by his own family, the Huallas:

Comadre, I'll tell you a sto— . . .
ah, I'll tell you about the Huallas:
They say that a man came, our ancient grandfather, from Santa Rosa.
And so, having come, he was supposed to pay taxes.
All the People had fled, fearing the taxes . . . .
. . .
he was Pedro Pari from the far high reaches beyond Santa Rosa.[10]
Only he remained
and he—that man—he didn't want to pay taxes.
"I won't give anymore, I don't want to pay anything, I don't—
let them cut off my head and take it!" he said.
He came from way off as a son-in-law, he did, our ancient grandfather.
And so then came his sons-in-law, the Huallas,
from Kallatiya, or who knows where the three of them came from!
For there were *three Huallas* there as well.
His wife had sent for papers (titles),
then he, too, worked in the fields.
. . .
And then the gentleman came, uhmm, from,
from Spain, to draw up the papers.
. . .
And he met up with . . . Pedro Pari's wife
and . . . said to her, "Well, Madam Woman!
So you want to form an *ayllu*? I'll draw up the papers for you."
So he spoke, seated on a horse, catching up to her as she herded her sheep.
"Yes, certainly, that's what I want!" she said.

"Okay, good, I'll do it," he replied.
"What are the names of these bordering hills? How far does your land extend?
. . .

And so that's how they drew up the titles on Puka Qaqa,
written with a chicken's feather, the *three* of them:
One was a copy . . . no, two were copies and one the mother.
. . .

and so with the titles the *ayllu* came into being FOREVER,
not as an hacienda or anything else.
And so there were those Huallas
who came from somewhere to live as sons-in-law.
. . .

And *we're three*, the Huallas,
three . . .
"Are there still three?" I asked.
Now we are three, but our own very ancient grandfather
was *just one*, that Pedro Pari.
And his wife was a Yuqra.
What Yuqra that would have been I don't know, I, too, am forgetting how to
tell it.
And so [now I'm telling you, Comadre],
Comadre Catalina.
"Thank you!"
. . .

From three Huallas we've multiplied into many, from three branches we've
become many,
but we are three, three parts.
"Three parts?"
Yes, we're children of three people, their very own grandchildren.
And so, Comadre, that's how it was,
all the people had run off to avoid paying their taxes of thirty-five centavos.
But, exclaiming, "I don't want to pay!" — standing alone, our old grandfather,
that Padro Pari, refused to pay them.
"Let them chop off my head!" he said.
And this: "I'm staying right here!"
He had dogs, *thirty* of them,
and with those dogs he chased off [the tax collectors].
"Whatever the Government does with me," he said, "I won't pay!"
"They can take my head, I'm staying right here!" he said.
He stoned them with his sling.
That grand old man with all those dogs.
And so that's how it was.
That's all I know, Comadre, thank you.

Erasmo's narrative pulls together four themes common in mythic histories: the natural claim of the earth-borne forebear; the practical claim made by cultivating land and grazing flocks; the legal claim substantiated by documents defining a territory's boundaries; and the validation of these claims by distant government authority. The narrative shows us the document coming into existence, the chicken feather imprinting its validation on the mother title and her two offspring. The title passes through the Yuqra woman's daughters to the three Huallas, "who came from somewhere to live as sons-in-law." By implication, that was the beginning of a tripartite Hualla lineage that passed through the generations. Erasmo expresses a vague sense of lineage solidarity but is uninterested in describing the Huallas as a corporate reality.

By the time Erasmo told me his Hualla-centric narrative in 1984, I had heard—several times over—a different version of how the Sonqo *ayllu* came into being. This version has little in common with Erasmo's, except for the number three. I published it in my ethnography of Sonqo,[11] so I only summarize it here. Luis told it to me in order to explain the meaning of *ayllu*.

In a previous age, Sonqo was inhabited by the *machukuna*, a race of giants who lived in moonlight on Antaqaqa Hill. They are said to have had three authorities and to have raised only three kinds of potatoes (for seed, for cooking, and for storing in freeze-dried form as *ch'uño*).

As the Sun rose for the first time, the fierce heat and blinding light drove the *machukuna* underground into caves, and eastward into the jungle. At this moment, the first three ancestors—Puma, Chura, and Yucra—sprang out of Sonqo's soil, each from a distinctive named place. That was the beginning of human society, of Sonqo *ayllu*. The three families multiplied and the *ayllu* flourished—until a terrible plague arrived, and in this Pisti Timpu, Era of the Plague, the *ayllu* was destroyed. This episode probably "telescopes" a long history of recurrent epidemics into one great plague. It was also, Luis added, a time of devastating taxation. Eventually this terrible era came to an end.

> When the Pisti Timpu ended, then again there was another kind of People. And it took that [same] form: THREE Anton Quispes! Ayapata Anton Quispe. Pillikunka Anton Quispe. Pakupuhru Anton Quispe. And so they were like the Old Ones. And that was later yet.

In this vision of history, time unrolls in a repetitive three-fold pattern of ancestors—*machus*, *runa* ancestors, and Anton Quispes—each triad intrinsically connected with Sonqo's territory. Each triad in the two human eras breaks into a group of two against one: the Puma and Chura stand against the Yuqra who left Sonqo for Kuyo Grande.[12] In the triad of Anton Quispes, Ayapata Anton Quispe was not originally named Anton Quispe (nobody remembers what his original name was). He came from the outside (nobody remembers where) as a *qatay* (son-in-law) to marry Juana, sister of Pillikunka Anton Quispe. Thus the Anton Quispes, who reestablish the triadic leadership, are distinguishable from each other only in terms of the neighborhoods, or *ayllus*, where they lived. Quispe is now the most prevalent surname in Sonqo.

| STABILITY Three Machukuna *Ayllu* ★★★ |
| APOCALYPSE First Sunrise |
| STABILITY Three Runa Ancestors *Ayllu* ★★★ |
| APOCALYPSE Plague and Taxes |
| STABILITY Three Anton Quispes *Ayllu* ★★★ |

The populous Huallas are conspicuously absent from Luis's telling. Erasmo Hualla's version is so different because it's told from a *qatay*'s (son-in-law's) perspective. His proud forebears, he tells us, rescued an *ayllu* left desolate, not by plague but by its inhabitants' cowardice in the face of the tax collectors. Only a woman is left—a chthonic Yuqra—whose claims to the land are accepted unquestioningly by the title-giving Spaniard. Pedro Pari occupies the woman and the land, and defends them from the predacious government. In the next generation this victorious couple acquires a trio of sons-in-law, the in-marrying Huallas, who thereby "get hold of lots and lots of land."

What Luis and Erasmo agree upon is the *ayllu*'s tripartite nature. Pedro Pari defends the *ayllu* with thirty dogs and perpetuates it with three sons-in-law. Even the land title comes in threes. In Luis's account, three *machus* give way to three original *runa* who give way to three Anton Quispes, who bond themselves to the land by absorbing place-names into their own names. Three Huallas establish a similar and rival bond by absorbing women whose earth-born origin gives their *ayllu* unquestionable legitimacy, even (they say!) in Spanish eyes.[13]

Competing factions use the model contextually in different ways according to their own purposes. A message coming through in both Luis's and Erasmo's narratives—different as they are—is that Sonqo's current population is intermediate, neither original nor alien. Its bond with the land comes not from earth-generated ancestors but from more recent forebears who allied themselves with the last remnants of this original group; and who claimed the land as their own by working and defending it.[14]

The *ayllu* is triadic because three is the perfect number—and three is the perfect number because it is balanced and unbalanced at the same time. The triads break down into dyads of *two* against *one*. The *one* is an outsider who receives his identity through women. The triadic *ayllu* is, from this perspective, a male-female dyad—a married couple. And married couples are dynamic, *yanantin*; they reproduce themselves (unlike a balanced pair—*masintin*, comrades of the same kind—that reinforces itself but does not reproduce). This is powerfully and wordlessly expressed by the triad of drinking vessels—two vertical *qeros* and a low horizontal *puchuela*.

The tripartite, two-against-one pattern surfaces again in an origin myth from Qaqachaka, an Aymara-speaking herding community in

> ## THE LOOM
> is a tangible expression of how
> *Two* and *Three* contain each other.
>
> *Weaving*
> needs two sets of yarns,
> the warp and the weft.
>
> Yet for each pass of the (*one*) weft,
> the warp yarns divide into *two* sheds
> that open and close
> —"eating"—
> as the weft passes through them.
>
> Every weaver feels this two-against-one play in her body and fingers as she weaves, and every child, bundled on its mother's back or hanging at her side as she works, absorbs this experience.
>
>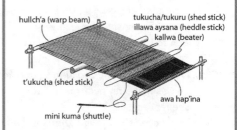
>
> hullch'a (warp beam)
> tukucha/tukuru (shed stick)
> illawa aysana (heddle stick)
> kallwa (beater)
> t'ukucha (shed stick)
> awa hap'ina
> mini kuma (shuttle)

Bolivia.[15] As recounted to Denise Arnold and Juan de Dios Yapita by Bernaldita Quispe, Qaqachaka's ancestresses were two gigantic women, sisters named Inka Mariya and Juana Doña Ana. Originally they went naked. Then the male sun rose into the sky for the first time, clothing the ancestresses in blood-red dawn. As the sun rose higher, the two ancestresses and their fellow mountains (for they were mountains) beat on drums and danced together in a circle. In this way, they defined the *ayllu*'s boundaries, finally settling into place as the mountains that ring Qaqachaka today. The blood-red light gave rise to dye of all the different colors; from that time on, Inka Mariya and Juana Doña Ana learned to weave.[16] Without Father Sun, there were no colors and no weaving. Red in Qaqachaka is the female color, while white is the color for males. In marriage, they say, the "red and the white paths meet," just as they do in Qaqachakan weaving with its predominately red-and-white color scheme.[17]

Ayllu as an entity, and as a process in time, is symbolized by the interplay of dyads and triads—but what does this have to do with those three baby foxes born from a human mother, and with Erasmo's story that we left hanging quite a while back?

Why *three* baby foxes?

To emphasize the *wrongness* of their very existence.

Hinaspas, papanqa nin: "Imaynapitaq khaynatari"
    "Well, how on earth did this happen?" says the father
—chay qusanqa nin, chay p'asñakunaq papanqa
    —says her husband, the girls' (step)father—
"Imaynapitaq khayna atuq uñachatari wachakunki?" nispa.
    "How can you possibly have given birth to baby foxes!"
"Chay, chay kunkan aycha tarikamusqan takasqay wiqsayman pasayun, anchaymi.
    "It was that stray neck meat that entered my body when I pounded it,"
    she replied.
Chaychá chhayna riki unquq rikhurkani," nispas nin.
    "I must have gotten pregnant from it," she says.

"Chayqa atuqpa pichikunyá karan chay!" nispa nin.
> "It must've been a fox's penis!" she says.

Chaysi,
> So then

yásta chay atuqchakunaqa riki
> from the first those little foxes

aycha-a-ata waputa munan. Chaysi,
> are cra-a-azy for meat. And so

ubihatachá ñak'akunku, imanankuchá-á!
> whatever [the family] slaughters—a sheep or whatever—

chaytapas totaltas, karahu! manañas dihanñachu, chay p'asñakuna
> [the foxes] devour totally; not a bit remains for the girls,

iskay p'asñakuna intinadan p'asñakunata
> those two stepdaughters,

wasipi saqeyuqtinku.
> when they leave meat in the house.

AychaLLAAman tirayshan!
> [The foxes] just go after MEAT like crazy!

For a human woman to bear three offspring at once is excessive and animallike. The fox cubs, too, are excessive in their appetites. All they do is consume. What this does is to emphasize how wrong everything is going. I've finally arrived by a circuitous route to this simple point, one that a native listener would recognize intuitively. Three is the ideal social number, yet the three fox cubs can't be socialized. Those intolerable cubs don't belong inside the household, but there they are, eating it up from within.

CHAPTER SIX

"CHAYRÍ?"

"AND THEN?"

Renegaypis chay p'asñakunaqa, karahu,
> In their fury, damn it, the girls
atuq uñata sipirqarinku, karahu!
> murder the baby foxes, damn it!
P'unchay saqiyusqa,
> If they leave meat at home during the day,
manañataq dihanñachu riki aychaman riy;
> there's nothing left over, (the foxes) get it;
aycha ñak'akusqanta tukurapullantaq, tukurapullantaq.
> whatever the family slaughters, (the foxes) just finish right off, finish right off.
Maqanachipun imañayá—
> This sets the family fighting like anything—
warmiqharita, p'asñakunatapas yastá k'amichipun riki.
> the couple beating up on each other, the girls trading insults.
Mana aguantaspas, karahu, SIPIrun kinsantinta, iy!
> The girls just can't stand it, damn it, so they KILL OFF all three,
atuq uñachakunata,
> the little baby foxes,
mamanpa wawanta.
> their mother's children.
Hinaspas, iy "Imanawasuntaq kunanqa taytanchisri, mamanchisri?
> Well then! "Whatever will our parents do to us now?
Hakuyá ripusunchis maymanpas chinkapusun kunan unchay aswan;
> Let's get out of here, we have to disappear right away,"

qoqawunchista ruwarukusun," nispas p'asñakunaqa rimanaykuspa.
    the girls say to each other, "as soon as we prepare some food to take."
Pasapunku, iy!
    And they really do leave
wayk'ukuspanku, ari.
    once they've finished cooking.

Suddenly, a crossroads in Erasmo's *karu kwintu.* Up to this point we've been listening to a familiar off-color fox story, but this new ending changes everything. Erasmo's substitution of a vulnerable girl for the funny old lady comes as a surprise and opens up a new domain of possibilities. With this episode he creates a central juncture, drawing the two stories together so that each draws out the other's hidden potential.[1]

In other words, this narrative move is interpretive. In a characteristically "Andean" way, Erasmo interprets a story with yet another story. His new episode offers an implicit commentary on "The Fox and the Woman," affecting our perception of what comes before and after—much as Inucha's choice of a new color affects our perception of the colors that precede and follow it. Consider the five versions of "Fox and Woman."[2] In the three "stand-alone" versions, the severed penis fails (as it were) in its quest for fulfilment. In the Q'ero, Coaza, and Ambaná versions, the "found-penis" episode dangles as a comical coda at the tale's end:[3]

Stand-alone versions of "The Fox and the Woman"

Ending as dangling coda:
• **Coaza, Puno**: The woman surreptitiously throws the penis away, and Fox is left to bewail his lost "candle."
• **Q'ero** and **Ambaná** (Aymara): An old lady finds the penis, mistakes it for food (neck meat or an oca) and takes it home. Eventually she recognizes it (*"Hey! But this is a penis!"*) and throws it away. As the story ends, Fox is frantically searching for his lost member.

Ending as interpretive frame:
• **Arequipa**: In Don Alejo's version, the husband actually ends up siding with the fox. He tears the "oca" from his wife's vagina and throws it back to Fox before beating his wife to death. Fox glues it back on with his own saliva and takes off for parts unknown. The narrative turns into a just-so story explaining the estrangement of Fox from human domesticity. *"Never again was he a dog for humankind."* This last statement is interpretive and transforms our understanding of the tale.

That leaves us with Agustín Thupa Pacco's version (Usi).[4] Like Erasmo, Agustín offers a *karu kwintu* fashioned from two well-known folktales. Erasmo and Agustín begin in the same way and don't diverge until the critical juncture when the penis is found. While Erasmo pairs up "The Fox and the Woman" story with "The Condenado Household," Agustín aims to pair it up with "The Fox in Heaven." This is how Agustín joins up the two narratives (my translation of his Quechua):

> So (the old lady) took (the "oca") home to cook it. When she put it on the mortar to smash it, it flew between her thighs.
>
> "What a swinish oca!" she exclaimed and threw it away.
>
> Later Fox found (his penis). So he picked it up and went off.
>
> Then he went way up to a hilltop and there he kept trying to put it back on. A condor was flying in the sky and as he flew past the hilltop he asked,
>
> "Hey, Lari, what are you doing?"
>
> "My mother sent me out for firewood. I cut off my penis with the hatchet and now I can't get it back on," (answered Fox).
>
> "Bring me a lamb and I'll refasten your penis," said the condor.
> So Fox caught a lamb and gave it to Condor to eat. Then with his excrement Condor refastened Fox's penis.
>
> "And where are you going, Malku?" Fox asked Condor.
> "I'm going to heaven. There's going to be a banquet there, and I'm going to attend," answered Condor.
>
> "Oh, won't you take me with you?" asked Fox.[5]

And Fox is off to gorge himself at the heavenly banquet. Unlike Erasmo, Agustín keeps Fox in the foreground; human beings reappear only at the end when—

> Instead of stretching out a thick blanket, the people set up stones and thorns on the plain. And that's where he landed. That celestial fox exploded and his shit went flying everywhere, winking and blinking in little pieces. And that's why Fox multiplied. That's all.[6]

Agustín keeps our attention on Fox's onanistic, endlessly self-propagating drive. Erasmo—who recorded his story at home with his wife and children gathered 'round—chooses to stay focused on the family. He is exploring the ramifications of domestic discord, and for that his narrative needs a child to find the penis and bring it back inside the home.

The fact that hidden discord can ramify from one household to another is an important concern in Andean communities. Secret violations of moral order have consequences for a whole kin group or community. Erasmo is constructing his narrative to explore these consequences.

> Remember the rich man in *Huarochirí*, whose mysterious malady was caused by his wife's indiscretion.

Actually, he's been working up to this narrative junction by weaving in a second household so quickly and naturally that it feels like the story of a single family; in fact, on my first listening I missed Erasmo's offhand qualification that this was a different household, and I thought the events were befalling the same family—that the same woman who was seduced by Fox eventually gave birth to foxes. The story of the scavenged penis and mother's impregnation with foxes, too, can stand independently as its own story. This is how ten-year-old Cirilo recounted it for me one afternoon, picking out just the one episode of the *karu kwintu* that he could relate to most easily. In other words, what I've been calling "Part I" is already a composite made up of two stand-alone stories.

By implication, the two families are close neighbors who draw their water at the same spring. When the wife in the first household surreptitiously drops the evidence of her indiscretion by their water source, she sets in motion her neighbors' dissolution. For, what comes of leaving that stray penis lying around the neighborhood?—An impossible set of siblings. And an unviable sibling group is social disaster indeed, for ideally brothers and sisters should be the foundation of social life.[7] As little children, they eat and play together, and they sleep snuggled together like puppies. As adults, they share a common inheritance and depend on the labor pool constituted by their spouses, the *qataymasis* (co-brothers-in-law), and *qachunmasis* (co-sisters-in-law). In practice, however, these sibling groups are often fragile. As siblings establish their own families and look ahead to their own children's inheritance, bitter quarrels may erupt, and the ideally indissoluble bonds fray and break. This structural contradiction is a driving force in Erasmo's narrative.[8]

Having foxes for brothers puts the girls in an impossible lifelong bind, for the fox cubs do nothing but consume. The give-and-take of work, advice, and emotional support—in other words, human reciprocity—is beyond their capacity. As the already dysfunctional household collapses in a spiral of abuse, the girls discard their own self-control and sense of duty. They murder their brothers.

This is what propels us into the *condenadu kwintu*.

It's time to take a closer look at this narrative strategy of combining stories within stories. It seems like a natural outgrowth of the old custom of round-robin storytelling. Aymara speakers have a word for this narrative practice: "This process of intertwining distinct themes in a story is *k'anata*, 'braiding.'"[9] There are, moreover, two modes of narrative braiding. The teller may either string together many small tales or join up two relatively long stories as sections within a larger narrative.[10] My acquaintances in Sonqo did not use the term "braiding," preferring the terms *topay* (meet up with) and *tukuy* (turn into, finish up as), to refer to the process of joining stories. Luis narrated Sonqo's mythic history in the first mode, *topay*, as a series of episodes. (I doubt that he would have told it spontaneously this way, as a chronological narrative, but when confronted by me and my tape recorder, this is the strategy he chose.) Erasmo (in Sonqo) and Agustín (in Usi) each used the second strategy, *tukuy*, to join up "The Fox and the Woman" with another familiar tale.

SONQO	
(Cuzco, Peru)	
Erasmo Hualla Gutiérrez	
EPISODE ONE	**EPISODE TWO**
THE FOX AND THE WOMAN	THE CONDENADO HOUSEHOLD

USI	
(Cuzco, Peru)	
Agustín Thupa Pacco	
EPISODE ONE	**EPISODE TWO**
THE FOX AND THE WOMAN	FOX IN HEAVEN
	(as origin of foxes)

Arnold and Yapita recorded a similar two-part story in Qaqachaka (Oruro, Bolivia), narrated in a mixture of Quechua and Aymara by Enrique Espejo Sepera.[11] Like Agustín's story, Enrique's second section tells of Fox at the heavenly banquet. But it's preceded by "Fox and Condor Make a Bet," the same story Don Crisólogo told me back in Chapter Two about Fox and Condor on the glacier. But in this version, Fox doesn't die on the glacier and Condor doesn't eat him. No, Condor carries him—fainting and complaining—up to heaven. And then we're into the "Fox in Heaven" story, ending as the parrots bite through Fox's rope and—splat!—down he goes with a belly full of seeds. This, comments Don Enrique, is the origin of domesticated plants. Fox droppings, he adds, prognosticate the coming year.

QAQACHAKA
(Oruro, Bolivia)
Enrique Espejo Sepera

EPISODE ONE	**EPISODE TWO**
FOX & CONDOR	FOX IN HEAVEN
COMPETE IN THE COLD	as ORIGIN OF FOOD CROPS

It's not hard to find examples of other composite stories. There's Angel González's composite story from the Colca Valley, recorded by Escalante and Valderrama, which we encountered back in Chapter Two.[12] Here is my summary:

To recapitulate, it begins in Hanaq Pacha (Upper World; Heaven) where Fox is God's spoiled little son. Left alone, he overboils the quinoa one day, and gets scorched by the sun on the next.

The narrative moves on:

God evicts Fox and his brothers from Hanaq Pacha. They descend by a rope to Kay Pacha (This World) in rank order from youngest/lowest (i.e., Fox) to eldest/highest (Condor). Bratty little Fox can't help but insult his brother Parrot, who follows him down the rope. So Parrot bites through the rope and sends him splattering to the ground. From the pieces grow more foxes and hairy cacti.

This would seem to be the end, but Don Angel continues with another episode that switches the focus from Fox to Alqamari (a kind of Falcon):

Once they've descended to Kay Pacha, Condor, Puma, Alqamari, and Fox (yes, he's back!) present themselves to four sisters for marriage.[13] Puma gets chosen first; the next sister picks handsome Alqamari because he's dressed in lovely blue clothes and has little white feet. But she comes to regret her choice because the other three husbands (even Fox!) provide good meat for their wives while the Alqamari brings only lizards, animal guts, and worms.

Don Angel backtracks to explain:

Alqamari was always a lazy good-for-nothing, even in heaven. He clamored to be served first at the table, and when God replied, "No, son, one must always serve from elder to younger," the Alqamari smashed his plate in a tantrum. Then God threw him from the table, saying, "Eat what you like. There will be days you have to eat human excrement!"

Don Angel seems to be braiding together several small tales, unifying them within a story of *taytacha* (God the Father) and his animal sons in heaven. The episode of Parrot biting through the rope functions as a link between Fox's amusing antics in heaven and the four brothers' marriages on earth.

Fox, God's Favorite Son
Fox overboils the quinoa
+
Fox is scorched by the Sun
(origin of Fox's scruffy appearance and shy manner)

+

Fox Falls from Heaven
As Fox, Parrot, Alqamari, Puma, and Condor descend by rope from heaven
(origin of foxes and hairy cactus)

+

The Marriages of Condor, Puma, Alqamari, and Fox
Alqamari is handsomest, but his wife gets the worst food
+
(why Alqamari eats disgusting food)

Behind the image of Fox descending from the banquet with a full belly is the shadow of Fox-the-youngest-brother descending first down the rope followed by Parrot. Parrot surfaces in the "Heavenly Banquet" story, not out of the blue, but out of the parallel story.

Once we've heard this story, we can't listen to "Star-wife" without hearing echoes of Fox, for the second half of "Star-wife" parallels "The Fox in Heaven."

CALCA	USI
(Cuzco, Peru)	(Cuzco, Peru)
Carmen Taripha	Agustín Thupa Pacco
Star-wife	**Star-wife**
Includes	Includes
Husband as Celestial Fox	Husband as Celestial Fox
(origin of quinoa)	(is scorched by the Sun)

And let us not overlook the most widespread composite story: "Ukuku-manta," "About Bear," which we met a few chapters back. This narrative divides naturally into two parts, the story about the bear and the shepherdess and the story about their half-bear/half-human offspring. The second half itself consists of several parallel episodes (to which we'll return in the next chapter).

A curious twist on the "Ukuku" story comes from Don Florencio Flores in Coaza, Puno (recorded by Alain Délétroz Favre).[14] Here's a summary:

> A priest becomes enamored of a pretty young witch. He follows her to hell and watches as she braves Satan's disgusting flatulence to win a prize of silver and gold. He tries to follow suit, but Satan lets go with an incredible fart that overpowers the greedy priest and leaves him engulfed in a malodorous haze. Desperate, he sees light through a small aperture and squeezes through it only to find himself in a cave inhabited by a female bear.

And here begins a variant of the old "Ukuku" story, curiously inverted:

> The she-bear keeps the priest prisoner in the cave, all the while providing him with plenty of meat and other food. She herself consumes immense amounts of beef, and after a while she gives birth to a son. As in the

familiar "Ukuku" story, the son frees his captive parent (in this case the priest) and kills the bear when she pursues them. Once home, the priest finds himself totally incapable of managing his half-bear son — and the story continues with their struggle for mastery.

Analysis à-la-Lévi-Strauss would treat these as transformations of each other, but I prefer to explore how the stories draw out different aspects of each other, and how a skillful teller finds creative ways of moving from one to another, of twisting together old themes in new ways so that the paired stories complete and complement each other as a married couple does. Paired stories aren't transformations of each other, but rather are transformers of each other.

And so, back to Erasmo as he moves ahead to unpack that hidden baggage, to draw out elements of pain and horror hidden in the bawdy comedy of "The Fox and the Woman":

Maytachá seqayunku riki?
> (The girls) set off—for who knows where?

"Ripusun, amaña kasunñachu," nispa.
> "Let's leave, we can't stay here anymore," they say.

Huqñintas maranpataman thallarachinku,
> It seems they spread out one corpse on the grinding stone,

huqñintataqsi punkupataman,
> another on the door step,

huqñintataqsi chawpi panpaman;
> and another in the middle of the patio;

qati usullamanta atuq uñata wachurparinku wañusqata.
> they leave the baby fox corpses scattered one after the other.

Wasita wisq'arunku
> [Then] they lock up the house

tira pasapunku.
> and hurry away.

Chaysi, tardin chayapunanpaqqa,
> And so, when their parents come home that afternoon,

taytamamanpa chayananpaq, atuq uñakunalla wañu wañu!
> there are the baby foxes all dead!

Aychataq yásta sarwirusqa.
> And the meat all torn up.

P'asñakunataqsi tiira pasakapun, maytachá.
> And the girls gone off somewhere in a te-e-earing hurry.

Chinkapun,
> They disappear.

Chinkapun riki.
> Really, they disappear.

CHAPTER SEVEN

AT THE BASE OF A BOULDER

Hinaspas,
    Well then,
maypiñachá tutayanku riki,
    when night falls, [the girls are] someplace far away,
karutachá p'unchayqa purinku ch'isiyaqqa riki.
    for they've been traveling all day until evening.
Chaysi, tutayakunku yastá.
    So there it is, nighttime.
Hinaspas, tutayakuqtinkuqa,
    They're caught, then, by nightfall,
mana mayman haykuyta atinkuchu, karahu, ch'in lomapi.
    and, damn it, they've no place to go in that vast empty plain.
Hinaspas, qaqa sikipi puñunku.
    So, they go to sleep at the base of a boulder.

The base of a boulder is a tricky place to sleep, especially in the high no-man's-land they call *loma* (or *puna*). The *loma* is where things happen that don't belong in normal human society. It's a place of adolescent sexual experimentation. (*"We would never do that in the village!"*) More than sexual reserve breaks down there. *Loma* is the frontier of normal experience. In the *loma* one may encounter saints or, more likely, souls of the damned. One might even hear the animals talk to each other. The poor homeless man in the *Huarochirí Manuscript* was asleep on a mountainside when he overheard the Fox-from-Above and the Fox-from-Below conversing about the rich man's illness. This mythic episode still turns up in contemporary stories.

Don Pacco Santos Ccama of Usi tells us (via César Itier) of a mail carrier who fell asleep *qaqa sikillapi*—right at the base of a boulder. Here is my summary.

> A mail carrier was overtaken by nightfall and fell asleep at the base of a boulder. And there he heard a skunk talking with a small falcon.[1] The animals are speaking of a wealthy man who is deathly ill. No one, it seems, can cure him. But the animals know the cause—a swollen serpent is lurking in the man's pillow. As the serpent swells up, so the sick man swells up, and when finally it bursts through the pillow, the man will die.
>
> The mail carrier sets off right away for the sick man and pretends to divine his illness from coca leaves. Then he kills the snake and the sick man recovers. The mail carrier goes home laden with gifts and respected as a great man.

Don Valeriano Puma of Coaza tells (via Alain Délétroz Favre) of a *kuraka* (wealthy authority) who fell strangely ill (the indented portions are my translation of the Quechua; the rest is summary):

> . . . He's getting weak and yet weaker; day after day after day he's fading away to skin and bone. There's nothing to be done.[2]
>
> But here comes our mail carrier again, overtaken by nightfall in the *puna*. It begins to snow and he seeks refuge in a cave (*qaqawasi*: house of the rock). As he sits there at night chewing coca leaves, he overhears a fox talking with a skunk about the *kuraka*'s illness.
>
> > "And you, Tía, you know what to do," said the fox to the skunk—for the fox called the skunk "Tía": "You, Tía, you know what to do; you should extract the illness [from the *kuraka*]."[3]
> >
> > "I'd like to but I can't," replies the skunk.
>
> She explains that the *kuraka*'s former lover has put three toads in his bedstead:
>
> > Those toads are devouring a heart, a replica of the *kuraka*'s heart, devouring it in his name.[4]
>
> What's more, the lover has put a snake in the rafters as well. Skunk explains that the snake could be lured into a pot of milk. She goes on to tell how to dispose of the toads and heart as well. Both animals then set off for the *kuraka*'s house, the fox to raid the sheep pen and the skunk to kick up dirt behind the house and then go to sleep.

"They say that when we are *layqasqa* (cursed by a sorcerer), the skunk kicks up the dirt behind our house," explains Don Valeriano.

Well, you can guess the rest: The mail carrier follows the fox and skunk to the *kuraka*'s house, pretends to divine from coca leaves, and cures the sick gentleman. The grateful *kuraka* gives the mail carrier half his land, horses, and fine clothes.

Luis Gutiérrez of Sonqo told me a short version of the same story. This time it's a foolish lad (*sonsu*) who goes to sleep in the *loma*.

In his sleep, he overhears condors convening for a banquet. They wait courteously for their chief to come before starting their meal.

"Condors really do that. They even take turns. I've seen them," Luis commented when I visited again and played back the tape.

Once the chief condor arrives, the birds begin to gossip: A wealthy man is ill; no one can cure him because they don't know that there's a toad under his hearth and a snake in the thatch. Of course, the foolish lad goes right off and performs the cure. And thereafter he's rich and respected — silly fool though he may be.

Finally, a most curious variant of this tale comes from Tiburcio Lobón of Coaza.[5]

A desperately poor man leaves his family to look for work. Unsuccessful, he lies down to die on the crest of a hill. Condors gather around him; as they wait for him to die, they gossip about a king's daughter who has fallen so deathly ill no one can cure her. But of course the condors know the cause: "She's sighing for the lack of a man." She'd be cured if only a man would go to bed with her and have sex repeatedly for a week, they say.

After a while, the condors get tired of waiting for the man to die, and they fly away. Well, off goes the man to the king. He puts on a big act, claiming to be a diviner, and manages to get left alone with the princess for a week to perform the cure.

He sleeps with her the whole time — it's a real banquet![6]

Then off he goes, home to his wife and kids, loaded with gifts.

But meanwhile his wife has given up on him and taken a new husband. She doesn't even know him until he plays a guitar behind the house and one of the children recognizes his voice. Then, joyfully reunited, they

> murder the other husband and settle down to live happily ever after, as it
> were.
>   "Sometimes God's just looking out for us, y'know," comments Don
> Tiburcio.[7]

Yes, the *loma* can be a miraculous place. Understanding the speech of animals is only one of the extraordinary things that happens there. It's said that the Christ Child appeared to a little llama herder in the high *loma* near the snow fields above Ocongate. The Christ Child gave the herder marvelous white clothing, and the two boys played together until a delegation from Ocongate came to investigate. Then Christ Child disappeared into a huge boulder, leaving it imprinted with his likeness. This miracle is said to be the basis for the Qoyllur Rit'i pilgrimage, which today draws tens of thousands of pilgrims to the chapel built around the miraculous boulder at the foot of the glacier of Qolqepunku.[8]

In *kwintus*, the *loma* has these same otherworldly qualities. Star-woman appears in the high potato fields or by a mountain lake. In Erasmo's version of the story, one of the deserted children sorrowfully goes and sits weeping on a boulder until he turns into a bird.

Extraordinary experience in the *loma* may prove terrifying and even fatal, for things may not be what they seem. Jorge Lira recorded an account in Calca of yet another traveler in the *loma* who seeks shelter for the night at the base of a boulder:

> Lo and behold, he suddenly sees a little hut with a man inside cooking his dinner. This man invites the traveler to spend the night, and the two of them eat and go to sleep. But during the night, the traveler is awakened by agonized screams. His host is suffering terrible pains. The frightened guest tries to help to no avail.
>   It seems the host was a deer. He said to his guest, "What can I tell you, sir, the flag's flap-flapping, the snare drum's rat-a-tat-tatting, the flute's toot-tooting; they're chasing me, they're surrounding me! Ay! Ay!" he said. "It seems, sir, I can't possibly escape!"[9]
> Finally, the traveler sleeps again, and in the morning he awakens to find the hut gone and himself lying at the base of the boulder. As he continues his journey, he notices something next to the road—a simple deer, dead, with an aborted fetus.
>   The previous day a band of Carnival merrymakers had gone out hunting deer and had chased this one, a pregnant doe, until she aborted and died.

"Ah, it seems it was a deer (*Tarukamá kasqa*)," said the man, and went on his way carrying his mail bag. Deer were originally human beings. That's why it's bad to hunt them. They say that God turned a jealous man into a deer as punishment. From that (deer), the deer have descended (multiplied).[10]

There's a similar but less traumatic story from Usi about a wandering orphan girl who seeks shelter in a lonely house where she finds a nice old lady cooking dinner.[11]

The old lady greets her kindly, feeds her dinner, and urges her to stay and meet her son.

Uh-oh! This sets off our warning bells. But surprise! It's going to be okay.

As soon as the young man arrives, the old lady cries, "*Kuwis kuwis kuwis*" and disappears under the bed. It seems she was a *qowi* (guinea pig) in disguise—and the young householder, like the girl, is actually a mother-less orphan. Brought together by the benign old *qowi*, they settle down happily to live as man-and-wife.[12]

But not everybody escapes so easily or even at all. Basilia warned me that nighttime travelers may encounter a "*saqra tinda*" (demon store)—where else but at the base of a boulder? Suddenly the boulder opens to reveal a se-ductive store, well stocked, brightly lit, and full of music and laughter. He who yields to its allure will eventually find himself back on the dark road, deathly ill.[13] And of course there's the *condenado wasi*—house of damned souls—but that will have to wait for the next chapter.

All this explains why Quechua listeners will prick up their ears at the phrase "*qaqa sikipi*." Yet why should the base of a boulder be a place of danger, miracle, and transformation? Boulders are all over the place in the high Andes, and it's not as though people can avoid them, or would even want to. Boulders provide refuge in bad weather—shelter from wind, shade from merciless sun, sometimes even cover from pouring rain. Boul-ders are landmarks; a singular rock is as good as a street address when one is far from roads and mailboxes. Yet mail carriers and other travelers need to keep their wits about them if they seek a boulder's shelter while cross-ing the treeless *loma*.

Why? To appreciate how this motif presages transformation — to enter into the listening of the stories — is going to require *an excursion into Andean modes of thought about time and consciousness.* You may have to suspend some cherished categories of thought, like the distinction between animate and inanimate objects.

Boulders — not just boulders, but all landscape features — stand midway between the *kwintu* dimension and this world of normal, that is, clear, present, and "true" experience. The *kwintu/chiqaq* distinction I introduced in Chapter Two differentiates states of consciousness. Let me explain: In my original project of asking people to record *kwintus*, I discovered early on that not all narratives qualified as *kwintus*. When I asked Erasmo to tell me a *kwintu* about the origin of nearby lake Qesqay Qocha, he hesitated and turned nervously to his wife. In their whispered conversation, I overheard Cipriana cautioning, "*Manan munankumanchu*" ("They wouldn't like it"). Turning back to me, Erasmo said that what I asked for was not a *kwintu*. He was willing to talk about the lake and how it came to be — but not for the tape recorder. The little black machine was for *kwintus* only.

A few days later Luis told me — again unrecorded — about a lake near Sicuani where an old man was pulled out of his boat into a beautiful submerged city. At the end of the day, he emerged from the lake and died. Luis commented that although this seemed "like a *kwintu*" ("*kwintu hina*"), it was not. On the contrary, it was *chiqaq*, true.

As time passed, Erasmo grew more relaxed about talking for the tape recorder. Shortly before I left Sonqo in 1976 he recorded what he called a *kwintu* about how a wandering *runa* — dressed purely in traditional *runa* clothing — met an Inca who showed him the secret city of Paititi from a hilltop and gave him golden corn. Later I played this tape for Luis, who was enraged. That wasn't a *kwintu*! It was "*chiqaq*" he said, and "*timpunchismanta*" ("from our *timpu*" [world-age]). In fact, he insisted, it had happened less than twenty years earlier.

This piqued my interest in the *kwintu/chiqaq* distinction, and I started a little experiment in which I played back tapes and asked listeners to tell me which ones were *kwintus*. I felt rather pedantic, but my friends took to it enthusiastically. Whether or not the distinction was salient before I arrived with my tape recorder, it was obviously something many of them found relevant and interesting. Sometimes they discussed the problem among themselves. Luis and his family began to preface or end new recordings by announcing whether the narration was a *kwintu*. These conversations revealed an overriding concern with how narrative events are located in time. *Kwintus* tell of events that pertain to another *timpu*; these things *could* happen or *did* happen in a different *timpu*, but not in our own.

I also learned that whether a narrative is *kwintu* or *chiqaq* depends on the context and situation of its telling. Erasmo pushed this realization on me in 1978 and again in 1984 when—rather to my dismay—he reversed his stance on the Lake Qesqay narrative and talked about it for the tape recorder. Not only that, he introduced the recording with, "*Kunan kwintuta willasayki*" (I'm going to tell you a story now).

"I thought you said that wasn't a *kwintu!*" I protested, feeling my nice classification of genres slipping out from under me.

Unfazed, Erasmo explained that he'd been afraid to talk about Sacred Places on tape while I was still new to Sonqo. Since it was now clear that the Places had accepted me and my recording activities, Qesqay wouldn't mind being discussed on tape. In other words, his reversal reflects not a change in his own belief, but a changed perception of *my* relationship with the local Places.

Here is a summary of the Lake Qesqay origin story as I heard it from Erasmo and several other people, including Luis and Basilia. It crops up all over the Andes, even as early as the *Huarochirí Manscript*.[14]

Qesqay, a lake in the high barren plains above Sonqo, was once a city, and that city would have been Cuzco if only it hadn't gotten swallowed up in a great flood after a *misti* marriage feast. Why? "*Qanqalla*" (It just did), answered Luis. Erasmo and Basilia were more expansive: the stingy celebrants had turned away a ragged beggar from the marriage feast. Of the whole city, only one woman invited him to rest and eat. As luck would have it, that begger was Diosninchis (God) in disguise.

(I backed up this recording at least twice, yet for some reason it was never transcribed and all the copies have gotten lost. Perhaps Qesqay didn't like it after all).

Furious, God sent away this one generous woman, warning her not to look back. But she did look back, for she had to stop to urinate and she turned her gaze backward as she did so. At that very moment, that city was flooded with water. The woman became Sipas Qaqa (Girl Rock), a huge boulder with a meandering stream of water running from its base. The marriage party

> also turned to stone, and the fleeing priest was petrified in his tracks, becoming that Pari Qaqa (Priest Rock) that Ana pointed out to Pedro and me as our truck lumbered up the road from Colquepata.
>
> During the dark of the moon, it's possible to hear the submerged church bell ringing: "*Kunan timpu kunanpiña uyarisqanku*" (In time present, right in the present it's said to have been heard), added Luis. And Don Inocencio Quispe, a traditional and self-righteous man, is said to have seen the church spires in the depths.
>
> If only that woman hadn't urinated, mourned Basilia, Sonqo would have been right on the outskirts of Cuzco instead of the rural backwater it is today.

"This must be a *kwintu*," commented Erasmo,

"because who knows in what *timpu* all that happened? Certainly not ours."

And yet, he added thoughtfully, it must be *chiqaq* because the lake and rocks are really there, *sut'ipin*. They clearly exist:

" . . . you can go up and see them. And some people really have heard the bell ringing."

It must be a *chiqaq kwintu*, he decided.

Who knows in what *timpu* all that happened? Time moves in fits and starts, a sort of indigenous catastrophism. "History" is a series of more or less static worlds, each of which is destroyed to make way for the next one. A world is called *pacha*; or, in some contexts, *timpu* (from Spanish *tiempo*).[15] *Pacha* has spatial and temporal aspects. The word refers to the earth in its materiality; and it refers to a moment in time. The cataclysmic event that ends one world and begins the next—like the first sunrise that burned up the *machukuna*—is called a *pachakuti*, or world-turn. While successive worlds differ from each other qualitatively, they parallel each other in terms of structure. For example, *machukuna* lived in the cold moonlight while *runakuna* (human beings) live in warm daylight. Nevertheless, the two worlds parallel each other, for *machukuna* had a society like that of *runakuna*.

To say the anterior worlds are "destroyed" doesn't mean that they no longer exist; it means that they influence our world by indirect means. They continue to exist, but not "in clarity" (*sut'ipi*). Thus the *machukuna*,

Sipas Qaqa, the girl who was transformed into a boulder when she turned aside to urinate. A resting farmer (not in the photo) has left a *chakitaqlla* (footplow) standing upright in wet, fertile soil below her. Photo by the author.

those dried-up remnants of an anterior age, come to life on moonlit nights and work their potato fields. Their fields *"are just where ours are,"* yet they aren't the same fields because they exist in different *timpus*. The *machu-kuna's* moonlit labors make our potatoes grow nice and big, like fertilizer working from below. But when they visit us in wind or dreams, the *machu-kuna* bring illness and birth defects.

Similarly, the twelve Inca authorities who fled from Pizarro over the paths of Sonqo are no longer of this world, yet they still exist. They are *past-as-potential future,* dwelling inside the depths of the forest, waiting for their time to come around again. The boulders, springs, and footpaths they left behind testify to their abiding, if hidden, presence.

Are accounts of the Incas *kwintu* or *chiqaq*?[16] *Chiqaq*, said Apolinar, because the events happened in our *timpu, "in our sun."* Alcides disagreed. It must have been a different *timpu*, he commented, because Incas could do remarkable things, like herding stones into walls.

They agreed that the Incas' *return* will be a *pachakuti*—then there will be lightning, wind, and earthquakes. Amarus will come roaring out of An-taqaqa Hill and all the mestizos will be chased away. The Incas will return, and they will recognize as *runakuna* only those people wearing traditional clothing woven only of llama and alpaca wool. Similarly, they will reject anyone who speaks or reads Spanish.

None of the men in Sonqo and fewer and fewer of the women would meet the Incas' stringent criteria. The messianic ideology stipulates that they remain loyal to their heritage by marginalizing themselves to the na-tional society. As they experiment with cash crops, send their children to school, and acquire television sets, the old ideology no longer holds much relevance to Sonqueños' lives. Their uncertainty about how to classify the Incas—*kwintu* or *chiqaq?*—expresses their ambivalence about maintain-ing social and moral continuity with the Inca past.

This explains why Luis got so upset when he learned that Erasmo had recorded the anecdote about the gold-bearing Inca from Paititi—not only recorded it but called it a *kwintu*! It turned out that the two men had been together when they heard the anecdote from a fellow traveler on the path to Paucartambo. Each evaluated it differently. Luis was deeply affected and obviously had an emotional investment in accepting the true and contem-porary nature of this extraordinary meeting. Erasmo, on the other hand, was fascinated but skeptical.

Contrary to what we might expect, Erasmo was the more traditional of the two, deeply invested in his identity as a *qawaq* (diviner) and curer. He seldom visited Cuzco and usually traveled on foot. His eldest son married young and lives in Sonqo. Luis, on the other hand, was both attracted to and repulsed by the mestizo world of commerce, and took pride in his sons who moved to Cuzco. Nevertheless, he yearned for the Incas' return and worried that he was "ruined" (*malugradu*) for the *pachakuti*. In effect, his shaky cultural faith needed to be reaffirmed by miracles; he needed Incas to emerge into the clarity of his own time and place.

While Erasmo could afford to feel skeptical about anecdotes heard secondhand on the road, he exhibited no such casualness concerning the Sacred Places in his immediate vicinity. Only when he and Cipriana felt reassured about my relationship with the lake and the rocks (the *chiqaq* aspect) were they comfortable treating the deluge story as a *kwintu*.

I've been translating *chiqaq* as "true," but perhaps "straight" would be a closer approximation. A *kwintu* is not untrue; rather, it's not straight ahead of us. It draws on dimensions of experience different from that of human beings. *Kwintus* are displaced to one side, as it were; they exist in the periphery of our vision. Thus Basilia ends the "Star-wife" story—a *kwintu*, no question about that!—with a brief disquisition on the heavens:

> And when Venus comes out bright in the evening or the morning, a mother with her child, a young woman with her child, then there's really hard frost, y'know. "Frost!" they're saying (when) she comes out splendid in the evening. "There's the star-girl!" they say, watching her.
> And that's all I know. [laughing]
> I've never been in the star-time (Ch'askaq Timpunpi).

Fox-time
Atuq Timpunpi:
"Let me tell you about my walk in the loma. I found Young Pascual (Fox). I was out there in the fox-time."
(Alcides Mamani)

Her comments show how inadequate is "time" as a translation for *timpu*. The Ch'askaq Timpu is equally present with Timpunchis (Our Time). Star-woman can be located; we can even see her, and the clearer she is, the more she affects us in the form of frost. Ch'askaq Timpu exists far away and beyond what Basilia can claim to understand, but it is neither of the past nor the future.

In the *kwintu,* these parallel dimensions are safely separated from our own and don't intrude on us. The potential for intrusion is there, nevertheless; alien dimensions can and sometimes *do* intrude: when frost forms at night, when the ancient dead seduce solitary sleepers in erotic dreams, when travelers encounter *kukuchis,* even when a fox gets into the corral. And this brings us back to the girls, asleep at the base of a boulder.

Hinaspa, chaymantaqa,
> And after that,

qaqa sikipi puñushaqtinku "puñusun" nishaqtinku,
> As they're settling down to sleep at the base of that boulder,

alqu kanikamusqa,
> a dog suddenly barked,

waka waqaramusqa,
> a cow mooed,

nina k'ancharimusqa.
> and a light shone out.

Chaysi: "Haqaypi tiyaq kasqataq, qhaway, qhaway" nispa TIRAYUnku iy?
> And so, "Look, look!" they cry! "Somebody seems to be living over there!" and OFF the girls run,

p'asñakunaqa. "Chaypi puñukamusun, haku" nispa,
> saying "Let's go, we can sleep there!"

"Alohawasunyá riki" nispa
> saying, "Surely they'll take us in!"

tirayunku phawaylla.
> They rush off.

CHAPTER EIGHT

HOUSE OF DAMNED SOULS

Hinaspa, tirayuspanku, karahu, chayarunku chay wasiman: "Mamay,
hanpusqayki!" nispa ninku.
>So off they rush, *karahu*, and arrive at the house: "Mother, we've come
>to you!" they call politely.

Chaysi, "Pasaykuy, pin chay?" nispas mamakuchaqa nin,
>Then, "Come in, who's there?" answers a little old lady,

tarpan!
>and meets them in the door!

Hinaspas, tarpaspa, pusaykun
>Then, having met them, she shows those girls in,

p'asñakunataqa sumaqta, iy!
>oh so nicely!

Chaysi, pusayuspa, karahu,
>And after showing them into the house,

senayta inbitan, waputa mihuchin aycha sapata!
>she invites them to dinner, feeds them grandly with many kinds of meat—

Uha, llama, waka. Hinas, chayqa, paqucha kashasqa kanchakunapi.
>lamb, llama, beef. And her corrals are full of alpacas.

"Yaw, allin uywayuqmá kay mamaku kasqa. Kaypi tiyakusunchis, karahu,
uywanta michiysisun," nispa p'asñakunaqa
>"Wow, this old lady's rich in animals. Let's stay here, *karahu*, and herd
>for her," whisper the girls to each other

—kuntentu!—
>—contented!—

haykunku wasiman.
>as they enter the house.

The girls are too inexperienced (and greedy) to distrust this ready welcome. Listeners, on the other hand, feel a shudder of dreadful anticipation: The girls are in for something now! But what?

Hinaspas . . . mmmm . . .
  Well . . . hmmm . . .
Chay p'asñakunaqa haykun wasiman.
  Those girls enter the house.
Tiyanku.
  They settle down.
Hinaspas, senarachin, mihurachin.
  Then [the old lady] gives them dinner, feeds them well.

We can't trust this old lady—there are too many gruesome tales about an ogre woman (*saqra warmi*) who greets travelers nicely, feeds them a hearty soup (which all too often turns out to contain bits of human flesh), and puts them to bed only to eat them up during the night.[1] In a version from Cuzco, told to Johnny Payne by Inés Callali, a little boy and girl went out looking for firewood and wandered far into the hills until nightfall caught them. Indented phrases are Payne's English translation.[2]

> They spied a light inside a cave. A cave with a light inside. They called out, "Excuse us, ma'am, excuse us. Can we stay here?"
> Then an old woman, an old crone, came out. "Huh? What do you want, children? What do you want? . . . Come on in. Sit down here," she said.
> The old crone fed the children "potatoes and meat" (which were really stones and toad flesh). She sent the skinny brother to sleep in the corner while she shared her bed with the nice chubby sister. In the morning the boy asked, "Where did my sister go?"
> "Oh, your sister went off to get water." The crone wasn't just a crone. She was a devil-witch (*diabla*). She was a troll-witch (*saqra paya*). And she'd eaten the little girl . . . since she was nice and chubby, the witch ate her. While they were in the bed, the witch ate her all up.
> And she sent the boy off to fetch water in a "gourd" (really his sister's skull). At the river's edge, he met María the Toad:
> "Creak, Creak, Creak, Creak, Creak, Creak. You're carrying water in your sister's skull," she croaked . . . "Don't go back there." That's what María said.
> So the boy ran away in terror, and the crone rushed after him in pursuit.

Finally he outran her and reached his father's house (no mention of a
mother in this story). There he told his father everything. He said:
"Night overtook us. We were looking for wood. We saw wood on a
hillside. We went up the hillside. We saw wood there. But it wasn't
wood. It was horse bones. It was cane reeds. Then it turned to night.
And when it turned to night, we slept in an old crone's house. While
we were sleeping in the old crone's house, that devil-crone, that dwarf
crone ate my little sister. Then she sent me off to fetch water in my
sister's skull. Then María said to me, "You're carrying water in your
sister's skull. Don't go back there. She also wants to eat you."
Horrified, the father told the boy to lead him to the crone's house.
They went to the house of that crone, that witch. There wasn't anything
there. It had turned to nothing. It didn't exist anymore. That witch ate
his sister.

Given this sort of precedent, we can expect at least one of the sisters to
meet her doom in short order. But then again, maybe not. Old ladies in
the *loma*, though seldom what they seem, are not always malevolent. The
crone could turn out to be a benevolent *qowi* (guinea pig), or even a deer in
disguise. Or she might be Old Lady Lake. Gregorio Mamani of Acopía tells
us about a traveler who happens upon a lonely house occupied by a similar
hospitable old lady.[3] She turns out to have three rowdy sons — Wind, Frost,
and Hail — who come roaring into the house at night and leave again. Next
morning, the traveler awakens next to a glacial lake, surprised and cold but
otherwise none the worse for wear. If this is Old Lady Lake, our runaway
girls will probably be okay.

But these benign possibilities are eliminated as soon as the Old Lady
mentions her son — "your brother," as she refers to him:

"Turaykichiswan manachu topamurankichis? Turaykichis hamuran ñak'ana maskhakuq,"
    "Didn't you meet up with your brother? Your brother was out there
    looking for animals to butcher,"
nispas nin mamakuqa.
    says the old lady.
"Manan tupamuykuchu, Mamay,
    "We didn't meet him, ma'am,
mayniqpichá, may lawtachá hamuranpas?" nispas nin.
    not anywhere. Which way did he come?" they answer.

"Chay loma larukunallatan hamuran," nispas nin mamakuqa.
"He came over that side of the high plain," says the old lady.
"Tarikamunqachus manachus ñak'anata," nispas.
"I wonder whether he found anything to butcher," she says.

Did he find *ñak'ana,* she wonders—creatures destined for slaughter?
Ñak'aq is a "butcher," *ñak'ay,* "to butcher" or "to slaughter": a normal and
necessary activity for herding folk, though never a pleasant one. But herders don't just "find" animals; they birth them and nurture them through
their lives—so when the Old Lady says her son is "looking for animals
to butcher," she implies that he's a cattle rustler. This dubious occupation
seems not to trouble the girls at all, and indeed it's not all that rare. The
whiff of horror that rises from the word *ñak'ay* comes not from the idea of
cattle rustling or even animal slaughter, but from the terrifying possibility
that this "brother" might be a slaughterer of human beings—a *ñak'aq.*

The *ñak'aq* (slaughterer; called *pishtaco* in northern Peru and Ecuador,
karisiri in Bolivia) is a preternatural creature of darkness who feeds on human fat.[4] If you travel alone at night, a *ñak'aq* might mesmerize you with
his blazing eyes, put you to sleep, and extract your fat and even your vital
organs. Or, disguised as a regular person, the *ñak'aq* may befriend you,
waiting until you sleep to practice his nefarious calling. Afterward, you'd
awake as though nothing had happened. Only later, as you sicken, fade,
and die, would you understand what must have happened to you.

Hinaspas, ah,
    Then . . . ah . . .
hinallamanqa, senay pasayta hinallaqa,
    it's like this—dinner's all finished,
puñunata mast'arikuspa puñushaqtinku hinaman—
    they've spread out their bed, they're falling asleep, when—

But wait, this can't be a *ñak'aq,* for *ñak'aqs* don't live in high, lonesome
huts. A *ñak'aq* looks like a prosperous mestizo or white person—an en-
gineer, military man, or wealthy show-off with a leather jacket, heavy
boots, a horse, or even a fancy car. *Ñak'aq* is monied, a rich ethnic Other.
In Sonqo, I seldom heard the word *ñak'aq* used without *misti* (mestizo) in
front of it; it was always *"misti ñak'aq."* As I learned most uncomfortably,

every newcomer potentially falls into this *"misti ñak'aq"* category. I well remember a mother pointing out to her children one market day in 1980—*"Misti ñak'aq!"* Today Sonqo is less isolated and less in thrall to the mestizos of the district capital, so the *runa-misti* opposition is less salient for younger Sonqueños than it was for their parents. Times have changed, yet the horror of the *ñak'aq* is still very close to the surface. In 2001, two bicyclists from Cuzco prevailed on Esteban to shelter them for the night. Esteban—who no longer calls himself a *runa*—remembered the old horror stories and stayed awake all night, frightened and watchful.

But this is not a house of monied mestizos. Old Lady and her cattle-rustler son aren't *misti ñak'aqs*. Then what are they?

. . . puñushaqtinku hinaman
    [The girls] are just falling asleep, when—
chayarachimun, iy!
    —hey!—he arrives with his cargo,
punkutas choqaYAmun K'IRRR nishaqta:
    SHOVES the door open with a CRE-E-EAK, exclaiming
"Chayqa ñak'anata chayachimuni, ñak'ay tarimuni, karahu.
    "This is all I could get, I hardly found anything, damn it!
Alqu karahu utiypas, runaraqtaq iskapawan" nispas, iy!
    Settle down, dog, damn it, the human being escaped me!"
Chayqa kundenaduyá kasqa chay!
    You see, he was a condenado!
Kundenadu wasillamantaqchá riki chayarusqa.
    It seems a condenado had come home to that very house.

We all gulped nervously . . .

Condenados, kukuchis—the undead. After death, they say in Sonqo, our flesh "washes away into the earth," leaving our bones behind, hard and dry. Some people—the incestuous, the suicides, the adulterous, the unremittingly selfish—are unable to complete this separation of flesh and bone. They remain imprisoned in rotting bodies, condemned to roam high glaciers, mountain peaks, and featureless *lomas*, filled with insatiable longing to feed on human flesh. They are horrible, terrifying—and yet vulnerable creatures. Unlike *ñak'aqs*, they suffer and can be defeated. Two interchangeable terms name these creatures: *kukuchi* and the Spanish-derived *condenado*. I, too, will use the terms interchangeably in the pages that follow.[5]

Christian images of a blazing inferno don't figure much in Andean stories. As Benito Narezo of Coaza tells us, *condenados* suffer a different fate:

> I'm told that those who die with many sins upon them wander as *kukuchis until the end of the world. Their hands and feet get completely worn out, their clothing turns to rags, they're nothing but bones, they've no flesh left to walk on the ground; I'm told their feet, too, wear down to nothing.*[6]

How do you recognize a *kukuchi*? They take many forms—a strange dog, or a horse or llama standing alone in a deserted place.

> *That's why they say, "That's a kukuchi," because they can take any form: sometimes a man, sometimes a dog, sometimes a horse. If a dog runs out from inside an empty deserted house, they say "kukuchi!" Around sunset, when the orange sun is sinking behind the hills of the loma, that's when they come out.*[7]

Another inner thread—remember how Fox bursts right through the door when the woman cuts off his penis? It adds another dimension to her husband's horrified question, "What, did you have a dog in the house?"

In their human form, *kukuchi*s are full of lice and covered with mucous. Their skin is slightly greenish and they don't like to show their faces. Asleep at night, smoke and even flames issue from their nostrils. Their company—sometimes even their gaze—is deadly.

> Some travelers, overcome by nightfall and fatigue, lay down to sleep, some in the middle of the road, some beside it. Only one of them lays awake for a while, looking around.
> *All of a sudden he saw something, something like a shadow was coming, coming closer. That shadowy thing came closer, looking, looking, he came over to the travelers sleeping in the middle of the road. He had a hideous discolored face, his hair was all rotten, he kept fingering the cord of his habit as he gazed on the humans.*[8]
> Those travelers died "from the *kukuchi* watching them while they slept." Only the one who wasn't seen survived.
> *That kukuchi was absolutely real (chiqaq); it's not a kwintu.*[9]

Many Andean stories (though not ones I heard in Sonqo) describe *kukuchi*s as wearing monks' habits with cowls that hide their disgusting features. Benito of Coaza (via Alain Délétroz Favre) tells how his father encountered one of these cowls:

> During a lean period, his father was obliged to hire out as a shepherd, living alone with the herd in the high pastures. After a while, the food ran out, and his employer neglected to send him more. So he skinned a sheep that had accidently drowned and rather guiltily set to roasting it in his shepherd's hut (guiltily because by rights the meat belonged to the owner of the sheep). Then suddenly, "from beside an *apacheta* (a pile of rocks marking a pass or boundary) he heard someone howling, *"Waaaaaw!"* As the eerie voice came nearer, he looked out and saw a strange figure in monk's cowl racing toward his hut. A *kukuchi*! There was no time to run away, so he climbed into the rafters of the hut and hid there. In came the *kukuchi*; he tossed aside his cowl (crawling with lice), and sat down to roast the meat. Suddenly the rafters collapsed, the shepherd tumbled to the floor, and the startled *kukuchi* fled without his cowl.
>
> *Then once he was outside the* kukuchi *realized that he'd left his cowl behind. Crying, "Oh my cowl, my cowl!" he rushed around and around behind the house sobbing, "Oh my cowl, my cowl, oh my cowl, my cowl, oh my cowl, my cowl!"*[10]
>
> Finally Benito's father picked up the cowl on the end of the roasting spit and tossed it outside the door. The *kukuchi* grabbed it and ran off.

These *kukuchi*s are sounding more and more like Fox. This desperate damned soul "rushing around and around outside the house," calling for his lost property brings to mind the frantic Fox running around outside the house calling, *"Ocallay oca!"* (Oh my oca, my oca!).

Don Aurelio Cuentas, also from Coaza, told Alain Délétroz Favre of a young husband who came to grief in part because of those cowls.[11] The tale begins in a familiar way: Husband and wife are separated by economic necessity. This initial "error" puts the rest of the story into motion (the indented paragraphs are translated from Aurelio's Quechua; the rest is summary):

> A married couple lived happily together until the husband decided to go work for a while in the tropical lowlands. While he was gone, his wife took a lover. One night the husband returned and found the two of them cavorting in bed. He said nothing, only observed them through a chink

in the wall, plotting revenge. He decided to disguise himself as a *kukuchi* and make them sick with *uraño* (a debilitating weakness caused by being frightened by a *kukuchi*). He went off to a deserted hut and sewed himself a cowl. When it was done, he set off toward his own house,

> but all unawares he came face-to-face with another kukuchi. It seems the young man was coming down from above, dressed as a kukuchi, heading for his wife and house, ready to cause uraño; and it seems that coming up from below was another kukuchi—but a real one! And so the two kukuchis met up with each other.
> "Brother-in-law, where are you going?" said the real kukuchi.

And well,

> "It's like this, Brother-of-mine, my wife's living with another man, so I'm going to terrify her," answered [the youth].[12]

Well, the real *kukuchi* offered to come along and help. The betrayed husband—thinking his companion was just another costumed trickster—happily agreed. They surprised the lovers and terrified them indeed, "leaving them stretched on the floor as if dead." And then, "Now we're going to scare mine, too," said the *kukuchi,* and with this he took the young man away.

For a year they traveled until they reached a snowy mountain, and there, at the foot of the snowfields, they slept. Right at sunset the young man awoke. The cowl had slipped off his companion's face, and he saw that it was covered with snot. At last he realized that his companion was a real *kukuchi.* Terrified and sobbing, he quietly threw off his own cowl and crept away.

> When he came out [of the snowfield], he looked up and down. There were kukuchis as far as the eye could see. "They're going to wake up now, they're going to eat me, they'll never let me go!" he thought.[13]

But he did get away and asked a herder woman to help him. At first she was terrified of him, but after he told his story, she took pity and gave him shelter for the night. In the morning he continued on his way, but he was very far—impossibly far—from home.

As he journeyed along, almost overcome by hunger, he met a man by an *apecheta* (cairn of stones). He was a *misti* mounted on a fine white horse.

> "Young man, where are you coming from?" he asked. And the youth answered, "I did this and this . . . " He told the misti his whole story.[14]

The *misti* gave him some bread and told him to eat it continually until he reached home. And so the youth did this and eventually made it back to his village. His wife and her lover were dead. And he himself was pale and exhausted, like someone from another life; his own parents couldn't recognize him. And two days later, he, too, died.

*Kukuchi*s are insiders; they may be our nearest and dearest, may even be ourselves (so we fear in our hearts). *Ñak'aq*, on the other hand, is the quintessential threatening outsider. He doesn't belong in this intensely inward-looking narrative.

Hinaspas,
  Well then,
mamakuqa ñit'in, karahu, hap'in.
  the old lady squeezes the bundle of meat, *karahu*, and grabs it.
"Chayqá turaykichis chayaramusqa,
  "Look, your brother's home,
na, ñak'anata aswan tarirakamusqa!"
  and he found plenty to butcher!"
nispas uman qhororusqata warmita hap'in!
  she says, holding a decapitated woman's head!
Chaysi anchhayna paka k'uchullaman ñup'un
  Then she stuffs the head and body parts into the corner
p'achawan pakaruspa.
  and covers them with some clothes.
"Aswan tarirakamusqa turaykichis ñak'anata," nispa.
  "Plenty, your brother found plenty to butcher!" she says.
Chaysi, maqt'aqa haykuramun:
  Well, the youth comes in muttering:
"Wapu llasataqmá kasqa kay, alqu karahu
  "And it was so heavy, damn it, you dog,
utiypas, runaraqtaq ayqewan, karahu!" nispas iy?
  calm down, the human being got away from me, *karahu*!"
Chayqa kundenaduyá karan chay.
  He was definitely a *condenado*.

Ah! I exclaimed.

Yes, definitely a *condenado* (*kukuchi*). This is regular *condenado* behavior. The same description turns up, almost word for word, in a story from Samuel Pacco Thupa of Usi (via César Itier).

It seems there was a mail carrier who came across an empty hut. He noticed footprints and, deciding to wait for the hut's owner, climbed up to a storage compartment for dried cow manure in the rafters.
  No sooner had he fallen asleep than—
  Clomp! Clomp! Somebody's coming to the house.

"You skinny dog, karahu, *now let's see if you can escape!*
Thump! Somebody threw something heavy onto the floor. And then
somebody entered the house.
"I'm tired, karahu," *he said, sitting by the threshold.*
You see, it wasn't a human being, it was a condenado. *He got up and*
went outside again and — Chomp! Chomp! — set to eating the cadaver
he'd brought.
— Skinny dog, karahu! *And you don't even taste good!"*[15]

The *condenado* came back into the house holding a woman's breast. He
stuck the breast on the windowsill and ate the rest of her body, complaining, *"Only the breasts tasted any good, you skinny dog, let's see you get away*
now!" Finally he finished and sat gloating,

"Me, I'm not afraid of anything, not if it has a beard down to the
ground, not if it has horns, not if it has hair down to the ground. The only
thing that scares me is the little luwiskurkur. *Please no* luwiskurkur, karahu, *please not that!" he says. "Not the* luwiskurkur!"[16]

And then with a great gnashing of teeth, the *condenado* ate up the remain-
ing breast. The mail carrier watched in horror.

"He'll want to eat me, too!"

At that moment, the *condenado* started sniffing — he'd picked up the
mail carrier's scent. The mail carrier pulled himself together and began to
imitate the curious burbling sound guinea pigs make as they run around
at night under the family bed — *"Luwiskurkur! Luwiskurkur!"* The *condenado*
leaped up, bumping his head, and rushed out of the house.

"Luwiskurkur! Luwiskurkur! Luwiskurkur! Luwiskurkur!" burbled the man
more and more rapidly.

"AAAAAAYYY . . . !" the *condenado*'s screams faded away in the
distance.

The mail carrier packed up three pieces of cow manure, climbed down
from the rafters, and ran off as fast as he could, burbling all the while,

"Luwiskurkur! Luwiskurkur! Luwiskurkur! Luwiskurkur!"

When he got to the outskirts of town, he spread out the three pieces of
cow manure and lay down on them to sleep. In the morning he went on
his way.

And that's how he freed himself. That's the way it ends.[17]

Putting aside for the moment the curious finale of *luwiskurkur* sounds
and cow manure, this *condenado* behaves and talks just like the one in
Erasmo's story. And his prey is, very pointedly, female. The tasty breasts
in Don Benito's story bring out a sexual dimension hinted at in Erasmo's
story, where the hidden head and body parts of the female victim point
toward a dreadful fate awaiting the sisters.

Condenados are weighted down by *hucha*. The word is usually translated as "sin," but that doesn't convey how *hucha* violates carefully calibrated relations of give-and-take, and—in the worst offenses—does it secretly, so the imbalance can never be put right. Incest is one such unredeemable offense; suicide is another. Small-time *hucha* can have the same effect—the slow accumulation of unpaid debts over a lifetime sloppily lived makes a complete, clean death impossible. As Sara Vargas explained to Johnny Payne, even urban schoolgirls think in these terms.

> *A condemned soul said good-bye to a friend, but when it still hadn't died, y'see? . . . As [a girl] was going along the courtyard, she saw a dog with one eye . . . As she watched, it got bigger and bigger, and then, oh that one-eyed thing, it got huge . . . All at once, [the girl] fell in a heap in the kitchen . . . [Everybody] went outside to see . . . When they got to the corner, they heard that a friend had just died. The soul of the girl's school friend had come just at the moment she died.*
>
> *The girl said, "Yes, it must have been her soul that came . . . She owed me money. Because of that money, she was coming to say farewell." The girl started to cry. Crying, she said, "Forgive me. And I also forgive you." After that, no more soul, nor anything else, appeared to the girl.*[18]

Even the best of us has something in the balance to set straight on our journey after death. Erasmo's listeners will expect to spend days after death climbing through a rocky *loma* and passing through villages inhabited by creatures that, in the world of the living, are subservient and easily abused. Peter Gose tells us that in "Dog Town" (*Alqullaqta*), "Cat Town" (*Michillaqta*), "Chicken Town," (*Wallpallaqta*), "Guinea Pig Town" (*Qowillaqta*), and even "Pot Town" (*Mank'allaqta*), " . . . each of these beings punishes the *alma* [soul] for any mistreatment it may have given them in life."[19] Only when these punishing obstacles are passed do we poor humans finally reach Blood River and cross over to the afterlife, mounted on a black dog. And what is *that* like? Well, who really knows? Andeans guess that it's a place not so different from our world, only perhaps less filled with

> *Urañu*, the soul who walks before death and carries off the living, may take
> THE FORM OF A FOX.
> They are "souls who have been evil or sinful in life, who have set a bad example, especially envious people . . ."
> (Aquilino Thupa Pacco to César Itier)[26]

suffering. Or, it may be a huge subterranean lake that we enter in order to be reborn, the inner lake that gives rise to the springs and rivers of this world.

Well before death—as much as a year—we begin to exude a sickly aura. At first this *qayqa* is imperceptible, but—quite beyond our volition or awareness—it makes people around us ill. Gradually, *qayqa* builds up around us, and we die. As our soul sets out for the afterlife, our external body begins to rot; our flesh disintegrates and washes away into the earth. Only bones remain as, finally, accounts balanced, we cross the Blood River.

Moral disintegration may be kept secret in life, but in death it's unavoidably manifest in the *kukuchi/condenado*'s bodily decomposition and its inverted behavior. *Kukuchis* do things backward, like entering houses piecemeal, through the roof.

Returning to Erasmo's narrative, the girls' journey has a quality of moral death as they wander like dead souls in the *loma*, fleeing their own unredeemable crime. As for the *condenados*, they disguise their disarticulated quality from the start. It's their victim who arrives in pieces. A head here, a breast there. Chomp, chomp, chomp. Down goes their flesh into the ravenous maw—to no avail, for a *kukuchi*'s appetite is never satisfied. Only the bloody bones are left, and bits of tattered clothing, cast aside.

CHAPTER NINE

CANNIBAL LOVER

Chayqa, *mamakuqa nin maqt'ataqa:*
    Then the old lady says to the youth:
"Panayki chayaramusqa,
    "It seems your sister arrived,

"Your sister . . ." The old crone seems to be embracing the girls as new members of the household, answering their naive hopes for sanctuary and support with mothering solicitude. Like Fox with his deceptive whining—"But I'm used to sleeping next to my mother . . ."—the old *condenada* creates a false context to lull her victims into a sense of trust and intimacy.

To her son, the same statement bears very different connotations. *Condenados* prey on their family members. Their insatiable appetites crave the flesh of their nearest and dearest.

---

                              panaykikuna,"
                                  your sisters,"
                              nispa maqt'ataqa.
                                  she tells the youth.

For him, "new sisters" means "new victims."

Chaysi,
 And then,
maqt'aqa nin: "Baya, baya, allinmi chayaramunku.
 "Fine, fine!" says the youth. "It's good that they've come.
Kunan tutachá huqninwan uwihata belaramusaq,
 This very night I'll keep watch over the sheep with one of them,
paqarintaq huqninwan uwihata michimusaq" nispa nin maqt'aqa, p'asñataqa.
 and tomorrow I'll pasture sheep with the other," says the youth to the girls.
"Kuraqkaqwan kunan belaramusaq uwihata," nispas nin.
 "I'll keep watch right now with the elder," he says.
Chaysi p'asñaqa . . . p'asñataqa
 And so the girl . . . he makes the girl
SiQAYchin maqt'a
 get UP and go OUT
uwihiriya ch'uqllaman puñuqta.
 to sleep in the shepherd's watch hut.
Kan anchhayna patanpichá
 Y'know, in these homesteads there's always
uwihiriya ch'uqllachanku kan riki.
 a shepherd's watch hut.
Chayman pasachin.
 That's where he takes her.

There's always a shepherd's watch hut . . . Our mind's eye shifts to a new location. Erasmo's listeners will have no trouble locating themselves in a lonesome shepherd's hut, familiar since childhood as a place to watch for marauders—rustlers and predatory animals like foxes. Other thoughts will cross listeners' minds as well, for a shepherd's hut is rich in adolescent memories. Girls, in particular, have their first (and perhaps only) taste of independence in these high pastures. At thirteen, Inucha enjoyed her days away in the *loma* with her stepsister Dionysia. I asked her what they did there, but (I should have known better) she didn't tell me much. She did tell me that they practiced weaving. She and Dionysia wove long fine ribbons for their hats and borders for their skirts, showed each other their discoveries, criticized and helped each other. When I asked Inucha who was teaching them to weave, she replied, "No one, we learn it ourselves in the *loma*."

Budding adult competencies begin to bloom in the *loma*. As girls move further into their teens, they begin to meet up with their boyfriends there—boys who are themselves herders, or who find some other pretext to slip away. In lonely isolated watch huts, unmarried teenagers meet, play, and experiment.[1] Everyone knows about this, and everybody carefully ignores it. Premarital sex is forbidden yet fully expected; it is public knowledge that must not be recognized. The tension so created is a driving force in Andean storytelling.[2]

So many stories begin with a shepherdess in the *loma* who is deceived by a wild animal in the form of an attractive man (not only Condor and Bear, but Lizard and Snake pass themselves off this way).[3] On one level, of course, these are simply cautionary tales—don't talk to strangers! But the affairs' secrecy puts inexperienced youths at risk. Alejo Maque (nicknamed Khunku), our fount of information on Andean erotica, tells us a sadly comical anecdote from his time as a shepherd boy:

> Up in the pasture he used to meet up with a girl and share her picnic lunch. One day he saw her from afar, waving her arms up and down and calling,
>
>
>
> *HAMUY! HAMUY!*
>
> COME! COME!
>
>
> He thought she was inviting him to share her lunch, so he rushed to join her. But a disagreeable surprise awaited him:
>
> > *Would you believe that it wasn't her arms beckoning to me, but it was her two legs kicking up and down on a man's shoulders! That man was screwing her—Khunku's girlfriend—screwing like crazy. He was a cow seller, a bull seller, one of those they call* ganadero.[4]
>
> Khunku wrapped his face in his poncho and never spoke to the girl again.

Men as well as foxes prowl in the high *puna*. Lone girls in the pasture are vulnerable to male predation, especially from older men—peddlers, cattle sellers—who may be passing through the *loma* for some reason. We hear such a man's voice in this song from Ancash:

While Fox goes after sheep, the singer goes after men's daughters, and people hate him as they hate Fox. At the song's end, seducer and Fox are related in an inverse proportion—Fox returns the sheep diminished, only pelt and bones, whereas the seducer returns the daughters augmented, that is, pregnant.

And so, thoughts of a shepherd's watch hut lead us back to "the time of the foxes." As listeners' thoughts turn to the lonely watch hut, Fox hovers

Ay zorro, zorro,	Ay, fox, fox,
zorro de la puna!	fox of the highlands!
Qamtawan nuqatawanshi,	You and me both,
runa shikimantsi.	The people hate us
Qanta shikisunki	You, they hate you for
ushanta suwapti.	stealing their sheep.
Nuqata shikiman	Me, they hate me for
wawanta suwapti.	stealing their daughters.
Puiditsu,	I just can't.
sapalla punuyta puiditsu!	just can't sleep alone!
Tumarilla tikrarilla,	Twisting and turning,
manan kaqllamanmi	I can't keep still!
tikrarilla!	
Ay zorro, zorro,	Ay, fox, fox,
zorro de la puna!	fox of the highlands!
Qamtawan nuqatawanshi,	You and me both,
runa shikimantsi.	the people hate us.
Qamshi kutishinki	You, you'll give back
tullunta millwanta.	wool and bones.
Nuqapitam kutishisaq	And I, I'll give back
wawanta willkantin	daughters with grandkids.
Puiditsu	I just can't,
sapalla punuyta puiditsu!	just can't sleep alone!
Tumarilla tikrarilla	Twisting and turning,
manan kaqllamanmi	I can't keep still!
tikrarilla![5]	

again at the edge of the scene. Remember Alejo Maque's comment, "If you ever sleep in a herder's hut . . . [t]here'll be a fox watching you, saying, 'hah, hah, hah' and licking its chops . . ."

When a young man makes a girl "get UP and go OUT" to sleep in a shepherd's hut, we can guess that he has more than brotherly companionship in mind, and that any "picnic lunch" is likely to be the kind Fox found when he reached between his hostess's thighs. Erasmo tells us nothing about the drowsy girl's reaction to this summons, but one can guess that she was not too unwilling. She had no idea she was destined to be the meal herself.

With the shepherd's hut in the back of our consciousness, Erasmo quickly moves our attention back to the younger sister, braiding in an episode that surfaces in other stories as well.

Hinaspas sullk'akaq p'asñataqa mana puñuy chayanchu,
   Well, the younger girl just can't get to sleep,
mana puñuy chayanchu; yanqa rikch'apakushan,
   she just can't sleep; she's lying there wide awake,
yanqa rikch'apakushan.
   wide awake.
Hinas, "Puñukuy, puñukuy, wachacha" nispa.
   "Sleep, sleep, my dear!" says the old lady.
Chaysi, naqa, manapuni puñunchu, karahu;
   But the girl just can't sleep;
manapunis puñunchu p'asña,
   she can't sleep at all,
rikch'ashallansi. Chaymantas,
   she's lying there wide awake. And then,
yaqa illarimunña, wallpa waqayta aknata,
   just before dawn, at cock-crow,
"WAAW!" nispa qapariramusqa p'asña, ch'uqllamanta.
   it seems that the elder girl SCREAMED from the watch hut.
Chaysi, mamakuta nin chay sullk'akaq p'asñaqa:
   So the younger girl asked the old lady:
"Ñañaychu hina qaparimun, kuraqniychu hina?" nispa nin.
   "Wasn't that my sister who screamed, my older sister?"
"Manan, wachacha!
   "No indeed, dearie!
Animalmi hamun, chaytachá uksiyakushanku,"
   It's that animals come and they're screaming to chase them off,"
nispas nin mamakuqa.
   answers the old lady.

An almost identical episode occurs in a story from Usi about "Two Gad-about Girls," told to César Itier by Aquilino Thupa Pacco. This, too, is a composite story, but unlike Erasmo's, it begins with the "Condenado Household" episode. Here, adolescent heedlessness is enough to send the girls wandering, wandering in a moral no-man's-land.

 Two sisters, *chanchara p'asñakuna* (frivolous, gossipy girls), lost their way and arrived at the house of two *condenados*: an old lady with her son. The son took the older girl to sleep in a watch hut, and the younger one shared a bed with the old lady. It seems that the old lady started to grope around and feel the girl's body. Startled, the girl asked,

"*Why are you feeling my body?*"

"*I thought you might be cold,*" *replied the old lady.*

Meanwhile she could hear her older sister giggling hysterically with the young man.

"*Why is that silly girl laughing?*" *asked her sister.*

"*My son just laughs like that. He plays around for no reason,*" *answers the old lady.* "*They're guarding the sheep,*" *she says.*

And then, almost at the midnight hour, the older girl let out a single terrible scream. The laughter stopped—silence!

With this, the younger girl realized that somehow the youth had killed her sister.

At dawn the old lady got up and started boiling water in a big pot. In came her son, carrying a breast.

"Did you bring something yummy (*misk'itachu apamunki*)?" asked his mother as she took it from him.

The younger sister watched in terror. She crept out for a look at the watch hut and found only her sister's clothing, all torn up, and her hair strewn all over the floor. At that, the girl quietly ran away. She fled to a distant plain (*karu pampata*).[6]

Story characters meet *kukuchi*s when they are morally at risk. The two girls are frivolous in the version from Usi, and fratricidal in Erasmo's version from Sonqo. In the Hansel-and-Gretel-type story from Cuzco, the boy and girl are little children, apparently motherless and too small to take care of themselves. As for Don Benito's father, the reluctant shepherd—he was guiltily roasting his employer's sheep when the *condenado* appeared. And the mail carrier of the *luwiskurkur* story? Messengers are, perforce, crossers of thresholds, ever in transit as they carry messages from one place to another over the featureless *loma*. Theirs is a risky profession.

Adolescents are morally at risk because, as part-child and part-adult, they are more easily duped and slower to recognize danger. It's not hard for the young *condenado* to mask his cannibalistic intentions with an invitation to adolescent sex play.

Chaysi, chayaramun, naqa . . .

   Well, the youth comes home . . .

inti manaraq p'unchayamushaqtin maqt'aqa, haykuramun.

   and enters the house just before daybreak.

"Ñachu almusay? Kunanqa sullk'akaqwanñataqmi michiramusaq uwihata.
"Is breakfast ready yet? I'm going to pasture sheep now with the other sister, the younger one.
Tutallamanta qarqusaqku.
We need to drive them from the corral first thing in the morning.
Kuraqnin ñañanqa puñushallanraqmi. Hinaraq puñukushachun payqa.
The older sister's still sleeping. We should let her sleep in.
Illariqmi malanochewanku imachá kampas. Animalkuna hamun,
For some reason we were up 'til dawn; we had a terrible night. Animals came around
mana puñuchiwankuchu, chaymi malanusqa puñukushanraq"
and just wouldn't let us sleep, so she's exhausted,"
nispas maqt'a nin, iy? Chayqa mihuramusqañasyá . . . kundenadu
he says. But really, he'd eaten her up . . . that *condenado.*

"Iiiiy!" wailed CIPRIANA.
"Aaahtakáow!" I exclaimed. "How a-a-awful!"

A confusion of sensual appetites rushes to the surface once *kukuchi*s enter the picture. The erotic conflation of food and sex, an amusing undercurrent throughout the "Fox and the Woman" episode, emerges now in horrifying immediacy. In one way or another, this story has been about food from the beginning—or pretended to be about food when it's about sex, or, as now, pretended to be about sex when it's about food.[7] Sometimes the characters employ a figure of speech—"That's your father's picnic lunch!"—sometimes they mistake one for the other (penis for "throat meat"); and sometimes the deception is deliberate, as in the misleading insinuation "Tonight I'll keep watch with the elder."

Misdirected sexuality transmutes into insatiable cannibalism.

Erasmo leads his listeners through this trajectory, from the "incestuous" infidelity of the woman, to murderous quarrelling over meat, to ravenous all-consuming cannibalism.

Erasmo's listeners recognize and use tropes such as these with gusto, but they also experience the sex–eating equivalence as deeply and urgently real. Households form around food and sexuality, and they fall apart when these appetites run out of control. The *kukuchi* is no figure of speech for Erasmo's listeners: real incest creates real *kukuchi*s. They are aspects of each other in the world of lived experience.

The "Fox and Woman" episode has already added another bit of confusion to the mix—a confusion of species expectations. Erasmo's narrative violates the normal expectation that human beings should have sexual
relations with members of their own species and eat members of other
species. The bestiality of Fox and Woman is matched by cannibalism in
the *condenado* household. Fox embodies this confused mixture of appetites
and species identification; his appetite for sheep and chickens transmutes
into sexual lust once he nears a human female. As Alejo Maque comments, "If (a Fox) is male and it sniffs out a sleeping woman, then it really
wants to screw her." This is what our story Fox is after, but as he draws the
woman into his snare, their banter centers on food:

"Hey Mom, what's this?"

"That's your father's picnic lunch!"

"Oh, let me taste a little!"

Quqawa, which I translate as "picnic lunch," is a meal wrapped up in a
woven napkin. Sharing *quqawa* in the pasture is an integral part of courtship (which is why it properly belongs to the married woman's husband).
It's what poor Khunku was expecting when instead he saw his girlfriend
getting screwed by a *ganadero*.

From that erotic "picnic lunch," Erasmo's narrative moves on to "throat
meat" that the girl scrounges for the family dinner, adding gender confusion to the mix-up of food, sex, and species. Raw "throat meat" (an image
evoking both penis and vagina) resists being cooked or even tenderized. In
"stand-alone" versions of "The Fox and the Woman," the confusion ends
when the old lady recognizes the "meat" for what it is ("Hey, but this is
a penis!") and throws it away. Confusion clarified, the story is over. Not
so in Erasmo's story, where confusions multiply to propel the narrative
into another episode. The second woman's impregnation produces a two-
species sibling set composed of foolish human sisters and greedy fox
brothers with their insatiable appetite for meat. The sisters kill them, but
instead of getting the meat, they become meat for cannibal souls.

Aquilino's story about "The Two Gad-about Girls" diverges from Erasmo's when the younger girl realizes that her sister has been murdered and
she herself is in mortal danger. While Erasmo keeps the girl in the thrall
of the *condenados*, Aquilino's surviving girl is no longer heedless. His story
quickly moves on to meet up with another, less somber-hued version of
itself, already familiar to us as a stand-alone story (Chapter Seven).

. . . the girl quietly ran away. She fled to a distant plain (*karu pampata*). There she was overtaken by nightfall and, once again, came upon a lonely hut. An old lady sat in the doorway. The girl was frightened.

"The same thing's going to happen to me. A *condenado*'s going to eat me, too!" she said.

But the old lady just sat by the door, chewing coca. She gave the girl a key to the house and told her to go ahead and cook dinner.

"I don't eat, I only chew coca," she said.

The girl went inside and found everything she needed to cook dinner. And then a young man appeared, driving a herd of sheep, playing the flute, and with a dog at his side. Again, the girl thought this must be a *condenado*. But no, he really was a normal human being. He entered the house and—

"*Kuwis! Kuwis! Kuwis!*" exclaimed the old lady.

She turned into a *qowi* (guinea pig) and ran under the bed.[8]

This was one of Cipriana's favorites; she loved the idea of the old lady turning into a guinea pig.

Familiar threads surface in "The Two Gad-about Girls": the victim's breasts as a special *condenado* treat, underscoring betrayed sexuality; the guinea pig as benevolent and protective; the deceptive groping at night (this time it's not "son/fox" feeling up his human "mommy," but "mother/*condenada*" feeling up her human "daughter").

So far, Aquilino's two episodes—"Condenado Household" and "Old Lady Guinea Pig"—reflect each other, dark and bright. But he isn't finished yet. His story continues, meeting up with yet another somber—but inverted—version of itself. It will surface again in the next chapter.

But what happens to Erasmo's surviving girl? We left her at breakfast with the *condenados*. And she still hasn't figured out what's happening.

Hinaspas, mmm...
   And then . . . hmm
chayqa, mihuruspa, pacha p'unchay chayamuytaqa,
   so it was--once they've eaten breakfast and it's broad daylight,
yastá uwihantinta pasachin, iy? p'asñataqa, maqt'a.
   the youth makes the girl go out with him, see?—to herd the sheep.
Maytachá lumata qatinku riki,
   They drive the sheep out to a high distant pasture,
hinas, chaypi, purinku maqt'awan.
   and the girl's out there with the young man.

Hinaspas, chaypi, mana chay ch'uqllaman achhuychinchu;
> But out there he doesn't let her get anywhere near the watch hut.

Pakallanta, huq llarullanta pasarachin.
> He makes her pass quietly to one side of it.

Hinaspas, awispakushansiyá p'asñaqa.
> And this makes the girl feel uneasy.

As well it should.

CHAPTER TEN

MAMACHA

Hinaspas, ummm,
    Then, ummm,
maypichá lumapi, kanpu lumakunapi uwihata michispanku,
    in some high pasture, while they're herding the sheep,
huq señorawan tupasqa,
    it seems that she met up with a lady,
chay p'asñaqa.
    that girl did.
Hinaspas, chay señora nisqa . . . na . . . nispa,
    And it seems the lady spoke, saying,
chay señoraqa mana señorachu kasqa, mistisachu,
    for she wasn't a lady, it seems, wasn't a mestiza,
mamacha kasqa.
    she was a *mamacha.*

"*Annn,*" sighed CIPRIANA. "How wonderful!"

A miraculous face counterbalances the *loma*'s monstrous one. Doña Balvina, still a shepherdess at sixty, knew this face well. As a girl, she often had to spend days at a time alone in the high pastures, and, she told me, one day a mestiza girl appeared and offered to help with her chores. Together they watched the flocks and together they washed wool to marvelous whiteness. As night fell, the girls settled down to prepare dinner, and the new friend minced *ullucu*s unbelievably fine, almost faster than the eye could see. A few days later, Balvina's parents came to check on their daughter. Then Santa Isabel (for, it seems, that's who her new friend was) was nowhere to be seen. When the mayor of Colquepata came to investigate, she disappeared for good. News spread, and for a few years pilgrims came to visit the site, but interest eventually petered out. Apparently Santa Isabel caused no new miracles.

"*Sut'ipin chay*," commented Balvina, "*manan kwintuchu*": "This is true (in clarity), not a *kwintu*."

Not all miraculous visitors get away as cleanly as Balvina's Santa Isabel. In the church in Ollantaytambo, there is a Christ Child tied down by one foot. He's a little trickster who just wanted to play. One day he approached a shepherd boy named Kasimiro, way up in the pastures above town. María Laura Ugarte of Cuzco told Johnny Payne his story:[1]

> "Little Kasimiro, Little Kasimiro," [the Christ Child] said. "Don't you want to come play?"
>
> The boy answered, "I can't play, child. My mother would hit me for sure. I have a lot to do. I have to spin this yarn, and stretch it."
>
> But the temptation was too great, and the two boys played together all day long. Toward evening, Kasimiro remembered the unspun wool and started to panic:
>
> "*I can't go back to my house because then my mother will beat me . . .*"
>
> "*Don't fret, I'll help you,*" *the child said to the boy.* "*I'm going to feed the wool to one of the sheep. Then you'll pull it out of her behind and roll it into a ball.*"
>
> "*What makes you think a sheep would eat wool, child? Never. They only eat grass.*"
>
> "*I know what I'm doing. Just do what I say.*"
>
> *So the child caught hold of a sheep, and began to feed it wool. The boy pulled spun wool from its behind, as fast as he could, and rolled it into a ball. In that way, they finished it all, to the last little piece.*

Day after day they repeated this miracle. Kasimiro went home with his yarn spun so very, very fine that eventually his parents became suspicious and went to spy on their son. When they saw what was going on . . .

> . . . *[t]he parents ran to grab hold of Kasimiro and the other boy. But the child, at that instant, disappeared. He wasn't there anymore. He'd turned to nothing.* (Ch'usaqman tukurapusqa.)

That could have been the end of the story, but the little Christ Child couldn't stay away from his playmate and kept coming back. Eventually the parents caught him and closed him up in the church of Ollantaytambo. For a while he kept escaping, but eventually they tied him down.

 Today the child is in [the church of] Ollantaytambo, tied down by one little foot, shining like gold.

You can visit the church and see the child, evidence that this narrative, too, is *chiqaq*.

Another visiting Christ Child is enshrined in a high mountain sanctuary south of Cuzco, where pilgrims gather for the Festival of Qoyllur Rit'i, shortly before the winter solstice in June.[2] Long ago, it's said, the Christ Child appeared to a shepherd boy pasturing alpacas alone in the high *loma* at the foot of Mount Ausangate.[3] The two children played together, the herds multiplied marvelously, and the little visitor gave his friend food and beautiful clothes. Eventually the boy's parents became suspicious, and an official delegation came from Ocongate to investigate. As they approached, rays of light shone from the Christ Child's white clothes like light reflected from a mirror, momentarily blinding them. At that moment the child disappeared into a rock, which ever afterward bore his imprint. Now, during the Qoyllur Rit'i festival, when the sun is on the verge of renewal and its rays are especially potent, delegations from many communities bring their *taytachas* (little fathers), small icons of the crucified Christ, to visit this petrified Jesus in his chapel. For four days, groups of pilgrims climb toward the glacial sanctuary ringed by Ausangate and other powerful mountains. They come to absorb the sacred potency of the place, to petition for various kinds of help, and especially to sacrifice their energy in arduous climbing and long hours of ritual dancing.

There, pilgrims confront both miracle and monster, for they walk among souls of the damned. Glaciers around the Qoyllur Rit'i sanctuary are crawling with ravenous *kukuchis, condenados* too burdened by moral debt to die cleanly and completely. Wandering alone, a pilgrim would be eaten alive; safety lies in numbers and in the company of *taytachas* and priests with their crosses. This long, cold, exhausting trek is a penance; pilgrims ward off damnation by paying their moral debts in advance.

Like the crosses and icons of the pilgrimage, the *mamacha* in Erasmo's narrative stands protectively between a *kukuchi* and its victim. She shares this role with other story characters as well—we've seen her before as María the Frog and as Old Lady Guinea Pig. In one of the most widespread horror stories, "The Condenado Lover," she takes the guise of an old widow. Here's a summary of the version told to Johnny Payne by Juana Rosa Callo Paliza:[4]

A young couple loved each other deeply and eloped against their parents' wishes. Because they had no resources, the husband returned home at night to rob his parents:

The parents listened. "Who could it be? A thief, a thief, a thief." The father grabbed an axe in the dark and hit the thief in the dark with it . . . In the morning they went to see who it had been. And it was their son.

Meanwhile, the young woman was waiting. After three days, her young man came back to her. But he was already dead, y'see . . . He was carrying a bundle containing the food and corn beer that his parents had prepared for the burial.

He said, "Hurry up and eat this. We have to get walking soon. We've a long way to go."

And so they walked and walked until the wife couldn't go on, and they stopped at the house of an old widow with seven children. The husband refused to eat and insisted on sleeping outside. Later that night the widow went out to check up on them.

And while they were sleeping face up, a flame spewed from the man's mouth. Because he was dead. And the flame was going whooosh, from his mouth, when he snored, whooosh!

Fortunately, the old widow woman turned out to have some miraculous qualities. In the morning, she informed the young woman that her lover was a damned soul. Then she gave the terrified girl a rope, a needle, a comb, and scissors and said,

" . . . Later today you'll arrive at a river bank. Then and there, he won't want to cross the river. He'll say to you, 'Carry me on your back.' You should answer, 'I'll tie you with this rope so your feet won't slip.' Then, throw the comb like this . . ."

The young woman did as she was told. In mid-river she shrugged off the *condenado*, and he was swept a ways down the river. But he untied himself and came after her, shouting, "I'm going to eat you!" The woman threw down the comb and a wall rose up; she threw down the scissors and a huge boulder arose. Finally she threw down the needle:

. . . *it turned to water. He shouted, "I'll catch you, I'll eat you this time." She ran and she ran, without knowing where she ran. The con-demned soul couldn't cross over the river. In the place they went, there were no open fields. It was just river-cane and cold and wind . . .*

But as luck would have it, she stumbled upon a gang of muleteers who came to her rescue,

" . . . she can cook our meals for us. She can be of some service to us. That's why we'll save her," they said . . .

The muleteers fought and the *condenado* fought back. Eventually

. . . he was only a pile of flesh, but still moving. They thrashed it out near the woman. They said, "He's still alive. We can't kill him." So they tied him to the back legs of a mule . . . [and] she kicked him to pieces.

Then they gathered up the pieces and burned them in a fire of mule and horse dung. A white dove flew out of the fire.

The dove said, "Thank you all. I was a condemned soul. I made a promise to Emilia. 'If you die, then I'll carry you off. If I die, you carry me off.' But God sent me back here. Now you've saved me (salvawankin)," said the white dove, and flew away.

Like our girl in Erasmo's narrative, this young woman stumbles through a wasteland—"just river-cane and cold and wind." Trackless fen and featureless *loma* reflect the protagonists' moral confusion. The old widow, like a *mamacha* (though never described as such), foresees the young woman's peril and gives her what she needs to escape. Finally, beaten to a pulp and then burned by muleteers, the husband's soul is saved—and the wife? Apparently she ends up cooking for the muleteers, not an appealing fate but better than being eaten by a *condenado*.

The beautiful lady in Erasmo's story needs to save the girl from the same devouring peril:

Chaysi nisqa chay p'asñata:
   And it seems this is what she said to the girl:
"Yaw p'asña, yaw lonla p'asña,
   "Oh girl, oh foolish girl,
imamanmi qan hamunki?
   whatever did you come here for?
Kay mana runaq chayanan llaqtata.
   This is no place for humans.
Kaypiqa saqraq llaqtanpin kanki.
   Here you're in a village of demons.

Kunallanmi qantapas kunan mihurusunki, ñan ñañaykitapas mihupunña riki!"
> Right now he's about to eat you up, he's already eaten your sister!"
nispa nisqa.
> she said.
"Imamanmi qan hamunki?
> "What did you come here for?
Manachu kasqanta kutipuyta atinki?" nispa.
> Can't you go back the way you came?" she says.
Chayqa mamachasyá kasqa chay señora,
> That lady, she was really a *mamacha*
señoraman tukuspa.
> in the form of a lady.

"*Señoraman tukuspa,*"
"in the form of a lady,"
"changed into a lady,"
"converted into a lady,"
"finished up as a lady."

The verb is *tukuy*, "to complete," "to finish," "to be converted into some-thing." Lira's dictionary gives as an example, "*Allpaman tukuy: convertirse en polvo*" (to be converted into dust).[5] Condor and Bear *tukuy* when they want girls to see them as handsome young men; they appear "*maqt'aman tukuspa*" (changed into an adolescent youth). Condor "converts" back and forth between forms; he changes into a youth, back to a condor, into a youth again, and then finally ends up in the pot, converted not only into a bird but into food for his in-laws. And the Ollantaytambo Christ Child, it seems, "turned into nothing" (*ch'usaqman tukurapusqa*). Erasmo's narra-tive, as Don Luis commented, "turned into a *condenado kwintu*." All com-pletion, it seems, is relative; more transmutations are always possible.

Though female saviors take many forms in Andean stories—lady, crone, frog, guinea pig—there is always an element of sainthood, of *mam-acha*, about them. Little Mothers are kind, powerful teachers, wellsprings of female knowledge and skill. In narratives, they reveal hidden truths to people in trouble and help them escape predatory creatures. Sometimes they actively collaborate, like María, the wise helpful Frog who reveals

Condor's true nature and helps the girl escape by taking over the laundry. We meet her again in the Hansel-and-Gretel-type story as motherly Maria-cha who comes to the little boy's aid as he unwittingly draws water in his sister's skull. Frog María inserts an element of comedy as well when she tricks the impatient captor by croaking, *"Manaraq! Manaraq!"* (Not yet! Not yet!).

The savior in "The Two Gad-about Girls" story is a guinea pig in the form of an old lady, almost identical in appearance to the *condenada* crone of the first episode in that narrative. While the girl fearfully suspects the worst, listeners are soon put at ease:

"I don't eat, I only chew coca," she said.

No *condenado* would chew coca, a quintessentially humanizing practice invented by Santísima María. A moment later, Aquilino explains (using that narrative past *-sqa* we encountered in Chapter Two):

> *"Chay payachataq kasqa t'asa qowillataq."*
> "That little old lady was really (so it seems) a little guinea pig."[6]

Rather than revealing herself and advising the girl outright, Old Lady Qowi simply lays the scene, readying the girl for marriage. When the groom-to-be arrives at the girl's nicely prepared dinner, the old lady turns into a guinea pig and scampers under the bed.

Curiously, guinea pigs share some qualities with *mamachas*. Remember the *luwiskurkur* that terrified the *condenado*?

Why should these weak little creatures, destined to be strangled and eaten on festive occasions, have power in narrative to ward off *condenados*? Although guinea pigs are used in divination and healing elsewhere in Peru,[7] this association would be unlikely to resonate with Aquilino's listeners in the Cuzco area, where, as far as I know, guinea pigs have no such uses. Instead, Aquilino's narrative emphasizes the guinea pigs' vegetarian

The mail carrier . . . began to imitate the curious burbling sound guinea pigs make:
"Luwiskurkur! Luwiskurkur!"
The *condenado* leaped up, bumping his head, and rushed out of the house.
"Luwiskurkur! Luwiskurkur! Luwiskurkur! Luwiskurkur!"
burbled the man more and more rapidly.
"Aaaaaayyy . . . !" the *condenado*'s screams faded away in the distance.

habits. Their diet of grass and potato peelings sits at the opposite end of the alimentary spectrum from that of carnivorous, cannibalistic *condenados*. The peaceful burble of guinea pigs is a sound of prosperous domesticity. A "cold house," not regularly occupied, couldn't support these little animals that run out from under the family bed to scavenge around the stove at night. *Qowis* are appropriate nighttime occupants of a sleeping house. With this in mind, it makes sense that up in the high, darkening *loma*, Old Lady Guinea Pig prepares the terrified, chastened girl for marriage by telling her to go inside the house, light the fire, and cook dinner for a young man.

And thus the featureless *loma* is civilized. As the new *warmiqhari* settles into a household of their own, the featureless *loma* becomes a place of human habitation, an incipient *ayllu*. Human needs for food and sex lie equally at the heart of social order and moral chaos; human community is built around the same appetites that, unbridled, propel souls into a moral wilderness.

Old Lady Qowi is just one embodiment of the great paradox running through all these stories: a domesticating force resides in wild places and manifests itself equally in devouring ogresses and nurturing little mothers. Pacha, the Earth itself, has these two aspects; the other face of nurturing, protective Pachamama, is Pachatira, the face that "seizes" people and drains out health and energy; the face that causes landslides; the face we find in the black spots of the Milky Way. She is the opposite face of Pachamama, just as Achkay the ogress and the *condenada* crone are the opposite face of the *mamacha*.

That *mamacha* and ogress are opposite faces of the same entity is clearly expressed in an anecdote recounted to Johnny Payne by Sara Vargas de Mayorga:[8]

> A tomboyish girl, it seems, was leading a horse loaded with corn from fields to town. But she didn't distribute the load evenly, and, as she was passing through a gloomy ravine the horse threw off the corn, so there the girl was, struggling by herself with the spilled cargo. All of a sudden, a woman appeared. The girl asked her nicely for help, but the woman gave a surly reply: "Do you think I have time for this? Ask the river sirens instead!" But the girl stood her ground and answered fearlessly,
> 	"*Please ma'am, little dove, dear heart. It's getting late; I need to be going.*" *At that moment, in that deep, low place, the sun began to shine*

brightly. The sun became blindingly bright. The sun was really shining.

"There you go," the woman said. "So, now you don't have to go ask the river sirens, since I'm helping you."

The load flew onto the woman's shoulder, and in an instant she had it bundled neatly up on the horse. Amazed, but still unafraid, the girl thanked the woman and continued on her way.

Then she looked back. She looked all around on the ground, but the woman wasn't walking. Instead, she was flying in the air. And her head was ugly, like a hag's, and her hair like that of a crazy person.

The girl made the sign of the cross and called on the Holy Trinity. Then she continued home without looking behind her. At home, she explained what had happened:

"I didn't vomit up foam or get sick or anything like that . . . Good spirits appear to women who have been good, ones who haven't been bad or indecent, who haven't stolen, who haven't acted wrong, who haven't lied. And this spirit turned into a good one."

That was a close call. With her tomboyish attitude and unbalanced load in a nasty ravine, this girl was in a morally ambiguous situation. Fortunately, her fearless courtesy and religiosity were enough to bring her through safely. Thus witch women turn into *mamachas*, giving help and direction that, like the skills they impart, guide girls out of the wilderness and back to the cultivated land and well-grazed pastures of normal society. Lost in the *loma* at the mercy of a *condenado*, the surviving sister certainly needs this kind of help.

CHAPTER ELEVEN

INSIDE OUT

Chaysi, qosqa nata, ch'ankita, p'atakiskata,
    And so then she gave her a cactus branch, a spiny cactus,
ch'ankita.
    a cactus branch.

This is unexpected. Where are the womanly items—mirror, comb, needle—familiar from the other *condenado* story? Where is the house, the stove waiting to be lit, dinner waiting to be cooked? Why, of all things, a spiny cactus?

"Kayta apanki pakallapi,
    "Take this along secretly
hinaspa, apaspayki,
    and, having brought it with you,
'Umaykita qhawasayki,' ninki.
    say to him, 'I'm going to search your head [for lice].'
Sut'in mana much'unta qhawachikusunkichu,
    He definitely won't let you see the nape of his neck,
. . . uuh . . . much'unpin chay runa mihunan simin kashan!"
    . . . uuh . . . that's where he has a mouth for eating human beings!"
nispa nisqa chay mamachaqa.
    said the *mamacha*.

Valeriano Puma, a curer in Coaza,
explained to Alain Délétroz, that

WITCHCRAFT TWISTS
the thread of one's life the wrong way.

*Noqanchis layqasqa
lloq'eman puskasqa kaspa
chaywan mana imapis
ruwakusqanchis avanzakunchu.*[1]

When a sorcerer spins us to the left
then we can't make headway
in any of our endeavors.

A curer rectifies the situation
by straightening out the thread.

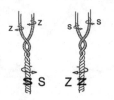

It seems our girl is in too deep for simple flight. Her only hope is to rectify the moral confusion of appetites, species, and genders that propelled her into the *loma* in the first place.

The *mamacha* prepares the girl for battle by revealing to her the secret of the mouth at the nape of *condenado*'s neck, the mouth he uses for eating people. She arms her with a *p'atakiska* cactus, the kind that grows in the *loma*, oblong and covered with spines. With the *mamacha*'s intervention, the inversion of sexual identity is complete: the girl now possesses a phallic counterpart to the *condenado*'s perverse orifice, like a misplaced vagina dentata. She is armed: gender perversion is matched by gender perversion.

When illness is caused by sorcery, Erasmo told me, the curer has to forcefully turn the spell back (*kutichiy*) on its perpetrator. Motivated by the same logic—what Gary Urton calls "the mathematics of rectification"[2]—the *mamacha* prepares our girl for a perilous encounter. She must force the evil back into the *condenado*.

Hinaspas, uwiha kutichisqanmanta rin, tarpanarukunku kaqta.[3]
So, once the girl had rounded up the sheep, they went on herding them just as before.
Chaypis, maqt'ataqa nin, por la fuerza,
Then she says to the youth, she insists,

CIPRIANA interjected, *"Umaykita, turay . . ."*
"Your head, brother . . ."

"Umaykita, turáy, qhawarusayki. Ch'eqñekikuna kashanpaschá, usaykikuna!" nispa qhawan.
"Your head, brother, I'm going to search your head. I'll bet you have nits and lice!" she says, looking at him.

"'Manan kanchu!'" coached CIPRIANA urgently. *"'There aren't any!'"*

"Manan kanchu!" *nispa nin maqt'aqa.* **Mana qhawachikuyta munanchu, mana!**
"There aren't any!" exclaims the youth. He really doesn't want her to search his head!

But of course he does have lice. *Condenados* are always full of lice. And of course he doesn't want to let on. This is where the girl has to muster all her inner resources and drive her courage to the sticking point:

POR LA FUERSApuni p'asñaqa hap'ispa qhawan.
Absolutely inSISTing, the girl grabs him and looks.
Hinaspas, much'unpi simin kashasqa, millay iy? yawarkama . . .
And there it was, a mouth on the nape of his neck—ugly, no? All bloody—

"Atakaaaw!" exclaimed CIPRIANA. "Oooh ho-orrible!"

—runa mihusqan!
—bloody from eating people!

"Ayy!" I gasped.

Huq simin much'unpi!
Another mouth on the nape of his neck!

"Agh!"

The monstrousness of the *condenado* is revealed in this misplaced all-consuming maw—manifestion of greed run wild, kin ties denied in incest and fratricide, species confused in bestiality, sex and food conflated, genders confused. All this taking without giving—which, finally, leaves a creature unable to die.

How does one kill the undead? In the back of their minds, Erasmo's listeners will recall other tales and other *condenados* who meet their dooms through fire and water or, as in the "Ukuku" story, by losing a fight. Here is the final episode of Don Aquilino's "Two Gad-about Girls:"[4]

First episode: The two straying girls chance on a *condenado* household where the oldest girl is inveigled into the watch hut to be eaten, at which point the other sister runs away.

Second episode: The surviving girl meets Old Lady Guinea Pig and marries a nice young man.

The *third episode* completes the composition by reversing the first one:[5]

Thrown together by the benevolent guinea pig, the young couple decided to live there together. After a while, they began to think about how they could avenge the older sister's death and destroy the *condenados.* "Let's kill the man and burn up the old lady," said the youth.

So they returned to the dwelling of the *condenados.* The young woman lured the young *condenado* out to the pastures by the shores of a lake. There she tricked him into a typical adolescent game of blindman's buff and pushed him into the lake, where he died. Then she rushed to the house, and found the old lady feeling quite ill. Feigning concern, she tucked the crone into bed and fussed around until her husband arrived, along with others, to set the house on fire.

Closing the door, they set fire all around the house. The old condenada *died screaming horribly.*[6]

After that, they helped themselves to all the *condenados'* things and went home to live as good upstanding people.

Her sister was gone, devoured by the condenado. *That's all there is.*[7]

Her sister had disappeared down that insatiable maw, into nothing. Her death cannot be rectified, but at least her sister can undo its cause and go on to live a moral life. No longer does she gad about heedlessly with her sister; now, part of a married couple, she can do away with the *condenados* and get on with her life. The doubling relationship, *masinitin* (sister/sister), is replaced with a paired relationship, *yanantin* (wife/husband).

Backed by husband and neighbors, the girl in Benito's narrative has no need of miraculous guidance. Together they employ one of the tried-and-true methods for destroying a *condenado*—trap it in a burning house. Here is another example of this strategy, told to Alain Délétroz Favre by Benito Nareza Calcina of Coaza.[8] The story of the *condenado* lover is braided together with another:

It begins with the story of the eloping lovers. Benito explains that the boy's family is rich and the girl's poor. The rich parents reject their prospective daughter-in-law, and this sets the story in motion.

The lovers elope, and the young man is killed while robbing his own parents. He returns to his still-living beloved, who is unaware of his nature. They sleep in the courtyard of an old lady who, realizing that the youth "is from the other life," alerts the young wife and gives her the means to escape. The wife carries her *condenado* husband across a stream, drops him in the water, and flees, throwing up obstacles behind her with the help of the old lady's brooch, comb, and needle.

Then Benito inserts an episode in which she meets another woman, a "señora," who reproaches her,

> *"Why did the two of you make such promises to each other? Now he's going to come after you, he's going to pursue you until you've fulfilled your promise."*[9]

This señora, too, gives her feminine objects—a mirror and comb—to throw behind her. The mirror turns into a lake (*qocha tukurqonqa*), and the comb becomes a range of steep, terrible mountains "full of thorns" (*kiska kiska*). With these obstacles barring the *condenado*'s path, the girl manages to rush into the sanctuary of a church. There she confesses everything to the priest. And the voice of the *condenado* is heard from outside the church door.

> *"I want to fulfill my promise," says the* kukuchi.[10]

The priest breaks off the center finger of the girl's right hand and presents it to the *condenado*, who seizes it and retreats into the distance. And so the girl is saved and lives on, multilated but in peace.

Here the story could end—and indeed in most versions it does, but Benito takes us back to the old lady and braids in her ordeal as well:

> The *condenado* returns to the old lady's house.
>
> *"Okay, you old lady, you advised my darling, my beloved to leave me—and sure enough, we've separated. So now you're going to dance with me!" he said.*[11]
>
> And dance they did. Every night he came back and forced the poor old lady to dance until her feet were completely worn out.
>
> One day a gang of muleteers passed by, and the old lady asked them for help, explaining everything that had happened. The muleteers agreed to help her in exchange for a cow, which they butchered and ate. Then they built a little house of dried cow manure, thatched it, and even made little windows and doors. They instructed the old lady that when the *kukuchi* arrived that night, she should take him to dance in her new house. Meanwhile they would bar the door and set fire all around the house. At their signal the old lady would come to the window and they'd haul her

out before the house burned up. And that's what happened. Dried cow manure makes a hot fire.

And so the kukuchi *burned up in there. He couldn't get out and was totally burned in the cow manure. And when that was finished, a white dove flew out and away.*[12]

Don Benito comments that there is a moral to the story: it's said that one should never make promises to last forever, because if you do, one of you will have to carry the other off to the other world. "*Anchaymi chay cuento*": "And that's [the meaning of] that story."

Many stories tell us that the burning saves the *condenado*'s soul. Penance completed, appetites finally quenched, the rotting soul changes to a white dove and flies away. So, too, does the *kukuchi* toward the end of the "Ukuku" story, for after the *kukuchi* drops through the roof in pieces,

The bear jumps up and GOES AFTER IT, *karahu*!

(fast) The iron doll and wooden doll are eating the boiled corn and they turn into people, see!

And so, *karahu*, when the bear man gets tired, the iron one jumps up, *karahu*, and he GOES AT the damned soul, y'see!

(soft) They hit each other, *karahu*, slam and slam each other

punch kick punch kick . . . go after each other like crazy.

The wooden one's eating boiled corn with the bear man, *karahu*!

When he says, "Now you go to it!" the wooden one jumps to his feet.

So they fight all night, and

. . . there we are, it's day already, it's getting light, *karahu*, and so he saves the damned soul, y'see, makes him yell, makes him talk.

And he asks him EVERYTHING, *karahu*!

"Where's your money? Where're your things?

These are your rooms, *karahu*! Get moving or you die!" he says.

The bear interrogates him,

makes him show everything, *karahu*, lead him to EVERYTHING, give him the keys, give him the money. EVERYthing, *karahu*!

his cattle, his goods, he has to give the bear EVERYTHING with the three of them slamming and beating him,

the damned one.

"I'll leave you my manor.

Thank you, you just saved me," and saying this, he turns into a white dove and flies off at daybreak.

The emergence of the white dove, the *condenado's* gratitude for his salvation and even at times his howling pursuit—*I have to fulfill my promise!*—produce a twinge of sympathy. *Condenados* were regular people once, and they need to die.

But no pity is due Erasmo's *condenado* with his rearward mouth and unrepentant butchery.

Hinaspas,
   Then
chayman chay p'atakiska qosqanta sat'irusqa aknata,
   she took the cactus branch the *mamacha* gave her and drove it [into the mouth] like this,
chay siminman, karahu, ch'ankiwan, iy!
   right into that mouth, damn it, with the cactus, y'see!
Chaysi, khamupakamusqaraqsi simin!
   And it seems that the mouth was trying to bite it!

CIPRIANA: *"Atakaaw!"*
   "Dr-r-eadful!"

Chaysi, chayman sat'iruspa, hinaspas, karahu,
   And impaled like that, *karahu,*
supayta . . . "K'ER, K'ER, K'ER"
   Like crazy . . . "K'ER, K'ER, K'ER"
t'ohapakunraqsi, iy? chay kundenadu maqt'aqa.
   he's groaning, no? that *condenado* youth.
Phawakachan. Romano saqrakunas waqwarin,
   Staggering around. Screaming like a black cat,
"Ch'sssss," ch'usaqraqsi tukun.
   "Ch'sssss," he deflated, collapsed into nothing.

No white dove here! Of the many tales that tell of defeating *condenados*, none in my experience expresses so clearly as this one how *hucha* has no substance once it's reversed on itself. Turned back on himself, the *condenado* collapses, converts into nothing (*ch'usaqraqsi tukun*).

Chaysi, uwihata wiqch'uspa, karahu, p'asñaqa tiira, karahu; mamakuq wasinta chayarun.
   And then, leaving the sheep, damn it, the girl rrruns, damn it, to the old lady's house.

Chaysi, mamakuqa nin...
   Then the old lady says ...
Chay wantuna ch'uqllatas chayarun...
   But first she stops at that watch hut,
"Uhalá hap'iramuyman," nispas; tullullanña p'achanpuwan kashasqa ñañanpa...
   "Oh, maybe I'll find her," she says, but there's nothing there but her sister's bones
   with her clothes

CIPRIANA: *"Eeee!"*

... yásta qhasu, qhasu.
   ... all tattered and torn.

Hoping against hope, she goes back for her sister and, finding only bones, gathers them up to bring home. This puts her in peril of pursuit by the old hag, just as the little boy was pursued by the old witch in "The Brother and Sister." But by this time, the girl has developed inner resources to make her escape.

Chaytas q'epicharukun, karahu, chaysi mamakuta yukarun:
   She wraps them up in a bundle and then, damn it, she hoodwinks the old lady:
"Uwihan tursonarusqa, chayman kachaymushawan... kuchillumanwan, mankamanwan,"
   "One of the sheep has colic, and [he's] sending me [to get] a knife and a pot,"
nisqachu hina.
   she said, adding,
"'Chayta aparamunki,' nispa, turay kachaymushawan," nispa.
   "'You've got to get them!' he says, and sends me off."

Bloat in sheep is treated by piercing the puffed-up spot with a knife and draining out the fluid. The old *condenada*, although amazed to see the girl still alive, is taken in:

Hinaspas, chaysi: "Hamuy, hinaspa apay, apuraylla! Phiñakunqa turayki, rinigakunqa, cheqaq renegusun" nispas nin,
   Well then, "Come and get them, hurry up! Your brother's going to get mad, he'll be furious, really furious," the old lady fusses,

kacharparin aphanllata.
    and sends her off anxiously.
Hinaspas kacharparin.
    So she sends her on her way.
Chaysi p'asñaqa seqayapun
    And the girl sets off
. . . khasssqanta . . . maymanta riran?
    . . . over the ve-e-rry same route . . . and where did she go?
Kasqan wasinman chayarapun . . .
    Home to her very own house . . .

RETURNING

Home to her very own house . . .

"Returning" puts me in mind of June 1978, when I made my first return trip to Sonqo. The rains were long past, and the road through Sonqo was briefly passable. I felt lucky to find a truck that would take me all the way there rather than dropping me off in Chocopia, ten kilometers away. Don Luis's house in the Pillikunka neighborhood was right next to the road, so, I thought happily, I could hop off right at the door. But I was wrong. The familiar ridges and boulders around Pillikunka had not even come into view when the truck stopped and the driver's assistant pitched my backpack over the side. It seemed that Luis had moved. I clambered down to join my backpack in the ditch by the side of the road, the driver pointed to a very steep path up what seemed like a vertical hillside, and my fellow passengers waved a cheerful good-bye as the truck continued on its way.

I set off in the deepening twilight, struggling along with my backpack. I could hardly see the path nor, in my heavy shoes, could I feel it. It was not one of those paths worn deep into the rocks by generation after generation of Andean feet, the kind that can guide you along even on pitch-dark nights. This was a newish track in dry, crumbling dirt and tough grass, and it gave me little guidance. It occurred to me that I might go right past the house in the dark and head off into the loma. The only hope of finding my way, it seemed, would be Luis's dogs, hungry, tough, snarling dogs that would come howling out of the night to chase me off. It was not a comforting thought. Those dogs can bite, as I knew from experience.

Peering into the dusk, I saw a small figure ahead of me—a dog? No, it had the triangular silhouette of a woman, but so small! A tiny woman.

It was Inucha. She had been three years old when I left; now she was almost six. Somehow she had seen me climb off the truck and start up the path to the house, and she had come down to meet me.

"Buenas tardes, Comadre," she greeted me with complete composure, betraying not a trace of surprise at my unexpected arrival. "Please come to the house," and she led me up the hillside. Now, indeed, the dogs came yowling down at us.

"Dogs, damn it, shut up!" yelled their little mistress and shut up they did. A yellow mongrel came scampering up and trotted happily along beside us. We walked along the edge of the corral. Six years later, returning yet again, I would watch her learning to weave there.

Just as I was about to beg for a rest, we reached the small thatched stone-and-adobe house.

"Pasakamuy, Comadre," Inucha instructed me. "Please do come in." I gratefully shed my backpack and ducked through the low doorway.

"Please, do have a seat, dear Comadre!" A new voice. As my eyes adjusted to the candlelight, I recognized Esteban, now nine years old, waiting with the same elegant, loving courtesy as his sister, with the Andean formality that contains such depth of feeling. I sat down and wept in exhaustion, relief, and amazement.

"Don't cry, Comadre dear, it's good that you've come. My father will be home soon. Just rest, nice and warm, and we'll fix you something to eat." Esteban tucked a poncho around my knees. Inucha started blowing on the fire. Within half an hour, I was eating warmed-over soup and boiled potatoes, with the guinea pigs nosing around my feet.

The dogs began barking. "Our parents," commented Esteban, and he stepped outside to alert them of my arrival.

Well, it seems his reserve fell away the moment he passed the threshold, for I could hear him squealing with excitement and running around the courtyard in little circles.

Inucha recognized me as she peered down the hill that evening, drawing less on her own hazy memories than on a picture of me derived from family conversation and reminiscence. It couldn't really have been that hard to figure out who I was—how many other backpack-toting gringas would come struggling up that hill?—yet her appearance in the twilight still seems tinged with the miraculous. No longer was I lost in the *loma*; she was taking me home.

But alas for the girl in our story. For her there is no recognition, and home is no longer home:

Chaysi, yásta yuraqchallañas chayarapun...naman, iy? . . . taytamamanman, iy?
Well, she arrives exhausted and all pale . . . where? . . . to her parents' house, no?
p'asñaqa.
that girl.
Chaysi: "Imanaqtin . . .?" mmm . . .
Well, "How come . . .?" mmm . . .
MANAS riqsinchu taytamamanpas, chaysi nin:
It seems her parents DON'T RECOGNIZE her, and say
"Wawaykuna chinkawaran, chaychus kawaqchis, sipas p'asñachakunallamá wawayqa chinkan,
"Our children disappeared, you couldn't be [one of them], they were still just little girls when they disappeared,
chaychu khaynaniraq yuyaq kawaq."
not like you, you're old and full of memories."
Nispa mamitanpas nipun, marastunpas.
Her mother tells her this, and her stepfather, too.

Yuyaq: remembered, full of memories. *Yuyaq* is the agentive form of *yuyay*, "to remember," "to think over past events in a contemplative way." In practice, it usually refers to a very old person, so I've translated it as "old and full of memories." With such memories, the girl is no longer a girl. Her passage through the *condenado* dimension has changed her as deeply as the passage of many years. Her mother perceives her as old and full of memories, impossible to recognize as the young girl who ran away only a few days earlier.

In other words, our girl hasn't yet truly returned home. Although she's physically present, she can't be recognized for who she is. Her identity is obscured by the hidden, experience-distant events of that terrible, distant *loma*. Her experience has to be shared, brought into clarity, before she can be truly said to return. Once clarified, she'll rejoin the human world as herself. And our story, by revisiting its beginning, will finally come to an end.

This reemergence is another recurrent theme in Andean stories. Listeners will recall other story characters who stray from the clear path into a dark, hidden dimension and emerge burdened as though by a lifetime of trauma and heavy memories. We've seen this before in the young man who played at being a *kukuchi* to frighten his unfaithful wife, and in the process got himself kidnapped by a real *kukuchi*: ". . . He returned pale and exhausted, like someone from another life; his own parents couldn't recognize him."

There's also a "true" (*chiqaq*) and frequently recounted anecdote about two boys who entered a *chinkana* (underground passage) on the hill of Sacsayhuaman above Cuzco. César Itier recorded a version told by Agustín Thuppa Pacco:[1]

> There was a **Stupid Gringo** who just couldn't resist climbing up the chinkana within the foundation of Chimor Bridge—and **!!!WAAAH!!!** he came high-tailing it out of there with **AMARUS** and **LEONES** right behind him! He got taken away in a medic's car and never was seen again.

Two boys dared each other to explore a *chinkana* that opens on the old Inca hilltop fortress of Sacsahuaman. Inside, they found themselves in the pitch dark. They lost all sense of direction and got totally lost. Day after day they wandered in the dark, exhausted and hungry, chewing on their own fingers for nourishment.

You see, those labyrinths were the Incas roads. They didn't have airplanes or trains; they just went straight underground, under rivers and mountain ranges, even to Lima and Cajamarca. So those boys just didn't know what they were doing and got totally lost. Slowly, slowly the boys made it back to Cuzco carrying ears of golden corn that they somehow found along the way.

A mass was going on in the Cuzco cathedral, and in the middle of the service there came a strange knocking on a little door. The boys were knocking with the golden corn.

"Who is it?" (the people) asked. "Are you of this life or another life?"

"We're of this life," they answered.[2]

So the people opened the door. In came the boys. They were completely pale, not at all as they once were. They collapsed, gasping, unable to walk . . . And after telling their story, they died.

Chinkana, "a deep crevice or labyrinthine underground passage," is derived from *chinkay*, "to disappear," a word we just encountered in Erasmo's narrative:

"Wawaykuna chinkawaran, chaychus kawaqchis . . ."
"Our children *disappeared*, you couldn't be (one of them)."

The *chinkana*, or interior passage, is both a physical place and a mode of experience. We make the same connection in English when we refer to subjectivity as "inner experience," but the Quechua language, with its emphasis on perception and states of consciousness, makes the equation more insistent.

Once again, it takes many words to explain what native listeners realize intuitively: For a native Quechua speaker, *any* movement into an interior location implies a qualitative change in consciousness.[3] Things that are inside (*ukhupi*) are hidden from view; one cannot perceive them directly without going inside. Even the interior of a house is a self-contained microcosm with its own state of consciousness. Sonqo's traditional houses are small, warm, windowless adobe structures; sunlight, air, people—all enter through the door. For those inside, the door is east because it is *inti haykuna*, the sun's entering place. In other words, if you're inside the house, direction is defined by the door, not by an absolute external reference point. When indoor rituals require that participants face east, they face the door (though to somebody standing outside, they might be facing, say, northwest). Because the house and the outside world have different orientations to the sun, crossing the threshold requires a reorientation of consciousness. People cross themselves, pray, and greet each other when the door is opened in the morning and again when it is closed for the night. A house, moreover, is a sentient being, formed from the living earth. While she warms and nourishes the people gathered around her interior hearth, she also watches and listens to everything that happens within her walls. For a person standing outside, what happens inside a house is hidden from direct perception or participation. Outsiders do not share the group consciousness, or intersubjectivity, created by the insiders' interaction within the vigilant *wasi-tira* enclosure. By the same token, outside events are not directly perceivable by those inside, nor do they share in the same subjectivity. Yet the difference is never absolute: one can cross the threshold from one (inter)subjective state to the other.

And this is exactly what our girl has to do as she emerges from the region of monsters and miracles into normal human society. For her, paradoxically, the high *loma* was a *chinkana*, a place of disappearance. For the young man who imitated a *kukuchi, chinkana* was a distant mountainside; for the young wife with the *condenado* husband, it was a marshy riverbed; for the two curious boys, it was an underground labyrinth. Deep interior and far exterior are the same when it comes to states of consciousness.

For listeners, this equation of interior and exterior will feel intuitively right because they are in the habit of thinking in terms of a circulating world in which every motion eventually returns, via an interior route, to its place of origin. Esteban explained to me that water flowing from Lake Titicaca eventually reaches Paititi, the hidden jungle city where the Incas are waiting for the world to reverse itself. From Paititi, the water flows back up underground and reemerges into our world through Lake Titicaca.

> That's where the water circulates to. The Sun just circulates around, and water does the same — just circulates. And in the direction of the sunrise there is a big mountain (Illimani), and the lake water is building up, and there it cascades out. Water, water, water is circulating.[4]

Water from Lake Qesqay (that lake with the submerged city) does the same; it flows into the jungle and then back underground up to the lake, to start the cycle anew. With the cycling of water goes a cycling of life, for community ancestors dwell in these mountain lakes. Rivers returning to their lakes via subterranean paths carry the recently dead to join the ancestral pool.[5] Water circulates around and within the earth, whose living body is carved with rivers and irrigation canals. K'uychi, the great two-headed rainbow serpent, participates in this circulation by siphoning water through its body. The Milky Way (called Mayu, "River") draws water from the Vilcanota River, which falls as rain and eventually flows back into the Vilcanota to renew the cycle.

When human beings fail to "go with the flow," they get into deep trouble. Denied their proper offerings, mountains may suck human blood to replace the water in their "veins." And one intrudes into that otherworldly dimension — through cracks in the earth, the base of boulders, the foundation of bridges — at peril of one's life. Sometimes this crack is an action: like the murder that propels our girls onto the high plains of damnation. They return, but not as themselves. The elder is just rags, bones, and hair. The other, hardly more recognizable:

. . . you couldn't be our child.
You're old and full of memories.

Hinaspas, WILLAKUN:
And so, SHE TELLS THEM,
"Chhayna chhaynata ruwaspataq riraykuqá; chhayna, chhayna wawaykikuna kaqtin,"
nispa.
"We went away after we did this and that; this and that, when we were your little
children."
Chay atuq uñachata sipisqankuta kaqta willakapun mamanman.
She tells her mother about how they killed the baby foxes.
Chayñas mamitan riqsipun!
Finally her mother recognizes her!

Willakun! She tells them! *Telling* is a kind of emergence, for words bring
interior experience into clarity. *Willakuy*, the recounting, is a familiar motif to Andean story-listeners. This is where
the far-reaching path of the story, like a
mountain stream, ends its underground
journey to emerge again at the beginning.
By *telling,* the girl comes out of the subterranean labyrinth of memory into the clarity
of shared consciousness.

> Diviners call out to the Earth and
> Mountains as they throw down the
> coca leaves:
> *"Sut'ita willawáy!"*
> "Tell me clearly!"

This homecoming confession that rehumanizes the teller after an encounter with entropic forces is another familiar motif in Andean narratives. Our Girl is in a large and varied company of protagonists whose direct speech within the quotation cuts through the story mode and drives
the tale to a new conclusion, as in this story, told to Jorge Lira by Carmen
Taripha:[6]

> There was a girl who had a snake for a lover. He came inside to live under
> the grinding stone, and from there he sucked up her life force. Although
> she was pregnant, still she kept him secret. As the girl faded away, her
> lover grew to monstrous size. No way could her parents find out what
> was the matter. Finally they went to a diviner, who consulted his coca
> leaves and learned the truth. Aided by their neighbors, the parents found
> the snake and smashed him to pieces. The girl, in hysterics, gave birth to
> a multitude of tiny snakes, and at that moment the snake lover finally ex-
> pired. Only then did she tell all:

> Then the girl spoke. About how she met the snake; she told her parents ev-
> erything. Then they understood it all. She clarified everything (sut'ichakun
> q'alas). And after that they were able to cure their child.[7]
> With her parents' help, she began again, married a nice man, and lived a
> normal life.

Judging by this tale, there's a chance that the girl in Erasmo's narrative
may end well after all. She may be like the young wife in the Coaza version
of "The Condenado Lover," who finally confesses everything to a priest.
After she gives one of her fingers to the *condenado*, she goes off to live a
normal life.[8] In the Hansel-and-Gretel-type story, the little boy runs home
and recounts the whole story to his father. While they never find the old
crone, the boy escapes safe and sound.[9]

But while *telling* may bring entropy to a halt, some damage is irrevers-
ible. The boys emerge from the *chinkana* into the sanctity of the cathedral
"not at all as they once were"; they tell their story, give up the golden corn,
and die. So does the Fake Condenado. His confession to the saintly gentleman gets him home, but once there, he tells his story and dies. The only
comfort is that at least he dies at home as himself, not in the company of
rotten creatures he once foolishly sought to emulate.

And such is our Girl as well:

Kayta willarukuspataqsis wañurakapun, iy?
    And when she finishes telling this, she dies, doesn't she,
chay p'asña?
    that girl?

"Ah!" I said.

Aknapi chay tukun.
    That's how it ends.

If this book were a weaving, a patterned shawl perhaps, I would be finishing it up now. I would have reached the taut end of the fabric where the
weft no longer can pass between the layers of warp, and I would have to

work the thread through with a needle. This would leave a rough line, like a run, in the fabric. "That's for your death," Gavina explained when I asked why she did that.

Some things you don't record, and you only write about them later, lest they stay buried too deep inside your thoughts. Such was my conversation with Balvina, I think it was in 2003, but she was thinking back to the San Juan P'unchay, St. John's Day, in June of 1985. At dawn, the dancing sun's rays strike the streams and turn them—momentarily—to holy water. The hills wake up, the sheep dance, and their people dance with them. Every household spends the day at home in the corral, keeping company with their own herds. And so on St. John's Eve, Santusa Nina's sheep needed to be separated from Luis's and taken home, for Balvina and Santusa pooled their flocks and shared the herding duties. Inucha, it was decided, would drive them back in the evening and stay to celebrate San Juan P'unchay with Santusa's family.

It was a "moon day" as Inucha set out with the sheep, a bright night of full moon and clear sky, when every boulder casts a shadow. Off she went over the old high path to Chocopia, dressed, I imagine, in her holiday best. Her skirt borders must have been shining and flickering around her knees. Red against black in the moonlight, red—and all the colors red brings with it—against black. Our wayruro, a pretty girl hardly fifteen years old, on her way to a party. But something strange was there as she threaded her way among the rocks, something coming around the base of a boulder.

When she tried to look, the kukuchi faded back into the rocks. When she looked away, it was there again on the margins of her vision. No matter how she went, it kept coming, slipping along after her from shadow to shadow. She rushed headlong down the hillside to Chocopia, weeping, shaking, coughing, beside herself with terror.

At Santusa Nina's, they gave her trago to settle her down; shot after shot of plain alcohol to ward off the pursuing terror and give her spirit a chance to return and recompose itself. Shot after shot, shot after shot, but she never came back.

* * *

Balvina and Luis were dancing in their corral the next morning when a small group of somber men made their way to Tawlakancha and reluctantly spoke words like thunderbolts that froze the dancers like statues for a moment *and then sent them running, barefoot and hatless, over the mountainside to Chocopia.*

"*Wawayki wañun,*" "*Your child died,*" *they said.*

Since *bright* follows *dark,*
and
merriment plays with *mourning,*

it's time for some brightness. If our story continued, what would be the next episode? Would Fox come nosing around again? Would our girl recover, marry, and raise a son who marries a star? Or who learns a unique method of spinning from an impish little Jesus? Remember how Jesus feeds wool back to the sheep? It goes in the front end as a hairy mass and gets pulled from the rear end as finespun thread.

But no, the girl is dead, and the story—come back around on itself—is over. Its two married episodes invert, reflect, and contain each other. And as the story is over, so is this book. If this were a weaving, dear Reader, only the fringe would remain to be finished:

Pedro pulled the blanket around his chin.

"*How long were you in Lima?*" *I asked him in Quechua.*

"*Six years,*" *he answered in Spanish.* "*I was twelve when I left Chocopia for Lima. My elder brother was already there.*"

His brother worked for a tailor and brought Pedro to help in the shop. It was exciting, and, what's more, the boy earned money. He learned to sew and life was good.

And yet, it seems that one day as he walked down a crowded street, the light seemed to change, the city noise receded, and he went into a kind of daze. All he wanted was to go home to Chocopia.

"*The Apus called me,*" *he said.*

So later that very day he was on a truck headed to Cuzco with hardly a good-bye to his brother and hardly more than the clothes on his back. For the whole ride he was wanting nothing but to arrive in Cuzco, to drink chicha *in Cuzco. But he had spent so long in Lima that in Cuzco he got terrible altitude sickness, and when he finally bought his big glass of* chicha, *he couldn't drink it. He just wanted to throw up.*

"*I'm still not adjusted after six months,*" *he said.*

But no, he wasn't planning to go back to Lima. He had plans in Chocopia — a little tailor shop! He knew how to sew, could make suits, he could set up a tailor shop right by the road.

"*All I need is the sewing machine,*" *he said, eyes shining in the starlight.* "*Lo único que me falta es la máquina.*"

The truck motor suddenly rumbled. Martín was awake. We recommenced our downward crawl out of the mountains to the valley of Cuzco. A couple of hours later, the switchbacks were behind us and we were whizzing (relatively speaking) along the paved road. About two A.M. *we approached the Guardia post outside San Jerónimo. The truck slowed, and we felt it pull over and stop. A breath of panic arose like frost in our nostrils. A Civil Guardsman stood outside the truck talking to Martín, saying something about* "*Aycha.*" *Meat!* "*Meat?*" *I thought. A few years later the Guards would be sniffing for coca leaves, but now it was uninspected meat, contraband meat destined to bypass the elite meat-sellers' union in the Cuzco market.*

Ana was whispering hysterically to Pedro. She shoved a poncho over his head, rummaged in her basket — and a sheep carcass was swiftly transferred from her bundle to Pedro's hands. He cradled it in his arms, hiding it under the folds of the poncho. I adjusted my mestiza-style hat and tried to become inconspicuous. Getting hauled off a truck to hand over my passport at two A.M. *was not exactly desirable. My companions quietly filled in the gaps around me. I remembered Basilia's advice a couple of years earlier:* "*You could pass for a* runa *woman! Just keep your mouth shut!*" *I kept my mouth shut. Still talking about meat, a Guardsman got on the truck and poked around in a (thankfully) desultory manner before dismounting.*

The frost-breath of panic softened. We were going to pass. But were we? The truck didn't move. There we sat until finally the man in the red poncho got off and struck up a conversation with one of the Guardsmen. After a while he got back on; whatever he did, said, or paid, it worked, and once again we were on our way.

About three A.M. *we pulled into the lower Cuzco marketplace near a bridge where the Avenida del Ejército crosses the railroad tracks. Nearby was the official* covered Cuzco market, and down the steps under the bridge, the "informal" markets continued along the tracks, rows and rows of shuttered metal kiosks. In a few hours, the market stalls would begin to open; vendors would emerge from little metal doors in the kiosks, open the shutters, and set out their wares: pans, towels, bags of noodles, cans of condensed milk, contraband radios, hammers and saws, maize, oranges, peppers, and potatoes. As Martín pulled to a stop, the only signs of life were a few dogs, too cowed and bedraggled to bark. The rest was silence.

I was staying only a few blocks away in an apartment shared by a couple of anthropology grad students. As I stood in a daze waiting for my backpack to emerge from the cargo, I wanted only to crash into bed and then, in a few hours, to heat up water on the stove (it was a cold-water flat) for a hot bath. Oh, a hot bath! My daze lifted enough to notice that I was the subject of earnest conversation among the market ladies. Where, they asked, was I going? It seemed there was no question of my walking off by myself, even for a few blocks. I would be set upon by thieves. It was impossible. I briefly thought that they were offering to accompany me home, but no, it seemed that they were taking me with them. "What a great opportunity!" I duly said to myself (I'm an anthropologist), but my sleepy heart was dreaming of a bed with clean white sheets and warm snuggly blankets.

Most of my fellow travelers, Pedro included, were disappearing nervously and quietly into the night. Much of the heavy cargo was going to have to wait until daylight, and a few worn-out travelers settled back into the truck to wait out the next few hours. Sra. Josefa hurriedly piled a huge bundle on her back and told me to follow her. I grabbed my backpack and trotted behind her down to the railroad tracks, too intent on staying awake and keeping my balance to pay much attention to where we were going. Eventually Josefa stopped to unlock a small metal door. Looking through the doorway, the interior was absolutely dark. I could see nothing, but a voice came from within, alarmed by my strange silhouette looming on the threshold.

"Is this a man or a woman?"

"I'm a woman," I answered.

Josefa hurriedly explained that I would only stay the few hours until daylight. Then, with a rapid good night, she ushered me inside along with my backpack. Before the door closed behind me, I realized that the room was about the size and shape of a phone booth, and half the floor was already occupied. There was no space to stretch out, so I curled up on the floor in the dark, feeling vaguely *that I was lying in some kind of puddle. Oh well. There was nothing to do but wait it out.*

I lay curled up in a ball waiting for daylight, and eventually a bit of light made its way under the door. My companion woke up and began to pray in a rapid and (to me) mostly unintelligible whisper broken by sobs and spells of outright weeping. She seemed to have forgotten my presence. It was still too dark for us to see each other as more than vague forms, and remembering her previous alarm, I whispered good morning as I eased myself into a seated position.

"Well, good morning!" No sobbing now. "Who are you?"

I explained as best I could, and my companion almost laughed in amazement. Hah! A gringa from the Estados Unidos! Hah! Here in the kiosk talking to her in Quechua! Hah! Happy curiosity infused her voice as she launched into questions.

What crops do you grow in the United States? What kinds of animals? Are there cities, or is it all countryside? Do people have money? Are you homesick? Where are your parents? Don't you have a husband?

We sat in the dark and talked. Her name was Teresa and she was from Sicuani. Why did she come to Cuzco, I asked. Oh, Sicuani was a dead town, nothing happened there, she had nothing to do. In Cuzco the streets were lively, people were everywhere, she loved it.

Anyway, in Sicuani she burdened her parents.

"Huchan kani," she said, "Maymaypa huchan." "I'm a sin, my mother's sin. My mother shouldn't have let me live." Why? "Because I am as I am."

Then quickly she turned back to the advantages of Cuzco. There was always plenty to do here. And people had money. And what did she do? "Oh, I go all around."

I imagined a street peddler, hawking whatever wares—from shoelaces to chocolate bars—the kiosk owner gave her to sell. We could hear people opening kiosks around us, calling out their good mornings, scolding children, and hauling out cargos of dry goods.[10] Light limned our doorway. It was time to go. She opened the door.

We looked at each other in daylight. She was gray (gray hair, gray eyes, gray face, gray ragged clothes), and she had no feet. She maneuvered a wheeled board, like a skateboard, out of the kiosk and took up two wooden blocks that she would use to push herself along with her hands. I felt hugely tall as I uncurled from my huddle on the floor and stepped out of the kiosk.

"Hah!" she said again, as I towered over her. *"Well, I'm off!"* she said, and rolled away for a day of begging in the streets of Cuzco. I picked up my backpack, which was covered with some kind of gunk, and headed away from the railroad tracks. Before I got very far, I realized that the gunk, which was also in my hair and clothes, was sputum and other indeterminate excreta from the puddle I'd just been lying in. I had a sudden hysterical desire to jump out of my skin. Nothing would do but an immediate bath.

"No hay agua." Rondi, my housemate, clattered past me on the stairs as I entered the house. *"There's no water."*

No water at all in the whole neighborhood. She was rushing out to buy bottled water. I hauled my stuff to my rooftop room and sat on the edge of the bed. In the market below, unwashed people busily went about their lives, but I couldn't go on without bathing. Where could I find water, hot water to wash in?

Then it occurred to me that my old graduate school mentor, Tom Zuidema, was staying in a different part of Cuzco in a boarding house that surely had hot water. I packed a change of clothes and some soap in a bag and set off, hoping that he hadn't already left for the day. To my great relief, he was just finishing breakfast when I got there. He seemed rather bemused as I explained my predicament.

As a boarder, Tom Zuidema is something of a catch. Not only does he bring his landlady the prestige of housing a local celebrity but — stoic and frugal as he is — he always takes cold showers. This means that he never asks to have the hot water heater turned on, which saves on the electric bill.

Thus, a few minutes after my arrival, Tom was introducing me to his landlady, who was sitting in a sort of drawing room next to a table piled with papers. She was a dark, stocky grim-faced woman whose cordiality toward Tom turned to cold refusal as he explained his request. She had no desire to turn on her hot water for a stranger.

This was when I exploded, words flying out of me like leones and amarus in the pachakuti. Miser! I screamed. People like you are what's wrong with the world, I screamed. I screamed about selfishness, exploitation, and — actually, I don't remember what all I said. I was, as they say, out of my mind.

I can sympathize with her now as I sit writing this, older now than she was then, and with a stack of bills on my desk. I must have seemed like the snotty old beggar at the wedding feast, uninvited and disgustingly filthy. And I, for my part, could happily have drowned her whole house in a flood of warm pee and *thought it poetic justice. But of course I was no deity, just a screaming gringa, and I needed Tom Zuidema's intervention to finally get my ten minutes' trickle of tepid water.*

Alone in the frigid concrete bathroom, I took off my gunky clothes, unbraided my hair, and washed away into the labyrinthian drains of Cuzco—

first, from the kiosk: snot and vomit;

then, from the road: dust;

finally, from Sonqo: smoke, soil, sweat.

Then I put on clean clothes, went off to a café on the main plaza, and ordered cake.

So that's how it was. I don't know what happened to Pedro. I asked after him when I returned a few years later, and nobody seemed to know who I was talking about. Probably he went back to Lima after all. At any rate, no tailor shop was ever set up in Chocopia.

I never saw footless Teresa again either. I came down sick a day or so after all this happened. For a week I ran the highest fever of my life. When I emerged from that hectic daze, I tottered off on my trip to Q'ero (a week late—but that's another story), so it was almost a month before I wandered back into the marketplace and down to the railroad tracks. Perhaps I lost my bearings in the labyrinth of kiosks, but I never found the little booth where I spent those cold hours waiting for the dawn to come. It seemed to have disappeared.

FRINGE

And that's about it.

The narrative "About a Married Couple" was composed by a creative individual using internal resources that were culturally constituted yet completely his own. Erasmo composed his story following the deep-trodden path of tradition, finding ways to make familiar things meet up well and transform each other in the meeting.

Language taps a marvelous synecdoche inherent in thought itself. Every word in every utterance contains the seeds of the words around it, and is itself enveloped by those very words that it contains. The meaning of any word looks outward to all the other words, and so it is with groups of words and stories. The Andean mode of patterning that I've explored in these pages exploits this characteristic. Storytellers set episodes against each other, juxtapose them to draw out hidden aspects of each other, and in the process create new stories.

A way of life, of thought, of being in the world goes into the listening of a story as much as the telling of it. This is, as Paul Connerton puts it, "how societies remember." I listened as an anthropologist trying to participate in an "Andean" kind of listening, to catch connections and relations and sense their emotional weight in what was for me a new context. In writing, I have followed Erasmo's lead and adapted his compositional strategies to this written medium, so the book contains the story Erasmo told me, and is contained by it.

Writing the book this way has been an act of appreciation, and also of cultural preservation—preserving the tradition by using it, making it part of my own—which means, of course, transforming and in a sense destroying it. The way of life in which these stories were situated is fast disappearing; the future of the Quechua language, though still spoken by millions, is far from clear. The ancient art of weaving persists while being transformed from a mode of subsistence in which people wove their own garments to a cottage industry producing commodities produced for sale to tourists and art collectors.[1] That's just how it is.

Inucha, Erasmo, Luis, and Basilia are gone, but Inucha's younger brother, Cirilo, has grown into a tall, handsome man, strong and slender, married with four children. He was only a little over one year old in 1975 when Erasmo started recording stories for me. He heard our story first as a cheerful round-faced toddler, running unsteadily between his parents as we huddled around the tape recorder. Growing into a little boy, he listened to it again in 1978, 1980, and 1984, giggling and shuddering with the rest of the family. As a ten-year-old youngster in 1984, he asked to record a story himself. We were sitting outdoors, leaning against the adobe wall of the little one-room house, not too far from the spot where Inucha worked on her skirt border.

> There was a little girl, he told me, who went out one day to fetch water from the stream, and there she found a piece of meat that she took home to her mother. Her mother tried to chop it up for the soup, but every time she whacked it with the hatchet, it jumped into her lap because —y'know what?—it wasn't really a piece of meat, it was a fox's penis! And so the girl's mother got pregnant and had [three] little baby foxes! Baby foxes! Three of 'em! And that's the end.[2]

Here was something Cirilo could imagine himself doing: scrounging some stray "meat" and taking it home to his mother. I wondered if he might someday braid this little tale together with other themes to make up a different *karu kwintu* of his own. Or might he use it as his contribution to a round-robin of storytelling, as the stories passed around the room like glasses of *chicha* or shots of *trago*? Perhaps. Certainly, if he had lived a couple of generations earlier.

Cirilo the married man of the twenty-first century owns a television and likes to spend his evenings watching travelogues, nature shows, and, of course, the ubiquitous soap operas. Cirilo the young father hardly remembers the stories he heard as a little boy. Perhaps Cirilo as a *taytakucha*—a little old man—will return to them, or maybe not (I won't be around to find out). Perhaps he may, with the childhood memories coming clearer as his short-term memory fails, remember how this image affected him, the image of a child finding, of all things, a fox's penis and becoming an unwitting agent of family disaster.

I may be a *mamakucha* (a little old lady) someday, but not an Andean one. I'll never weave as Inucha was learning to do, or tell *karu kwintus* in Quechua, as Erasmo did—nor would I want to. The best memorial to Erasmo and Inucha, it seems to me, is using what I learned from them in my terms, in my own medium, which (for better or worse) is expository writing in English. This way I contain them, and they contain me.

Erasmo said,

". . . I, too, am forgetting how to tell it.
And so NOW I'M TELLING YOU, COMADRE,
    Comadre Catalina."
"Thank you!" I said.

"KUNDURMANTA"

"About Condor"

Narrative by Erasmo Hualla Gutiérrez (Sonqo, June 1980)
Transcription and translation by Catherine J. Allen

Line breaks indicate pauses.

CATHERINE:
Ya'sta — willanaykipaq.
  It's ready for you to tell your story.

ERASMO:
Huq kwintuta, huq kundurmanta apachisaq Wiraqocha Ricardupaq.
  I'm going to send a story about Condor to Mr. Richard.
Yuu-yarinapaq.
  So he'll remember.

CATHERINE:
Gracias.
  Thank you.

ERASMO:
Yuu-yarinapaq.
  So he'll remember.
Huq kwintuchata willasayki kundurmanta.
  I'll tell you a little story about Condor.

CATHERINE:
Gracias.
  Thank you.

ERASMO:
Huqsi, kundur kasqa.
It seems there just might have been a condor.
Purimusqa, hinaspas, runa maqt'aman tukusqa.
He went wandering, and he changed his form to that of a human youth.
Hinaspa, huq uwihira pasñaman TARpan
And he went FOLLOWing a shepherd girl
sapa p'unchay.
every day.

CATHERINE:
Ay! Sapa p'unchay!
Ay! Every day!

ERASMO:
Hinaspas, ya'sta, puqllapayun, puqllapayun,
And so there it is, they just play and play
sapa p'unchay uwihaman tarpasqa, puqllapayun maqt'a —
every day while she follows the sheep she plays with the young man—
manan maq'tachu; kundur kasqa.
not a young man; it seems he was a condor.

CATHERINE: *Ay!*

ERASMO:
Hinaspas, puqllanku, q'epinakunku.
And so, they play piggyback.
"Haqay moqokama apasayki," nispas nin.
"I'll carry you as far as that hill," she says.
Chaymantaqa, q'epirusqa tirachin, pasña! primerta!
And then she carries him at a run, that girl does! She goes first!
Chaymantaqa, maqt'antaqsi nin, "Ñawiykita chillmimuy,
And then the young man says, "Cover your eyes,
noqapas q'episayki!" nispa.
now I'm going to carry you!" he says.
Hinaspas, qaqa toqomanñataq payqa q'epirakusqa, Kundur!
And with that, it seems he carried her off to a hole in the rocks, that Condor did!
Hinaspa, chaypi wachakapusqa kinsata
And so, there it seems she gave birth to three
uña kundurchakunata!
little baby condors!

CATHERINE:
Uña kundurcha!
Little baby condors!

ERASMO:
Uña kundurcha!
Little baby condors!

CATHERINE: *Ay . . .*

ERASMO:
KINsa yuraq kunkachayuqkama, kuskan runa kuskanta phuruyuq hina.
THREE of them, all with little white necks, half human and half feathered.
Mmm—chaysi,
Mmm—and then,
"Imaynataq chaynatari wachakunipas!" nispa pasñaqa,
"Whatever have I given birth to?" says the girl,
qaqa toqopin khuyaRAYshan—
she's MISerable in that rocky cave—
Kundurqa manas qacharinchu.
and Condor won't let her go.
Chaysi, listu, wawankuna allinñataq, chayqa akawarata taqsamun,
And so okay, the babies are just fine, so she washes their diapers,
watullayuq haykun.
goes out tethered to a rope.
Chaymantas, nisqa Kundurqa,
After a while, it seems Condor said,
"Ñachu? Ñachu?" nispa nin.
"Ready yet? Ready yet?"
Chaysi, "Manaraq, manaraq! Manaraq! Manaraq!" taqsan.
But, "Not yet, not yet! Not yet! Not yet!" She's washing.

(*Thump! Thump! Thump!*) (ERASMO thumps on pot to imitate the sound of washing.)

Anchaynata taqsayshan akawarata.
That's how she's washing the diapers.

HIPÓLITO (ERASMO'S SON):
Chaysi?
What then?

ERASMO:

Chaysi, "Ñachu?" nin. "Manaraqmi!" nin. "Ñachu?" "Manaraqmi!"
And so, "Ready yet?" he says. "Not yet!" she says. "Ready yet?" "Not yet!"
Hinaspa, waskata puntanta watarapusqa rumiwan.
Well then, it seems she'd tied the end of the rope to a stone.

CATHERINE: *Aha!*

ERASMO:

Chutarin, qaqasiya q'asan, chutarin qaqasiya q'asan.
He pulls on the rope, but it seems taut, pulls but it seems taut.
"Manaraqmi!" nishantaqsi.
"Not yet!" she's saying.
Chaysi, QAYRAllataq akawarapatapin.
But it's only a FROG there with the diapers,
"Manaraqmi manaraqmi," nispa tiyapushasqa.
sitting there saying, "Not yet! Not yet!"
Laq'arayshasqa!
It seems it was croaking.
(Laughter)
Hinataqsi, pasñataqsi pasakapusqa taytamamanmanmi
And the girl, on the other hand, has run away to her parents' house.

CATHERINE: *Ha!*

ERASMO:

Hinaspas, pasaqtin, hinaqa,
Well, after she's left,
q'entiqa muyuramun, iy?
there's a hummingbird hovering around, see?

CATHERINE:

Chayrí—?
And then—?

ERASMO:

"Pharr q'enti rrhirr! RRUN q'enti rrirr!
"Pharr! Whirr! RRUN Whirr!" goes the hummingbird.
"Piqpa maypi warmi munasqancha
"Somebody's little darling wife
qanchis apachitatanña wasaparushan," nispa.
is already crossing seven hilltops!" he says.

CATHERINE:
Ha! Chayri?
    Ha! And what then?

ERASMO:
Chaysi, q'entitaqa nin kondurqa,
    Well, Condor replies to the hummingbird,
"Q'enti imanawan, karahu, milpuruykimantaq!" nispa,
    "What's this, Hummingbird, *karahu*, I'll swallow you for this!" he says.

CATHERINE: Oh no . . .

ERASMO:
Chaysi, yapamantaqa,
    And well, yet again,
"Pharr q'enti! RRUN q'enti!
    "Pharr! Whirr! *RRUN* Whirr!" goes the hummingbird!
Piqpa maypa warmi munasqancha taytamamanman chayarapushanchá," nispa
    Somebody's darling little wife is just getting home to her parents' house!"
nillantaq.
    sasses (the hummingbird).
Chaysi . . ."Q'ENTI, karahu, millpuyman!" nispas.
    Well, "HUMMINGBIRD, *karahu*, I'm swallowing you!"
Phawarispa ayparun, millpurapun q'entita.
    (Condor) swoops in, catches the hummingbird, and swallows him up.

CATHERINE: *Ay!*

ERASMO:
Hinaspas, manachá riki karunpaschu
    Well, he doesn't even chew him,
interuta millpurapun!
    swallows him whole!
Hinaspa, hisparipapun kasqan interasllata q'entita—
    And so, it seems the hummingbird gets shat right out again, whole—

CATHERINE:(Laughs) Oh no!

ERASMO:
—kawsashaqta!
    —alive!

(Audience gasps, somone says, *"Manan allinchu!"* ["Not good!"])

ERASMO:
—kawsashaqllata!
—alive and well!

(Audience giggles)

ERASMO:
YAPAmantaqa phawanrishallantaqsi q'entiqa pharrpharriruspa!
And AGAIN the hummingbird's darting around, just whirring away.

CATHERINE:
Amayá!
Oh NO!

ERASMO:
"Kharr q'enti rrhir! RRUN" q'enti rrhir!
"Pharr! Whirr! RRUN Whirr!" goes the hummingbird!
"Piqpa warmi munasqancha taytamamanpi larupiña," nispa!
"Somebody's darling little wife is at her parents' house now!" he says.
Hinaspa, chaysi urayun kundurqa, riki,
So Condor goes down [to look], y'see,
chaysi, chiqaqpaq manan kapusqachu warmin.
and sure enough, his wife isn't there.

CATHERINE: *Ah . . .*

ERASMO:
Hinaspa, QAYralla kapushasqa,
There's only a FROG,
akawaranpatapi tiyapashaspa unutapi.
just sitting there in the water by the diapers.
Hinaspas, mmm,
And then, mmm,
CHAYmi siqaykun waqayuspa, Kondurqa.
WELL, Condor goes off crying,
"Q'enti karáy chiqaqtamá niwasqa chay q'entiqa," nispa.
"*Karáy,* the hummingbird told me the truth," he says.
"Maypipas kunan toparusaqpunimá, karahu!
"I'll find him somewhere, *karahu!*
Millpurullasaqtaq kunan, karahu!" nispa.
I'll swallow him this time, *karahu!*" he says.
Hinaspas . . .
And so . . .

CATHERINE:
Chayrí?
   And then?

ERASMO:
Chay q'entiqa ña taytamamanmanña chayarullantaq riki.
   That hummingbird's already at the girl's parents' house, y'see.
"Pharr! RRR q'enti RRUN whrrr," q'enti hina.
   "Pharr! Whirr! *RRUN* Whirr!" goes the hummingbird.
"Kundurmi qatayniykiqa manan runachu," nispa.
   "Your son-in-law's a condor, not a human being," he says.
"Kunanmi qatayniyki hamunqa,"
   "Your son-in-law's coming now,"
Chaysi, mmmm, consinanku anchaynata runa masinkuna.
   And so, mmm, the people set right to planning.
"Kundorta hap'isun," nispacha riki.
   "We'll catch Condor," they're saying, y'see.
Unuta rakipi, unu t'imputa listuta suyachinku sumaqta riki.
   They boil water in a big cooking pot, and when it boils, they wait, all ready
   and fine, and
hinas . . .
   ah
—punku urullanman llavesikiman nanku churanku,
   —they spread a sheep skin over the opening of it,
rakipi.
   of the big pot.
Hinas,
   So
chaYArun, lawantanta tokuyuspa wapuuu, na—
   he arRIVES as a young man, playing his flute so fine, ah—
yuraq sedanokantayuq maqt'aqa!
   with his white neck scarf!

CIPRIANA (ERASMO'S wife):
Suwigranman!
   To his mother-in-law's house!

ERASMO:
Suwigranman!
   To his mother-in-law's house!
Pasñaq taytamamanman, hinas,
   To the girls' parents house, and so

"PaSAYkuy!" nispas, sumaqta atindinku!
"DO come IN!" they say, greeting him so nicely!

CATHERINE: *Ay!*

ERASMO:
"Qanchu kanki qatay?" nispa.
"Are you (our) son-in-law?
Pay, "Arí, noqan kani Mamitáy!" nispa.
"Yes, here I am, dear Mother!" he replies.
Chaysi, tiyachinku, iy?
So they get him to sit down, no?
"Tiyaykuy," nispa sumaqta, "qarapatachapi."
"Do be seated," they say oh so politely, "right on this sheepskin."
Hinaspas, Kundurqa fuertepaqcha
And so down he goes — that Condor —
KHALLA! nispa pasakun unu t'impupi!
KERSPLASH! into the boiling water!

CATHERINE:
Aah! Pobre kundor!
Oh! The poor condor!

ERASMO:
Hinaspa wañupun Kundur
And Condor dies
PHAALLAQ! PHAALLAQ! PHAALLAQ!
Fff-LOPP! Fff-LOPP! Fff-LOPP!
sapakama listusu wañurapun unu t'impupi.
he's totally done for, and dies in the boiling water.
Pelarapunku lluyta.
They peel off everything.
Hinaspa, Kondurta mihuyapun swigran!
And then, his mother-in-law eats him up!

CATHERINE:
Ay! Swigruchu?
Ay! And his father-in-law?

ERASMO:
Arí, swegrun mihupun Kundurta, QATAYninta.
Yes, his father-in-law eats him up, his SON-IN-LAW!

HIPÓLITO:
Qatayninta mihurapun!
He ate up his son-in-law!

CATHERINE: *Ay!*

ERASMO:
HINAS!
WELL THEN!
Chaypi chay p'asña salvakapusqa taytamamanwan iskapapusqa.
That's how the girl was saved by escaping to her parents' house.

CATHERINE: *Ah-huh.*

ERASMO:
Manan chaymanta kutipunñachu.
He never returned from there.
Hinan chay . . .
And that's that . . .
chayta kwintuta apapuwanki riki Wiraqocha Ricardupaq.
You're to take this story for me to Mr. Richard.

CATHERINE:
Gracias!
Thank you!

ERASMO:
Kay kwintullata apachimusayki, Wiraqocha Ricardu!
Mr. Richard! I'm sending you this story!
Kondurmanta! Qonqarapusqankitaqsí!
About Condor! I'll bet you've forgotten it!

CATHERINE:
Manan!
No (I'm sure he hasn't).

ERASMO:
Annn, perdirapusqa, nnaa—sinta!
Ahh, and it seems it was lost—ah—the tape!

CATHERINE:
Ah, chay sinta! Riki!
Ah yes, that tape! You're right!

ERASMO:
Chayqa huqmanta willapushayki chayta!
> And so now I'm telling it to you over again!

CATHERINE:
Gracias! Huqmanta!
> Thank you! Over again!

ERASMO:
Yuyarinapaq!
> So he can remember!

CATHERINE:
Allinmi! Gracias!
> Very good! Thank you!

"UKUKUMANTA"

"About Bear"

Narrative by Erasmo Hualla Gutiérrez (Sonqo, 1975)
Transcription and translation by Catherine J. Allen with
assistance of Jaime Pantigoso

Line breaks indicate pauses.

ERASMO:
Kunan willasayki kwintuta, ukukumanta, Kumpadri.
　　Now, Compadre, I'll tell you a story, I will, about Bear.
Ukukus p'asñaman tarpasqa,
　　They say that Bear prowled after a girl
uwiha michisqanpin
　　while she pastured sheep.
Hinaspas, chay uwihas michisqantin
　　And so, as she pastured the sheep
maqt'amansi tukuspa, tukuspa, tarpasqa.
　　he turned into a boy and went after her.
Chay maqt'a tarpan, tarpan, hina.
　　He just followed and followed her.
Hinaspas, chaymanta q'ipirapusqa warmita,
　　And then he carried her off,
qaqa t'uquman!
　　off to a cave!
Hinasqa, qaqa t'uqupi, uywasqa.
　　And there in the cave he cared for her.
Hinaspa, uywasqa, tiyaykun, uywan—
　　There he cared for her—
uñayña tiyanku.
　　they lived there a long time.
Wawan kapunña.
　　Soon they had a child.

Hinas, chay wawanqa —ya'sta hatunchaña hatunchaña!
  And so that child—it's getting bigger and bigger!
P'asñataqsi kaqllata wisq'asqa tiyan qaqa t'uqupi,
  And the girl is still living shut up in the cave,
qaqawan tapasqa.
  closed off with a rock.
Hinas, chaymanta, purin ukuku, wakaman rin, maytachá, karuta!
  And so, then the bear goes off, goes after a cow, where to? Far away!
Chay wakata q'ipimun, sarakunata q'ipimun, IMAYNAta apan!
  He carries the cow on his back, lots of corn on his back, he'll carry ANYthing!
Uwihakunata . . .
  Sheep, too . . .
AsKHAtas chayachin!
  He gets a WHOLE LOT of stuff!
Taqantinta saratapas q'ipikun,
  He carries the whole corn crib on his back,
taqepi wakakunatapas palltarukun!
  and loads the cow on top!
Hina q'ipin!
  That's how he carries them.
Chaymanta
  So then
chayachin.
  he gets that stuff.
Chayqa, ña chay,
  And well,
wawachanqa hatunchaña aknanchaña.
  the baby is growing bigger and bigger and bigger.
Chay huq wawachan kallantaq, iskaypiña wawachankuna.
  There's one child . . . and then there're two children.
Chay warmitaqsi kaqllapin tiyan, wisq'asqa, qaqa t'uqupi.
  And the woman just stays there, shut up in the cave.
Uywashan.
  Caring for them.
Waputasyá mihuchinpis —
  And he sure feeds them well—
aychata, wakakunata apamun, uwihakunata, khuchikunata,
  he brings meat—cows, sheep, pigs—
IMAYMANATASYÁ apun!
  EVERYTHING you can think of!
Hinaspas, chaymanta
  And so, well then,

iskay wawan chayqa.
there are two children.
Ya'sta . . . Huq kaqqa allinchaña waynachaña.
The first one is already fine, a young man.
Huq kaqtaq tinkuchallaraq, ya'sta hatunchallañachá wiñashanña riki!
The second one's still kind of small, but it's growing up fast, y'know!
Hinaspas, mamanta yachachisqa:
And so, they instruct their mother:
"Machulayta pasakapusunchis.
"We're all going to run away to our grandfather's.
Papayta ninki,
You say to our father,
'Mana iMAMpi yuraqniyuq yana wakata aparamuway!' nispa Mamitáy ninki," nispa.
'Bring me a black cow without ONE bit of white on it!' that's what you tell him,
Mommy."
Papanta nin.
She speaks to their father.
Papanta qatisqaku.
They send him away.
Hinaspas,
And so,
rin papanqa,
off he goes, their father,
sirtupaq,
no doubt about it,
mamitan niqtin siqaykun.
the little wife told him to, so off he trudges,
manan imampi yuraqniyuqta maskhayaaamun wakata!
looking for a black cow without a bit of white on it!
Manan tarimunchu.
He can't find one.
Astatas puriyamun.
He searches all over.
Chayachimun ñak'ayta.
Then finally he manages to get it.
Chaykamataqsi, chikuchankunaqa
But meanwhile the little boys
HayT'Amun aknata chay qaqa wisq'asqanta.
KICK (like this!) the rock closing up the cave,
"Pasakapusunchis!" nispa.
saying, "We're going to get out!"
Hinaspas, kuyurachimunku rumita iy?
And so they roll the stone a little, y'know?

Qaqata, punkunta.
The rock, the door.
Chaysi, kuyurachimuqtinku,
And when they move it,
"Ya'sta, Mamitáy kaRÁY!" nisqa.
"Mommy, *kaRÁY!*" they say.
"Kuyurachiykun kunan, huqtaq wikch'usaqku," nispa nin.
"This time we rolled it over, next time we'll send it flying!"
Chaysi, iskayninmanta, chikuchakunaqa, karahu, hayt'amullantaq aknata iskay chakiwan hayt'an, riki.
(*fast*) And so both of the little boys, *karahu,* they just kick it like this, with both feet, y'know.
WAAQ! dalimun!
WAAQ! They go at it!
Wanturamun riki.
Push it away, y'know.
Hinaspa, papan hap'iramusqan, chay punkuntan kichashaqtin.
And so, they're opening that door, the one their father put there.
(CIPRIANA, ERASMO's wife, laughs.)
Papan machu ukuku!
Their father's an old bear!
Wiña ukukuchakunataqsi hayt'amushan!
And the little bear children are kicking at it!
Hinaspas
And so,
naa—chayqa
well then,
"Papay q'uñikuqmi lloqsimurayku," nispalla
"Daddy, we're coming out to sun ourselves!" they say
yukurunkunataqa machu ukukutaqa.
to fool the old bear.
Mamantaqsi hinalla tiyashan.
And their mother's just sitting there.
Yapamantaqa,
Once again
"'Manan iMAMpi yuraqniyuq uwihata apamuway,' nispa kachanki, Mamitáy," nispas yacharachinku.
"Send him away, Mommy," they tell her. "Say, 'This time bring me a sheep without ONE BIT of white on it!'"
Chikuchakunaqa mamitanta.
Little boys instructing their mother.
Chaysi, ukukutaqa kaq—nallantaq—warminqa kachallantaq.
And, well, so the bear's wife just sends him right off again,

"Manan iMAMpi yuraqniyuq uwihata maskharamuway!" nispas.
　　saying, "Go look for a sheep without ONE BIT of white on it!"
SiQAYkun ukukuuuuuuu . . .
　　He trudges AWAAAY! that bear!
Maypichá purimun? Loman-lomanta riki!
　　Roaming who knows where, way up in the mountains, y'know.
Uwihata maskhaspa.
　　Looking for a sheep.
Chaysi huq qhawayun uwihata
　　Then he sees one!
Yuraqllataqsi.
　　But it's got white on it.
Huq uwihata qhawakun!
　　Sees another one!
Yuraqllataqsi.
　　But it's got white on it.
Yana uwihakunata rikSIYshan!
　　He's looking out for a black one!
Manapuni ñak'aytas tarimun.
　　He just can't find one.
Mana imampi yuraqniyuq ñak'aytas tarimun.
　　But finally he manages to get one without a bit of white on it.
Maypichá riki?
　　Who knows where?
Hinaspas hamun ukukuqa chayqa q'ipiykuspa.
　　And so the bear comes carrying it on his back.
Chaykamaqa pasakapusqakun,
　　But it seems by that time they've gone away,
mamanta horquranpusqa, riki, t'uqumanta.
　　(after) taking their mother out of the cave, y'know.
Chaysi, mamitanta yachachin,
　　And they instruct their mommy,
"Kunanqa tarparamawasun papay chaypachaqa.
　　"It may happen that our father catches up to us.
Hayt'aspa choqasaq kunan maymampis.
　　We'll have a run-in with him somewhere.
Sichus nuqaykuta winsiruwanqaku, chayqa
　　If it happens that he defeats us,
sut'illan, puka q'osñi sayarinqa.
　　then very clearly red smoke will rise up.
Chayqa, Mamitáy, lakikunki," nispa.
　　And then, Mommy, you (can) grieve," they say.

"Si es papayta winsirusaqku, chayqa, azul q'osñi sayarinqa.
"And if we beat our father, then blue smoke will rise up.
Chayqa kusikunki, "nispas nin, mamitanta,
Then you can rejoice," they tell their mother,
uña ukukuchakuna.
those little bear children.
Hinaspas uña ukukuchakuna niqtinqa,
So after the little bear children say this,
purishaqtinkuña siqaykun.
off they go, wandering.
Hinaspas, karumanñas tarpan riki, maypiñachá?
And so they go a long way, who knows where?
Hinaspas, tarpaqtin mamitanña ñawpaqta pasashan, phawaiilla!
And as they follow him, their mother goes ahead, reeeal fast.
Ukukukunachataqsi taytan tarpaqtin, MAQANAkun,
When those little bears catch up to their father, they FIGHT
taytanwan!
with their father!
Hinaspas,
And so,
taytanwan maqanakuqtin,
when they fight with their father
taytanta winsirapun wiña ukukukuna, iy?
—whaddya know?—those little bear children, they beat their father.
Hinaspas mamitanta qhawarikunanpaq azul q'osñi sayarishasqa.
And so the blue smoke rises up to their mother's watchful eyes.
CHAYsi mamitanqa tuSUYkun, karahu! "Sipiramun alqu machuta ichaqa!" nispa.
Hahahaha!
(fast) And their mother DANCES, *karahu!* "I'll bet they've killed the old dog!"
Hahahaha!

(ERASMO's wife and children are laughing.)

Chaysi, tarparapun mamitanwan, wiña ukukuchakunaqa.
So then the little bear children meet up with their mother.
"Ya'sta Mamitáy, kunanqa machuta salvaramuykuña!" nispa.
"Okay, Mommy! We just saved the old guy!" they say.
Hinaspa, tarpan, chayqa tarpaspaqa, kunTINtu ripunku machulanman.
And after they meet up, they go off OH SO happily to the grandfather.
Chay p'asñaq mamitanmansi chayapun.
It seems the girl goes home to her mother.
Papanman mamitanman wiña ukukuchakunata pusan.
She leads her little bear children to her father and mother.

Hinaspas, chaymantaqa
   Well, so then
chayanku machulanpa wasinpi,
   they arrive at their grandfather's house,
chaypis purikachan purikachan
   at their grandfather's house, and there they have to do lots of chores,
uwihata michichimun.
   like herding sheep.
Uwihakunata LLUYta p'anaspa sipirapun, chikuchaqa.
   And they kill off ALL THE SHEEP, those boys.
Chaysi, manachá bawtisqapaschá karan, chaysi
   Then, it seems they'd never been baptized, so
kurawan bawtisachisqa, chayta;
   a priest baptized them;
machulansi bawtichishasqa.
   the granddad made them get baptized.
"Bawtisachisunman, manan bawtisasqa irqichakuna hina . . ."
   (Mumbling) "They ought to be baptized. Unbaptized kids are like this . . ."

(RICK, CATHERINE's husband, offers *trago.*)

ERASMO:
GRAsias, WiraQUcha!
   THANK you, kind SIRRR!

RICK:
Salud. Tomakuy!
   To your health!

ERASMO:
YusulPAYki urPÍY!
   You're SO very KIND!
Hinaspas, bawtisachisqa machulanña,
   And so, the grandfather had them baptized,
kura bawtisachisqa.
   baptized by a priest.
Kura padrinun kasqa chay chikuchakunaq.
   The priest was godfather for those boys.
Hinaspas, chaymantaq,
   So then,
bawtisachisqanmantaqa,
   after they were baptized,

hampun.
>they came back.

Hampuspaqa,
>After they came back,

tiyan wasinpi,
>they stayed in his house,

chay auluchanpapi.
>in their grandfather's house.

Hinaspas, irqichankunan kan chaychakunatas,
>Well, there are some other kids there,

puqllapayan, puqllapayan, tiruwan tirun.
>and the (bear) boys play and play with them, play at marbles.

SIpirapunsi t'inkashaspalla.
>And it seems they KILL them all off, shooting marbles.

Chaymantaqa, yapamanta
>And then, they just keep playing around—

puqllallantaq, wallpachakunata, aknata, ch'ankan, ch'ankan,
>they clobber all the nice chickens (like this!)

SIPIRAPUN pasaq pasaqta.
>THEY JUST KILL OFF everything everywhere.

Quwichatapis q'asarapun.
>Guinea pigs, too, they crunch them up

Imanampas sipirapullantaq, hina!
>any old way, like so.

Animalkunata tukurapushanña!
>They're just finishing off the animals already!

Yasta, "Imaynachá kay wawaqa, manan wawaqa kanmanchu!
>Well then, "What's with these kids! These can't really be children!

Comparimanya qopusaq aswan. Padrinu uywakapuchun," nispas.
>I'd better give them to their godfather. Let him bring them up!"

Kuraman apapun riki.
>Grandpa takes them to the priest.

"Manan awantaymanñachu," nispas.
>"I just can't put up with this!" he says.

Chaysi, padrinuman apasqa.
>So, they're taken to their godfather.

Hinaspas, padrinunpanpiqa kaqllataq . . .
>And there at his house, well, it's just the same.

Chay . . .
>There . . .

Impliadonkunachá kan,
>There are servant boys,

chikukunawan puqllan.
  and they play with the (bear) boys.
SIpirapullantaq . . .
  The (bear) boys just KILL them off,
sipirapun.
  kill them off.
Yapamantaqa
  Again they keep on
puqllan, puqllan, imakunatapis kamachin
  playing, playing, bossing everything around
sipirapullantaq imakunatapis!
  and they just kill off whatever!
Ya . . . . . .
  Ah . . . . . .
FAstidiYUsu, riki, chiku!
  WHAT BOTHERsome kids!

CATHERINE:
Manan allinchu!
  This is bad!

ERASMO:
Ukuku wiñacha, awír?
  Those little bear cubs!

CATHERINE:
Riki!
  That's right!

ERASMO:
Papantapis sipipunña! Ahh . . .
  Even killed their father!
Isti . . .
  Let's see . . .
Mamitanpis, ista . . .
  And their mother—
LlaKIsqa kapun!
  she's just MIserable!
"Imanataq kay waway khayna?" nispa.
  "How come my children are like this?"
Ñas nin nisqa.
  That must be what she said.

Kurapis phiñakapun.
    The priest is getting mad, too.
"Ima rusil chikutaqa kaytaqa pusamuwanku?"
    "What kind of troublesome kids have they brought me?"

(CIPRIANA laughs.)

"Bwinu, imaynapi kaykunata kastigasaq, imanasaq," nisqa,
    Alright, how to punish them then? What shall I do?" he says,
rinigasqa.
    furious.
Chaysi, iskwilaman churan, kuraqa.
    So, that priest, he sends them off to school.
"Prufisurkuna, maystrankuna kastiganqa riki.
    "The teachers will punish them for sure!
Wananchinqa!" nispa nin.
    They'll discipline them," he says.
Iskwilapis tiruwan puqllan puqllan chikuqa.
    And in the school those boys just go on playing with marbles.
SIPIRQARIPUN tiruwan t'inkaspallan alumnukunata.
    They KILL OFF THE STUDENTS by shooting marbles.
Sapanqata wañuchin.
    Each and every one.
Chaysi yapamantaqa
    So they keep on
puqllan, puqllan
    playing and playing,
hinas t'inkarapun,
    shooting marbles (like this!),
prufesur nintañataqsi sipirapullantaq.
    then they shoot marbles at the teachers! Kill 'em off!
Siku!
    Dead as doornails!
Chaymantas, rinigasqa khihacha imacha huwishutachu siginku, riki, kurawan.
    After that, the priest is pursued with squabbles and all sorts of lawsuits.
Chaysi, hinaqa
    Well, and so
kuraqa nin,
    the priest says,
"Ñachá allin waynañachá chaypiqa kashan, riki!"
    "Well, don't these seem to be fine young men!"
Chaysi, "Imanasaqtaq, kay wawaytari?" nispa nin.
    And, "What am I going to do! Oh what children I've got!" he says.

"Khaynananaq ricibiluri!" nispa.
   "Still such troublemakers!" he says.
"Weno ñataq edasninpiña kwartilman dispachasaq," nispa,
   "They're old enough to send to the army," he says,
kwartilman dispachapun.
   and sends them off to the barracks.
"Chaypiqa, karahu, ofishalkuna kastigamunqa allinta," nispa.
   "There, *karahu*, the officers'll teach 'em a lesson," he says.

(Audience laughter)

"Fusilayumunqaku, karahu, chhaynata ruwaqtinqa," nispa.
   "They'll shoot 'em if they act like that," he says.
"Sipipunqaku," nispa nin.
   "They'll kill 'em," he says.
Firru bastunchantas ruwarapun munayta ruwachipun.
   He makes an iron club, has it made very nicely.
Chaynintinta kachan.
   He sends them off with that.
Chay firru bastun aysasqa rin, kwartilman.
   They go off dragging the iron club to the barracks.
Chaypi . . .
   And there . . .
mayta . . . mmm . . .
   Well, so . . .
Chay kwartilmantaqa
   in the barracks . . .
risqamantaqa kwartilpichá,
   after they get there,
kamaaachin ofishalkuna imanachá!
   the officers order them arou—nd like anything!
Mana atinchu, mana atiqtinsi,
   They're just no good at anything, no good at all—
yasta, karahu, rinigasqa riki, paypis kastigasqa.
   until, *karahu*, they get furious and do some punishing themselves!
Q'ASUN, karahu, chay firru bastuninwan!
   CRACK 'em, *karahu*, with their iron club!
Wañurachipun ofisaltañataq.
   And so they kill the officers.
Sipipun.
   Murder 'em.
Chaymantas suldadukunas, "Lluy fusiliyasaq," nispa nin.
   And then it's up to the soldiers. "We'll just shoot 'em!"

Chaysi balata CH'AQLAN huqta CH'AQLAN, huqta CH'AQLAN—
But they just SLAP the bullets, SLAP the bullets, SLAP the bullets, SLAP the bullets—
kutichin, karahu, Q'ALATA mana balapi sipinku!
slap back ALL the bullets, *karahu!* The bullets can't hurt 'em, *karahu!*
Ukuku uña, iy?
Little bear cubs, y'know?

(Audience laughter)

Karahu, es firru bastoninwan hoqarikuspa Q'ASUN!
(fast and soft) *Karahu!* They grab the iron club and CRACK!
Batin, batinbi bin sipin—
Bam boom smash 'em good—
q'aLAta trupata chiriyarachimpun!
they ICE OFF the whole troop!
LLUYta matanzaruspas,
And when they've massacred EVERY LAST ONE of 'em,
kumpalinman kutiripun,
they go right back to their godfather,
—nnata—kuraman.
to the priest.
"Imapaqmi, Papáy, kwartilman churamuwanki?
"Papa, why on earth did you send us to those barracks?
Awír, baliyuwashasqakun noqata, fusiliyawashasqakun noqata!
They fought with us! They even shot at us!
Q'alata sipimuni kay bastunniywan q'asuspa," nispa nin.
We killed the lot of 'em, cracked 'em with our iron club!" they say.
"AY! Imaynasaqtaq, kunanri kay wawaaayqa! Hisus Maria!" nispa.
"AY! What am I going to do now? These CHILDren of mine! Jesus and Mary!"

(Audience laughter)

Kuraqa wañunraqsiyá!
The priest is just dying!
Pit'aykachanraqsi!
Jumping up and down!

(Loud laughter)

"Imataq kanqa?" nispa.
"What will come of this?

"Imanasaqtaq bueno, karahu?" nispas.
Whatever can I do?" he's saying.
"Huqkaqchanqa kashallansiyá sullk'a kaqqa!"
"And there's the other one, the younger one, too!"
. . . . (long pause)
Hinanspa, chaymanta,
And then
"Imapitaq wañurachipusaq, seq'urapusaqchu, imaynataq kay wawaytaqa,"
"How will I kill them, hang them?"
nispas nin kuraqa.
says the priest.
Chaysi, yuyakun kuraqa,
So then he thinks of something—
"Turrita karahu!
"To the tower, *karahu*!
Kachasaq kampana tukaqta," hinaspa
I'll send them to ring the bell," he says,
"ayllu runantinta, karahu, ayllu runa tanqayamunqa," nispas.
"and the townspeople, *karahu*, the townspeople will push them off the tower!"
he says.
Turri sikita khapuyachin ukhquta!
He has them dig a hole at the bottom of the tower!
"Chayman tanqayamunqa aylluntin runamanta," nispas.
"The townspeople together will push them into it," he says.
"P'anpapusaq chay uhupi," nispas.
"I'll bury them in the hole," he says.
Hinaspas
So
iskaychanta kachapun, iy?
he sends them both up there.

CIPRIANA (coaching):
Huqchampis chaynallataqchá . . .
The other one was about this big . . .

ERASMO:
Huqchampis hinallataq Sirilucha.
The other one was about as big as Cirilucha.
Hins, turripatata kampana tukaq rin.
And so they go to ring the bell in the tower.
Kampana runtutas waaaqharapun chaypi.
They slaaam the clapper.

Chay hoqna p'ananantin kampanamanta hurqurunkun!
   They pull the clapper right out of the bell!
Hinaspas, runakuna siqan.
   Then the people climb up the tower.
Rakhutaqsi khapu kashan turriq pachampi. Ankhayna uhupi!
   And the hole at the bottom of the tower is wide, and deep—like this!
Chaysi, tanqayunan kashaqtin,
   And then they start pushing—
runakunata tanqayamun,
   and they push the people,
runakunata llipinta hach'iyaramun aknata, iy!
   send them all flying—like this, y'see!
Chay t'uquman llipin runa—BUQH! BUQH!—pasakapun karahu!
   And they all fall—BOOF BOOF—into the hole, *karahu!*
Q'ala wañupun.
   They die, every last one.

CIPRIANA (coaching):
Qawashansi pay
   It seems he's watching.

ERASMO:
Qawashansi kuraqa.
   And it seems the priest is there, watching.
"AY, imasaqtaq! Karáy kunanqa! Manan kayqa allinchu kapun!
   "AY! What am I going to do? Damn it all! This is terrible!
Imaynasaqtaq aylluntin runatari!" nispas nin.
   What will I do about the townspeople!" he says.
Hinaspas, sullk'achantawan tanqarayakampusqa.
   Well, the younger one got pushed in, too.
Chay kuraq kaq chikullanña kapushan.
   Now the priest has only that one boy left.
Hinaspas, kura kaqqa kutirun . . .
   And so, that boy goes back again—
. . . nnaman . . . kuramanqa hayk'urun.
   . . . um . . . to the priest.
"Papáy, qhipaymanta runakuna yankapuni fastidiamuwashasqaku, chaymi rinagaypi wiqchuyamuni llipinta!" nispa.
   (fast) "Papa, people came after me bothering me for no reason at all and so I got mad and tossed them all out," he says.

(CIPRIANA laughs.)

Kutirqun, kutirun, iy . . . kuramanqa?
  He keeps on coming back, doesn't he . . . to the priest?
"AY WAWÁY! IMATAQ KAYKUNA khaynaniraqta sipirapunki aylluntin runata!
  "AY! MY CHILD! HOW COULD YOU KILL THEM, kill the townspeople
  like that!
Imanawanqakun noqata?"
  What'll happen to me!"
Wañunraqsiyá kura.
  It seems the priest is just dying!

(RICK laughs.)

"Imapin kasaq kunan?" nispa.
  Saying, "What's going to become of me now?"
Hinaspas, "Karáy! imapaqmi turiyawanku? nispas
  But—"*Karáy*, what did they tease me for?"
chay ukukuqa nin,
  says the bear,
uña ukukuqa.
  the little bear.
"Chay chayta ruwamuni!" nispa.
  "That's why I did it."
Kampana runtutapis aparikunraq aparikamusqataqraqsi wakharuspa.
  And he's still carrying the bell clapper he pulled out when he rang it.

(One of the children laughs.)

Hinaspas . . . nan . . .
  And so, hmm,
chaymantaqa kuraqa rinigasqa, riki
  then the priest is really furious.
Nispas kura "Karahu, imata ruwasaq?" nispa nin.
  "*Karahu!*" he says, "What am I going to do?" he says.
"Bwinu intonsis kaytaqa.
  "Okay . . . then this is what I'll do.
Muntita kachasaq, chaypi animalkuna mihunpunqa,
  I'll send him to the jungle; the animals there will eat him
ukuku—puma— tingri—imakunapis," nispa,
  —bears, pumas, tigers—whatever!
"MAchumaCHUNNta, PayapaYANNta!"
  "OLD and deCREpit ones, MALE and FEmale ones!"
MulakuNAta rantiruspas chaynintinta
  The priest buys some secondhand MULES—

Chaynintinta per—perdinan kwinta kachan.
and sends him off with the troop of them.
"Llant'aman haykuy!
"Go on and get firewood!
Montañatapuni haykunki!" nispas.
Go to the jungle!" he says.
Simana puriyta.
It's a week's trip.
Kachaykun maytachá? Muntita, riki!
Where to? To the jungle, right?
Chaysi, ukukuqa haychalla aysasqa, karahu, riyatakuna apariyusqa.
So, that bear sets out lugging an axe, *karahu*, and carrying ropes.
Tiraykun silbayuspa, uña ukukuqa,
Off goes the bear cub, whistling,
kaballukunapi, mulakunapi, hinasyá!
with horses, with mules like that!
Hinaspas, ichaykun hoq wayk'umanchá, imaynachá ichan, riki, mulakunata.
And then he leaves the mules, leaves his mules in a gully or someplace.
Paytaqsi llantata ch'iqt'aaaykun.
And he sets to cuu-tting firewood.
Mihunata wayk'uyuspacha,
Then he cooks himself some food,
rin chayqa mihunata quqawanta mihuy mihuspa.
packs it up, and goes along snacking on it.
Hinaspa . . . nnaqa,
And then . . . and so
huq qaway hamunanpaqqa
he goes to check on the mules,
mula kashaspa pisichallaña.
but there aren't many there.
Animalkuna mihurapusqa LLUYta mulakunata ch'ustirapusqa!
The wild animals have eaten them ALL UP!
Hahahaha!
Hahahaha!
Hinaspas, rinigakun ukukuqa!
Well, Bear is furious!
"Imanasaqtaq karahu mulayta mihurapusqa?" nispa.
(fast and soft) "What am I going to do now, karahu, now that my mules are eaten up?"
Kutirun, llant'ataqa peru llant'ayllashansi askhata.
He goes back for firewood and sure cuts lots and lots of it.
Huqta qawaq kutirun, Q'ALA mula mana kapunchu!
Then he goes back for another look, and the MULES ARE ALL GONE!

Lluyta tukurapusqa animalkuna.
The animals finished off every last one.
TulluLLAñas muntumuntun!
NOTHing but piles 'n' piles of booones!
Hinaspas, ukuku rinigakun, karahu!
Well, Bear is furious, *karahu!*
Muratas p'itirukun, rakhuta muntimanta.
He snaps off branches[?], thick ones from the forest.
Chayta, aysakuspas munti-muntinta,
Armed with them, he roams the whole forest
tukuruspa animalkunata huñiyamun:
and herds together all the wild animals:
tingri, ukukumasikunata, liunkunata, LLUYtas animalta huñiramun, askhata, iy!
tigers, lions, his fellow bears, he herds them ALL together, lots of 'em!
Chaypis, llant'ata liyaruspa, t'eqiyamun llipin animalta kargayamun.
And then when he's bundled the firewood, he loads up all the animals.

(A child laughs.)

P'ANASHASPALLA dalimun astala kuraq kasqa, kasa kuralkama.
And WHIPS 'em all the way to the priest's corral.

CIPRIANA (coaching):
Chayarachin . . .
He drives them there [to the priest's corral].

ERASMO:
Chayarachin. Pay, "Papáy!
He drives them there, and says, "Papa!
Khaynatan mulanchista tukurapusqa chay animalkuna, chay huchanmanta kayman kargamuni llant'ata," nispa.
these animals finished off our mules, and for that crime I made THEM carry the firewood!"
Patiyuman, qarkurun, karahu p'anashaspallas, iy!
He's beating them, kicking them right into the patio, *karahu!*
Wakinsi chakipaki, wakinsi makipaki,
Some with broken hindfeet, some with broken forefeet,
yasta wiqrukuna! Imaymanatas chayarachin!
exhausted and broken! That's how he drove them in.
Hinaspas, kuralman qayqoruspa llant'anta paskaruspa, P'ANAYkun chay uhupi!
And when they're all in the corral and the wood's unloaded, he GOES AT THEM in there!

Mula mihusqanmanta karahu! "MAYmi mula?" nispa.
Because they ate the mules, *karahu!* "Where're the mules?" he yells.
Hinaspas, kuraqa qaparillantaq,
And the priest is screaming,
"AY! Imaynasaqtaq kay wawaytaqa?
"AY! What am I going to do with this child of mine?
Karahu, Hisus Mariya! Khaynaniraq animalta maymanta aparamunki?
Jesus and Mary, damn it! Where did you bring all these animals from?
Kasqanta saqirampuy!" nispa nin.
Leave them alone!" he says.

(Audience laughter)

Hinaspas karáy, kuraqa niqtin, p'anashaspalla kallita, karahu!
And so, hell, when the priest says that he's just beating them down the street,
  karahu!
Qharkumun thuni-thunita,
They're caved in and collapsing,
laq'a-laq'ata wiqrukunata,
broken and twisted,
manan ñawiyuqta, pampasyá kay,
blind, dead, and done with,
animalkunata ruwaypun yasta.
[that's how] he does in the animals.
Mana chanintapuni ukuku p'anayun riki.
The bear beats them unmercifully.
"Imaynasaqtaq! Manamá chaypi mihumunchu chay chikutaqa! Imaynataq kasaqri?"
nispas kuraqa,
(fast) "What'll I do? They didn't eat the boy. What's going to become of me?"
  says the priest,
Lla KIsqa, iy!
REAL disappointed.
"Khaynaniraqta chayarachimullantaq chaytaqa!" nispa.
"Just like before, he's gotten away with it!" says the priest.
"Manaña wañunchu imapipis!"
"He just doesn't die!"
Llant'atapis, kullukunata kargayamun.
He's brought firewood, logs.
Waputasyá madirakunata ch'iqtayushan.
It seems that he's splitting it up like anything.
Chayta rawkhaykun chayqa chayllawanqa kuntintutaqsi kuraqa, llant'allawanqa.
But when he's got it all neatly piled up, the priest is happy, contented with his
  nice woodpile.

Hinaspas, chaymantaqa
  And so

(Audience laughter)

manapuni maypipis wañunchu riki!
  He sure doesn't die anywhere, does he!
Chaysi, asindayuqñataq wañusqa, llipin, warmiqhari, q'ala.
  Well, [there's a manor where] the hacendado died, and it's empty of everything,
  men and women.
Hinaspas
  And so
chaypi kundinakusqa asindayuq.
  the landlord is a *condenado* [damned soul].
Hinaspas, kundinakuspa tiyasqa
  So he lives on, that damned one,
q'alatañas runantapas tukun ch'usaqtaña.
  and [the hacienda] becomes uninhabited, absolutely deserted.
Manañas ima runapis kanñachu.
  Nobody lives there anymore.
Asindapi manañasyá imapis tiyaqpas imas kanchu.
  Absolutely nothing lives anymore on that hacienda.
Allin wasinchansisyá kasqa.
  There are nice little houses there.
Kundinadullas chaypi tiyan, karahu! Wapu chay asindayuq.
  (fast) Only that damned soul lives there, *karahu!* It's a fabulous estate!
Chaysi
  And so,
"Chaypiqa kundinaduqa salbanqa,
  "The damned one will save him!" says the priest.
chayman churasaq kaytaqa," nispas.
  "I'll send him there!"
WApu, sarapis, imapis mihuypis asindapi kashan.
  There's FABulous corn, every kind of food on the hacienda.
Hinaspas . . . nnaqa . . . churan!
  So, well, he sends him there!
Kuraqa chay asindamanñataq.
  The priest sends him off.
"Kundinaduqa mihunqapuni kaytaqa," nispa.
  "The damned one will eat him up!" he says.
"Chaypiqa salbakunqa," nispa.
  "That way he'll save him," he says.

Hinaspas,
  So
kuraqa
  the priest
qatin chayman.
  sends him away.
"Chayman, chaypin haykumunqa kundinadu ankhayNANta qhasuruspa."
  "In there, the damned one will break in like THIS—"
Huq imachá haykumunqa," nisqa, manan "kundinadu" nisqachun.
  Or he must have said, "Something will come in"; he wouldn't say it was the
  damned soul.
"Chaywan maqanakunki," nispa.
  "Hit him with this," he says.
Chaysi huq k'ullu wawata ruwarapun, wawata.
  Then [the priest] makes a doll out of wood, a doll.
Huqtataq hirumanta wawata ruwapun hinas.
  And he makes another doll out of iron.
Chaynintintas kachan, kumpañata churan riki, wawakunata.
  He sends him off that way, with the dolls as companions.
Chaysi, rin.
  Well, and off he goes.
Rispa, chaypi mut'ita t'impuyachin HATUN pirulpi, karahu, paylapin.
  And when he gets there, he boils corn in a HUGE copper pot, *karahu*, in a pail.
Chaypin t'impuyachispas, ukukuqa k'irayakuspas,
  In that way, when he's boiled it, the bear just stretches out and
aknata daLIIIYkun mut'ita.
  GOES AT the boiled corn, like this!
Wakatas ñak'aykun, chaytas ch'ustiruspas miHUYkun kankayuspa, iy!
  It seems he even slaughters a cow, roasts it, and PICKS its bones clean!
Hinaspas, chiqaqta,
  And then—really—
kundinadu haqaymanta qhasaramun wasita.
  the damned one breaks in, through the ceiling, up there!
Chaysi, aknata, makin alayriramun.
  First, like this, one hand appears.
"Yau! Imataq chayri?" Qhawan, hahaha!
  "Hey! And what's this?" He's watching. Hahaha!
Hinaspa, qhawan, iy? Hinaspa,
  Well, and so he's watching, isn't he, so,
"Ha karawchu!" nin. "HUQ!" nispas nin,
  "Well, *karáwchu!*" he says. "ONE!" he says,
huqta llamiyamuqtin.
  as one hand reaches in.

Chaysi astawan llik'iruspas kukuchun alayurunña makin llipinña.
And then another one tears through, the whole hand up to the wrist.
"ISKAY!" phasil ninmi.
"TWO!" he says casually.
Hinaspa yapamantaqa p'atatataspa
So then again, gnashing its teeth,
dalishan, karahu, kankayuqta, iy? waka kankayuq.
it goes after the roast—see?—the roast beef.[1]
Hinaspas, yapamantaqa astawanña alayrimun aknata korpunpuwanña.
And then, once again, more of the body appears—this much of it.
Isk— "KINSA," niñasyá.
T—"THREE!" he exclaims.
Chaymantaqa, yapamantaqa UMA alayrikun.
And then, there's more—the HEAD appears.
Ya'sta— "TAWA!"
There it is! "FOUR!"
Yapamantas chakantin alayrimun. "PISQA!"
And then more: the feet. "FIVE!"
Ya'sta, kuskan korpunñas! "SUHTA!"
There it is, its whole body! "SIX!"
Yupayshan ukuku.
The bear's counting.
Runapunisyá haykumushan.
It seems that somebody's coming in.
Yapamantaqa alayrimun, ya'sta, uma allintanña ukhumanña haykumunña, ya'sta!
More of it appears, there it is, the head's all the way inside now, there it is!
"QANCHIS!" nin.
"SEVEN!" he says.
Ya'sta, kuskan sinturonña alayriyamun. "PUSAQ!" nin.
There it is, waist and all! "EIGHT!" he says.
Ya'sta. Chaymantaqa, utra alayriramun llipinña , karahu, ya'sta!
There it is. Then the rest appears, all of it, *karahu*, there it is!
"CHUNKA!" pasayapun pampaman, iy!
"TEN!" It drops onto the floor.
. . . Kukuchi!
(soft) *Kukuchi.*

CATHERINE: (soft)
Aahtakáw!
Ooh my God!

ERASMO:
Arí.
That's right.
Hinaspa, P'ANAN karahu!
And so he SLAAMS it, *karahu!*
P'anan naqa ukukuqa, karahu. DALImun hatariruspa karahu!
Slaams it, *karahu!* The bear jumps up and GOES AFTER IT, *karahu!*
Chay hiru wawan k'ullu wawantaqsi mihushan mut'ita, y runaman tukurapun.
(fast) The iron doll and wooden doll are eating the boiled corn and they turn into people, see!
Chaysi, karahu, chay sayk'un chay runa ukuku, chay hiru kaqñataqsi hatarin, karahu, chaytaqsi DALINAKUN chay kundinaruwan, iy!
And so, *karahu,* when the bear man gets tired, the iron one jumps up, *karahu,* and he GOES AT the damned soul, y'see!
Maqanakun, karahu, p'ananakun, p'ananakuspa
They hit each other, *karahu,* slam and slam each other
saqman hayt'an saqman hayt'an supaytas dalinakunku.
(soft) punch kick punch kick go after each other like the devil.
K'ullu kaqwan chay runa ukukuwantaqsi mihushan mut'ita, karahu!
The wooden one's eating boiled corn with the bear man, *karahu!*
K'ullu kaqñataq hatarin, karahu, "Qanñataq daliy!" niqtin.
(fast) The wooden one jumps up, damn it, when he says, "Now you go to it!"
Hiru kaqpuwanñataq samanku, riki, chay mutita dalillantaq!
The bear man rests along with the iron one, snarfing down the boiled corn.
K'ulluwansi maqanaykun kundinadu, k'ullu wawawan.
(soft) The damned soul fights with the wooden one, *karahu,* with the wooden one!
Daliynakunsi, sayk'unchá chayqa runa kaqñataqsi hatarin ukuku, karahu,
It seems they go after each other, and when that one gets tired, bear man jumps up again!
dalillantas daliyu . . . !
—has at 'im—at 'im!

(Audience laughs loudly.)

SEKUTAPUNIÑAS hap'inaykushan.
They're caught in a stranglehold.
Ya'sta, ima urañachá kanman, ñachá tutaña, tutañakushansi.
Okay, so how late is it getting? It must be dark, getting dark already.
Yapamantaqa mihuyshallankutaqsi, karahu! Chay runa ukuku sayk'un, chayqa hiru kaq hatarillantaq utra vwilta karahu!
And they're still just eating away, *karahu!* When the bear man gets tired, then the iron one jumps up for another round, see?

Yapamantaqa karahu sayk'un chayqa k'ullu kaqqa utra vwilta hatarillantaq.
And when he gets tired, then the wooden one jumps to its feet again, *karahu!*

(Laughter)

DAAALIN karahu!
SLAAAMS him, *karahu!*
Paytaqsi t'ohachin!
And that one makes him yell!
K'ullu sayk'un chayqa runa ukuku hatarispa DAAlillantaq riki kundinarutaqa!
And when the wooden one gets tired, bear man jumps up and SLAAAMS 'im, see, slams the damned soul.

(Audience giggles.)

Ya'sta p'unchay hamushanñas, ya yuraqyaramunña, karahu,
And so there we are, it's day already, it's getting light, *karahu,*
chaypis salvan chaypi, qaparichisqa pacha kundinaduta riki,
and so he saves the damned soul, y'see, makes him yell,
rimarchisqa!
makes him talk.
Tapuyusqa LLUYTA karahu!
And he asks him EVERYTHING, *karahu!*
"Maypin qulqe? Maypin imakunan kashan?
"Where's your money? Where're your things?
Kay kuwartuykikunapi chaymi qan, karahu, purimunki wañusqaykimanta," nispa, iy!
Right here you are in your rooms, *karahu!* Get moving or you die!" he says.
Tapuyun ukukuqa.
Bear interrogates him.
Rikuyachikun, karahu, Q'ALAta pusakachayachikun, llawitas intrigayachikun, qulqikunatas intrigayachikun, LLUYTAS karahu!
He makes him show everything, *karahu,* lead him to EVERYTHING, give him the keys, give him the money. EVERYthing, *karahu!*
—wakakunata, kawsayninkuta, Q'ALAtas ukuku intrigayachin, kinsantinmanta p'ana-p'anashaspalla, iy,
—his cattle, his goods, he has to give Bear EVERYTHING, with the three of them slamming and beating him,
kundinaruwan.
[beating up] the damned one.
"Qanwanmi saqipusayki kay asindayta.
"I'll leave you my manor.
Gracias kunanqa salwawanki," nispas yuraq paluma pasapun p'unchay hamuytaña.
Thank you, you just saved me," and saying this, he turns into a white dove and flies off at daybreak.

(Audience laughs.)

Kundinadu, "Kunan ripusaq HANAN PACHAmanmi," nispa.
  "Now I'll go to HEAVEN," says the damned soul.
Hinaspas, ukukuqa karahu
  And so, Bear, *karahu,*
kuntintu qhipapun chaypi.
  he happily stays behind.
Mut'itapis, karahu, dalikun waqmanta, wakakunatas, karahu, mixuykun, ñak'aykun.
  He goes after the boiled corn again, *karahu,* eats more beef, slaughters more
  cows.
Kampanatas p'anaykun.
  He rings the church bell.
"Patrunaykichis kaPUU—NI, patruniykichis kapusaq,
  "I'M your master, I'll be your master!
HAMPUYCHIS, HAMPUYCHIS!" nispa waqachaykun turripatamanta.
  COME BACK, COME BACK!" he cries from the bell tower.
"Nuqan kapuni hasinDAyuq!" nispas.
  I'm going to be lord of the MAnor!" he says.
"Salbanin kunanqa chay kundinaDUta!" nispasyá!
  "I just saved that damned SOUL!" he yells.
Ukukuqa wahakachaykun.
  Bear's raising the cry.
Hinaspas,
  Well then,
Ukukuqa karahu,
  Bear, *karahu,*
chaypi asindayuq wapu sillapin puripun,
  so he's lord of the manor, goes around on a fine saddle
kawallukunata sipispa, imayá sillakuspapis manasyá atinchu,
  —and kills off the horses; they can't carry him in the saddle,
Ukukuta kawallu.
  Bear's too much for the horses.
Hinaspas, purin purin
  And so, he goes all over
runa huñuKUUUUNsi, chay asindaman, kaqta kutiyapunku.
  and GAAAAthers together the people, and they return to the manor just as
  before.
Chaysi llank'anku, karahu, supaytas runakunata qatin.
  And so they work, *karahu,* he drives them like the devil.
Manan chaypipis por fin wañunchu, riki, karahu!
  He sure didn't die there after all, *karahu,* did he?

Kundinaduta aswan sipin, salban riki.

He even finished off the damned soul, he saved him y'know.

Chayqa, "Manamá chaypis wañullataqsi!" nispas kuraqa rinigasqa, karahu!

And so, "What! He didn't die there!" The priest is furious.

(The tape ended. When a new tape was installed, ERASMO took up the story again.)

Chay ukuku kasqa asindayuq.

It seems that Bear is lord of the manor.

Salbaspa chaypi asinda runata huñusqa riki.

Saved, he rounds up the people of the hacienda.

T'uquspa p'anpapusqaku.

They dig a hole and bury him.

Anchaymi chay . . . na . . .

And that's that—ah—

Chaypi chay ukukuta salbapunku.

That's how they saved the bear.

Wañupun, anchay p'unchaymantaraqsi trankilu kapunku

He dies, and from that day onward they're happy,

chay asinda runapas,

the manor people are happy,

kurapas

the priest is happy,

lluy, imapis.

everybody's happy.

Kuntentu qhipapusqa chaypiraq.

They stay on contentedly.

Kurapas chaypiraq.

The priest stays on, too.

Trankilu kapusqa chay hushukunamantapis lluy

He's tranquil, freed from the lawsuits

librakapusqa ñak'ayta.

after all that trouble.

Manaña priukupakuñachu sinchitañachu ni imakunamantapis llakikapun, sinchitañachu.

They don't worry about anything, or get mad or sad, mad or sad.

Maypachachus chay ukhuman p'amparapunku ukukuta, anchayña susiyukapun.

From the moment they bury the bear deep in the ground, everything settles down.

Chayña runakunapis trankilu llank'ariyapusqaku trankilu purikachakusqaku.

And then the people go to work happily, contentedly go about their business.

Nishutasyá ukukuqa frigasqa.

That bear just screwed up too much.

Chayqa, chayñas chay kurapis trankilu karikapun.
   And so, well then, that priest he's real happy.
"Kunaqa wawayta salbapuni, chaypi salvupuni kashan,
   "Now I've really saved my child; this way, he's saved for sure,
asinda runaraq mana pinsasqapi," nispa nin.
   without the manor people realizing it," he says.
Runaraq aswan chayta sipin—kurapunisyá kunsihasqa chayta.
   The people killed him—but it was the priest who advised them to do it.

CIPRIANA (coaching):
Manan unas kanchu . . .
   It seems there's no water . . .

ERASMO:
"Manan unu kaqtin, chhaynata t'uqunkichis,
   "Since there isn't any water, dig a hole over there
*chayqa chaypi intirarapun chayqa salbapunkis ichapas chay patruniykichista," nispa
kunsihasqa.*
   and bury him in it, and maybe that way you'll save your master," he counseled
   them.
Anchaypi chay, salbakapun, chayqa kuntintu chay kapun kurapis.
   And so they save him that way, so the priest is delighted.
"Vaya, kunanqa sipipunqa chay wawayta malhishuta," nispa.
   "Excellent, that'll be the end of my troublesome child," he says.
Hina kapusqa, chay tukupun.
   So that's how it was, that's the end.
Ankayllan tukun chay.
   That's how it ends.
Chayllatan yacharani!
   That's all I've learned!

"CH'ASKA WARMI"
"Star-wife"

Narrative by Basilia Gutiérrez Chura (Sonqo, August 1975)
Transcription by Jaime Pantogoso M.
Translation by Catherine J. Allen

Line breaks indicate pauses.

BASILIA:
Runa maqt'awan riki, ch'aska tiyasqa, riki . . .
    Well, it seems there was a star living with a young man.
Imaynapi ch'aska tiyaran runa maqt'awan?
    How did a star come to live with a human youth?
Runa maqt'awan tiyasqa riki . . .
    It seems that indeed she did live with him—
kay pachapi, riki.
    in this world.
P'asña kasqa,
    She was a young woman,[1]
hinaspa runa maqt'aq churinta riki
    and so it seems she bore sons for that human youth,
wachakusqa, kinsatañayá riki!
    three of them!
Hinaspa riki kay runaq p'achawan churakusqa . . .
    And she wore this human clothing
churapusqa chay p'asñata.
    that (star-)woman did.
Hinaspa mana munanchu:
    But she doesn't like it:
"KHALLKIwashanmi! KHALLKIwashanmi!" nispa.
    "It's ITCHING me! It's ITCHING me!" she says.
"Achakáw!" nispa. Runaq p'achanta mana munasqachu;
    "It's awful!" It seems she didn't like human clothing;

paypa p'achan mana khallkinchu.
    her own clothes never itch her.
Hinaspa, chaymanta riki,
    And well, so then, y'know
manan chay p'achanchista awantasparipusqa, riki,
    she couldn't stand our clothing, so it seems she left,
chinkarakapusqa chay maqt'amanta, kinsa wawayuq riki!
    abandoned that youth with three children already!
Hinaspa, iskay . . . na . . .
    So, two—na—[hesitating]
Wawachanta llapanta saqIRPArispa iskapapusqa, riki.
    All her little children, she left them BEHIND, escaped y'know!
Hinaspa maqt'aqa chakra ruwaq rishanankama—
    And all the time that youth (has been) working in the fields . . .
hina . . .
    well . . .
Maqt'aq chakraq ruwasqanta muHUtas kapasta wayK'UYunnn
    All the SEED potatoes the youth raises, she COOks
p'asñaqa!
    that young woman does!
Mankatas khapurullantaq—mankata
    She puts the pot on the fire—and it breaks—
mankatas khapurullantaq—mankata
    puts the pot on the fire—and it just breaks again—
yapas churpun mankata khapurun.
    puts the pot on the fire again—and it just breaks again.
Muhuta tukun q'ala p'asñaqa.
    She completely finishes off the seed potatoes.
Chaymanta pasakapusqa muhu—
    And then she takes off, when the seeds [are all gone]
mankata p'akita tukuruspa, Hanaq Pachaman.
    and the pots are finished off, takes off for heaven.
"Maymi mamayki?" nispa maqt'aqa chakranmanta chayan.
    "Where's your mother?" asks the youth, home from the fields.
Chaysi nin: "Mamayqa pasan ankita 'llikwww' nispa.
    And (the child) answers: "My mother took off like this *'llikwww'*!
Pasarun haqaychi—
    She just went away up there!"
"MayMANmi mamayki pasarun?
    "WHERE has your mother gone?
ÁY! MAYtan pasan, maytan—!"
    OH! WHERE has she gone, where!"

Phawakachansi maqt'aqa!
    The youth's running around in despair.
Wawachakunataqsi iskay kinsantin chawaman—tiyashan.
    And it seems the three little kids are just sitting there in dismay.
Mana kanchu.
    She's gone.
MANA maqt'aqta—maqt'a tarinchu,
    The youth just CAN'T FIND her.
Hinaspa—p'asñaqa—
    And so—the (star-)woman—[hesitating]
"Haqayllatan mamayqa chinkarun."
    "My mother disappeared right up there."
Chaysi chakra ruwasini—
    Well, there's work to be done—
Mana manaPUni tarispa ripun ripun chakra ruwachiqsi.
    When he just can't find her, he goes, goes back to work the fields.
Kutiramoqtinqa, wawakuna:
    And when he comes back, one of the children tells him,
"Papay! Mamayqa chayaramusqa,
    "Papa! Mother came back from up there,
haqayninta 'chikkk-chikkk-chikkk' nispa, haykuramun kunan—
    arrived with a sound of 'chikkk-chikkk-chikkk'—
chaymi huqchayta aparikapun kuraqchayta!"
    and then she took away one of us, my big brother!"
Chaysi nin, "Maytataq aparikun!"
    So he exclaims, "Where can she have taken him?"
Huq p'unchayqa saqiyllantaq—
    He leaves them for another day, saying,
"Maytataq intunsis mayta rispa maskhamusaqchá, riki!" nispa.
    "Where oh where shall I look for her?"
Maskhaq rin.
    He goes to search.
Hinaspa mana kanchu. Mana kaqtin—
    But she's not there, and meanwhile,
wawaqa, huq wawatañataqsi haykuramuspa p'asña,
    the young woman's come back for another of the children,
chikkk-chikkk-chikkk
    [with a sound of] chikkk-chikkk-chikkk
huq wawata, mana iskaychanta aparin, mana kapunchu.
    the child's gone. She took one, not both, of the (remaining) children.
Anchaymanta tutamantawan ch'isinwan qoyllur riki,
    And that's why in the mornings and evenings there's a star,

qoyllurqa riki,
   y'know, a star
iskaynin ch'askata, huq wawachantin ch'isin ch'aska lloqsimun—
   who has two littler stars. She comes out with one of her star-children
   in the evening—

ALCIDES (BASILIA's son, interrupting):
Tumay, Kumpari, tumay, Kumpari!
   Drink up, Compadre! Drink up!

BASILIA:
huq huq wawachantaq riki
   and the other, she comes out with the other
tutamanta illarimuyta lloqsimun, riki.
   as the morning is dawning, y'know.
Iskay wawachanta, huq wawachanta—
   Just two little children, the other child—
Huq wawachantataq saqirparipusqa.
   It seems she left the other one behind.
Chayqa chaymanta riki
   And therefore
chaypi maqt'aqa riki maskhaq rin . . .
   that's where the youth goes to look for her . . .

ALCIDES:
Tumay, Kumari!
   Drink up, Comadre!

BASILIA:
Intunsis
   So then
Hanaq Pachata rin.
   he goes to heaven.
Chaysi aktual wapu "llip-llip-llip" nispa
   And the moment he arrives, [there she is] gorgeous—going **"llip-llip-llip,"**
misamanta p'asña lloqsiyamushasqa.
   the [star-]woman's coming out of Mass.
"Kaytaq warmiyqa! Ay! Imanasaqtaqri!
   "Is that my wife! AY! What am I going to do?
Manan noqaqa awantaymanchu,
   I can't possibly support her,
manan noqaqa awantaymanchu p'achachina!"
   I can't possibly afford her clothes!"

ALCIDES:
Sirbishu, sirbishay!
  Service! Let's have some service!

BASILIA:
. . . *CHHIW kallitaraq k'anchayshasqa.*
  . . . *CHHIW* her clothes are shining all to way to the street!
Chay iskay—iskay wawacha.
  Those two—(hesitating) the two little children. . .
Ya'sta! Chayllan!
  Okay, that's it! I'm finished!

ALCIDES:
Tumaysunchis! Serbesa askharaq,
  Let's drink up! There's plenty of beer left,
kinsa kashan kaharaqchushina kashan!
  about three whole cases!

BASILIA:
Macharunkichis, pantarachiwankichis,
  You all made me nervous and made me make mistakes,
pantarachiwankichisyá!
  really make mistakes!

ALCIDES:
Yuyarisunchis chaymantaña, nusierto, tumayuruspaña!
  We'll remember [the story] later, won't we? When we've had enough to drink!

BASILIA returned to the story and finished it in a different session:

BASILIA (beginning hesitantly):
P'asña kasqa . . . llank'aq maqt'a.
  There was a girl [and a] peasant youth.
Chay llank'aq maqt'amanyá chask'a sapa . . .
  The star [came to] the peasant youth every . . .
Haykun sapa kutillan qasan.
  She came down every time there was frost.
Chaypi p'asña ikhuripusqa llank'aq maqt'aman.
  There she appeared to the peasant youth.
Hinaspa munakuspa kay pasñawan tiyakuyta . . .
  And because he was in love with the girl, [he wanted] to live with her.
"Tiyakusaq," nispa nisqa.
  "I'm going to live with her," he said.

Llank'aq maqt'ataqsi muhunta llank'asqanta tukuraysipun!
But it seems that she finished off all his seed potatoes!
Wayk'uspa wayk'uspa.
Just cooking and cooking.
Chayqa unayñachá tiyanku riki,
But they lived together for a really long time,
chaychá wawachakunayuq kan riki.
and, sure, they had children.
Wawachayuq kapun riki
They had children
chay wawachayuq hina uywashan, tiyashan.
and lived together raising those children.
Sumaqtasyá p'asñawanqa tiyaykushankupas.
They lived together blissfully, he with the young woman,
Hinaspa manasyá phiñanakunkupaschu.
and they didn't quarrel with each other.
Hinaspa p'achanta mana awantaspallapuniyá, ripusqa p'asñaqa!
But then the young woman left because she just couldn't stand the
[human] clothes!
Uuuuu! *P'achanta mana awantaspallapuniyá!*
Ewwww! She really just couldn't stand the clothes!
Hinaspa pasapusqa: "Manapuni kay maqt'awanqa . . ."
And so she left: "No way [am I staying] with this fellow!"
Muhutapis tukurusqa, mankapis p'akirakapusqa, wayk'un mankata!
And it seems that she also finished off the seed potatoes, and broke the pot,
the cooking pot!
Winashaqtin hina takatakayuspas winan, takatakayuspa papata winayshan.
She shoved them roughly [into the pot], like this, just shoved the potatoes!
Papata muhullantas wayk'unsi, iso siqa, manan nataqa . . . papallata!
It seems she cooked only seed potatoes, nothing else, only potatoes!
*Papallata takayuqtin—**phuq!**—pasayrachin!—**phuq!**—pasayrachin!*
When she shoved the potatoes in the pot—**poof!**—it made the bottom fall
out—**poof!**—the bottom fall out!
Raqrallataq!
All smashed up!
Chayqa manchakapunñachá p'asñapis riki.
So the girl must have gotten worried, too.
"Imanaqtintaq p'akinkiri, p'akinkiri mankatari?" nispachá maqt'a nin.
The young man must have been saying, "How come you're breaking,
breaking the pots?"
Chaysiyá, "Ankayllamanta ripusaq muhu tukurukuqtin!"
And she's saying, "As soon as the seed potatoes are finished, I'm getting
out of here!"

"Muhullatataq wayk'unkipis.
  And he's saying, "You cook only seed potatoes.
Imaraykutaq muhullatari chakra ruwanaypaq kashaqtinri wak'unki?" nispa nin.
  And how come? Why are you cooking the seed potatoes I need for my
  planting?"
"Intonsis pasapusaq!" nispachá pasakapuran p'asña.
  "Then I'm leaving," the young woman said, and off she went.
"Pasapusaq," nispa wawachakunata . . . manan kapunchu!
  "I'm leaving," she told the children . . . [and] she was gone!
"Maytataq rin, maytataq rin chay p'asña p'as- p'asñayqa?" nispa nin.
  "Oh where did she go? My girl, d-dear girl, where did she go?"
  says [her husband].
Hinaspa, "Imanasaqtaq kunanri?
  And then, "What will become of me now?
Maytataq maskhamusaqri?" nispa.
  Oh where can I search for her?" he says.
"Maytan mamayki purin, maytan mamayki rin?"
  "Where did your mother go off to, where did she go?"
Wawachakunalla mamantinsis, mamantinsi kasqanku mamantin.
  It seems that [some of] the children were with their mother, they were with
  their mother, with their mother.
Maman chinkapun, pay wawan chinkapun, mana kapunchu.
  Their mother disappeared and they disappeared, too; they were gone.
Mana tarispa huq: "Mamayqa pasapun, 'manan manan maytapaschu risaq,' nin,
  There was one left who didn't go [who said], "Mother went off saying,
  'I'm not going just anywhere,
'manan maytapas risaqchu,' nin, "llaqtayta ripusaq,' nin.
  not just any place,' she said. 'I'm going to my own country,' she said.
*Kayatataq—**chikk-chikk-chikk!**—mamayqa ankaypa saruspa pasan.*
  And right here, standing here going—**chikk-chikk-chikk!**—she left.
*Huq qonqayllan mamayqa—**llikww**—nin, kayqa pasarun!"*
  All of a sudden she took off—**llikww**—off she went!"
*"Imaynapitaq chaytari—**llikww**—nin, imaynapitaq?*
  "However could she go—**llikww**—like that, how?
Imataq kanmanmi warmiy? Wañunchu, imanantaq?" nispa.
  What's become of my wife? Did she die, or what?"
Manapunichá yachanchu riki maqt'aqa,
  That young man really didn't know [what she was],
runa p'asñataq tiyakushan, ankhayna.
  [he thought] he was living normally with a human woman.

CATHERINE:
Aha!
 Aha!

BASILIA:
Sumaqahá tiyakushanpis riki nispa, manan riki hina.
 He thought they were living together just fine,
Mana kaqtinyá riki,
 [but] as she was really gone,
imaynapichá ispiritu riran Hanaq Pachata,
 since [as a] spirit she'd gone somehow to heaven (Upper World), to heaven,
riran Hanaq Pachata, riran riki maqt'a.
 he went to heaven, the young man went [too].
Tapukachakun . . . Huqtan . . .
 He kept asking around . . . and again
wawaraq chinkapusqa, wawa, huq wawachakuna:
 it seems another child disappeared, and another one said,
"Mamayqa haykuramuspan kunan unchayqa hamusqan mamayqa chaymi,
 "Mother came in today, she came and asked me,
'Maypin taytayki?' niwanmi," nispa nin.
 'Where's your father?'
"'Chakrata rin,' ninin," nispa.
 'He went to the fields,' I answered.
'Chayqa wayway haku pusapusayki,
 'Then come on, my child, I'm taking you with me,
haku . . . ripusunchis,' nispa niqtin
 come on, let's go,' and saying that
kuraqchaytaqa . . . kuraqchaytaqa pasachipun!"
 she took away my big brother [older sibling]!"
Huq wawachallaña tiyashanku, iskaychallaña wawachakuna tiyashan.
 Only one child was still left, or [maybe] just two were left at home.

CATHERINE:
Aha! Chayrí?
 Oh! And what then?

BASILIA:
Kutiyaramuspataq, huq p'unchayqa kaqllataq kutiyaramullantaq,
 And when she returned, one day she returned and it was just the same,
wawachakunata pasachin.
 she took away another child.
"Maytan mamayki pasarun? Manan!
 "Where did your mother go? No!

Munaymi kasqa! Akna sumaq!"
She was beautiful! She was so wonderful!" . . . (inaudible . . .)

(The tape was interrupted briefly here.)

Imamantan maqt'a chaypiña kasharan chay ura riki?
What was the young man doing right there at that time?
Hanaq Pachataña chayasqa ña.
It seems he made it to heaven.
"Kay kallillata haykunki," nisqa. "Kay kallillata haykunki," nispa nin.
"Go down this street," [someone in heaven] told him. "Go down this street."
Chiqaqpi chay kallita haykun.
So he went straight down that street.
Chay kallita haykuqtin,
While going down that street,
"Ña misa tukuruqtin riqsinki,
"Now when Mass lets out, you'll recognize her," said [his guide].
riqsinki warmikita," nin, "riqsinki."
"You'll recognize your wife, you'll recognize her."
WISCHHH *Hanaq Pacha kalli **aaa**!*
"Wow, heaven's streets were— **WISCHHH**
LLEQQ ishallantaqsi, sumaq inlishapis sumaq!
They were just FULL UP, and the church was splendid, just splendid!
Hina mamantinsi lloqsiramun kallita!
And then [when Mass was over] people came out into the street, his wife among them!
Mundutas(?) chipipín maqt'aqa! Ñawinraq chipipichin.
The young man was overwhelmingly dazzled! His very eyes were dazzled.
"Anchay kaqmá riki warmiyqa!"
"This surely is my wife!"
Mamachan, wawachanta riqsirapun
He recognized his little wife and child,
iskaychanta wawachanta riqsirapun.
recognized his two little children.
Hina qatikun, maqt'aqa rimayurun.
So the young man followed them, and spoke out to them.
Paypis rimaychikullanchá, rimaychikun.
And she, too, consented to speak with him.
Wasiman pusanku. Misa tukuyta wasinman haykurapun.
She led him to her house. As Mass was over, they went to her house.
Muhulla wayk'uyta qallarirun, muhutas winayrullantaq.
She set to cooking seed potatoes; it seems she put seed potatoes (in the pot).

Muhutas wayk'uruspa impitaramun maqt'aman.
   When the seed potatoes were cooked, she invited the young man to eat.
Mihuchimunsiyá riki, mihuchimunsi.
   She sure fed him, it seems she fed him.
Mihuychispaqa, "Ripusaq,"
   When he'd finished, she told him, "I'm leaving,"
ima nispaña, manañachayá chaypiqa rimaychipunchu ni.
   and whatever she said, there was no answering her back.
Ya'sta, "Manapuni p'achaykiwan awantaymanchu;
   That was that. "There's no way I can stand your [human] clothing;
manan chay p'achan kurpuyta phaqtiwan,
   those clothes don't fit my body,
qhasqan p'achaykichis, khallkin p'achaykichis," niyamun.
   your clothing is hard, your clothing is scratchy," she declared.
Hina maqt'aq waqakuspa,
   So, with the youth weeping,
muhullata wayk'uruspa mihuyachimun, khuchita mihuyachimun
   she fed him boiled seed potatoes, fed him pork,
kachayanpun!
   and sent him away [back to earth]!
Anchaypi ni maqt'atata . . . ni mamantin kakusqapis,
   And in that way the young man—no . . . he wasn't together with his wife,
mamantin, iskay wawachantin maqt'aqa hina khuyay kirapun.
   he was left grieving for his wife together with two of his children.
Anchayllapin tukukun, mana chaymantaqa yuyapunichu, arí!
   And that's the way it ends, I don't remember anything more.
Imaynapiyá chay maqt'a kutiyanpuran,
   How the young man returned,
aswan mana yuyanichu.
   I don't remember that either.

CATHERINE:
Kutipuran?
   He returned?

BASILIA:
Umm. Imaynapi Kay Pachaman chayapuran?
   Uh-huh. How do you suppose he got back to earth (This World)?
Chaymantayá chay chask'aqa sirtupaq, chisin lloqsimun,
   And yes, for sure, when that star [Venus] comes out bright in the evening
tutamanta lloqsimun, maman huq wawachantin,
   or the morning, a mother with her child,

p'asña huq wawachantin,
   a young woman with her child,
kapasta qasa qaqasayamushan, riki.
   then there's really hard frost, y'know.
"Qasa!" nispa nishan, chay—
   "Frost!" they're saying—
ch'isinta wapu lloqsimun
   [when] she comes out splendid in the evening.
"Haqaymi chay p'asña ch'aska!" nispa qhawakunku.
   "There's the star-girl!" they say, watching her.
Chayllatayá noqapis yachani.
   And that's all I know.
Manayá Ch'askaq Timpunpi qaqraqchu kaniqa.
   (laughing) I've never been in the star-time.
Tutamantan ch'isinwan wawacha pusayusqapuniqa
   Morning and evening, accompanied by her little child,
huq huch'uy ch'askachayuq riki lloqsimun rikinacha . . .
   she comes out along with a little tiny star, y'see . . .

CATHERINE:
Ch'isinpis tutamantapis . . . lloqsimun.
   Morning and evening . . . she comes out.

BASILIA:
Anchay kaqchá chay chay p'asña, runa p'asña maqt'awan tiyaq riki.
   So that must be that girl, who lived as a human girl with the young man.

APPENDIX D

"HUALLASMANTA"
"About the Huallas"

Narrative by Erasmo Hualla Gutiérrez (Sonqo, August 1984)
Transcription by Jaime Pantogoso M.
Translation by Catherine J. Allen

Line breaks indicate pauses.

ERASMO:
Noqa Kumari willasayki huq kwin . . .
 Comadre, I'll tell you a sto— . . .
nata . . . Huallamanta:
 ah, I'll tell you about the Huallas:
Huqsi hamusqa machulaykuraq Santa Rosamanta.
 They say that a man came, our ancient grandfather, from Santa Rosa.
Hinaspa hamuspa dikuntribushunta pagana kasqa.
 And so, having come, he was supposed to pay taxes.
Chayta manchakuspa lluy runakuna ripusqaku . . .
 All the people had fled, fearing the taxes . . .
Sonqo Ayllumanta
 from Sonqo Ayllu
Sipaskanchamanta ima.
 and from Sipaskancha, too.
Sipaskanchay wasapana Muruwisa sikipi tiyasqa Roq'a Roq'api . . .
 He lived beyond Sipaskancha, beyond Muruwisa, in Roq'a Roq'a . . .
Pedro Pari wichay larumanta Santa Rusa kasqa.
 He was Pedro Pari, from the far high reaches beyond Santa Rosa.
Chayllañas runa tiyasqa, hinaspa chay runa
 Only he remained, and he—that man—
mana kuntribushunta pagayta munasqachu:
 he didn't want to pay taxes:
"Mana yapaymanchu ni imatapis pagaymanchu noqaqa, umayta wit'uspa apachuku!"
nispa.

"I won't give any more [taxes], I don't want to pay anything, I don't, let them cut off my head and take *it*!" he said.

Wichay larumanta qatay kasqa chay, antis machulaykuraq chay.
He came from way off as a son-in-law, he did, our ancient grandfather.

Chayqa chaymanta chaypa qatayninqa hamusqa Hualla
And so then came his sons-in-law, the Huallas

Kallatiyamanta chaymanta, maykunamanta hamurankupis kinsa!
from Kallatiya, or who knows where the three of them came from!

Chaymanta Huallakunaqa chaypi kaypi kinsataqa.
Then there were Huallas here and there, three of them.

Chay runataq . . .
And that man . . .

siñuran ruwachisqa papilista.
his wife had sent for papers [titles].

Dispues paytaq chaqrapi llank'asqa.
Then he, too, worked in the fields.

Askha uywayuq! paqochayuq, wakayuq, llamayuq, uwihayuq hina chaypi . . .
They had lots of animals—alpacas, cows, llamas, sheep!

namanta kasqa Sipaskancha chay q'asa muyurina uhumanta Muruwisa sikinmanta asta Paucona hawakama.
. . . let's see . . . all the way from the pass to Sipaskancha, turning toward the inside behind Muruwisa all the way to the outskirts of [Hacienda] Paucona.

Chaypi huq hamusqa wiraqocha namanta
And then the gentleman came, uhmm, from

Ispañamanta papil ruwaq.
from Spain, to draw up the papers.

CATHERINE:
Ispañamanta?
From Spain?

ERASMO:
Ispañamantaraq hamusqa Kapon Estrada.
He came all the way from Spain, Capon [Captain?] Estrada.

CATHERINE: *Estrada.*

ERASMO:
Kapon Estrada chay . . .
[Yes,] that was Capon Estrada . . .

chay siñurantaq, chay Pidru Pariq siñuran
and he met up with that woman, Pedro Pari's wife,

uwihata michisqa,
herding sheep

hinaspa chaypi tupasqa Puka Qaqapatapi Pauconaq hawanpi.

   on Puka Qaqa (Red Rock) on the outskirts of Paucona.

Chaypitaqmi nisqa:

   And there he said to her:

"Ayllukayta munankichu, yaw Siñura Warmi,

   "Well, Madam Woman! So you want to form an *ayllu*?

ruwapusayki noqa papilsta."

   I'll draw up the papers for you.

Nispa nisqa, sillapi kawallupi tarpaspa uha michisqanpi.

   So he spoke, seated on a horse, catching up to her as she herded her sheep.

"Arí, munanin!" nispa nisqa.

   "Yes, certainly, that's what I want!" she said.

"Entonce ruwapusayki weno," nispa.

   "Okay, good, I'll do it for you," he replied.

*"Imakuna sutin chay kulindaykikuna, maymanta kananta allpaykis kananta
munawaq ayllu kananta," nispa.*

   "What are the names of these bordering hills? From where does your land
   extend; which land do you want for your *ayllu*?" That's what he said.

Hinaspa willasqa.

   And so she told him.

"Talmantan ka-an noqaq allpay.

   "My land does exte-e-end from such a place.

Chayta noqaqa ayllu kananta munayman uywaypaq purinanpaq," nispa.

   I want that for my *ayllu*, for my animals to graze on."

*Chayqa hina ruwachisqa papilista Puka Qaqapatapi, wallpa phurullawan
qelqachisqa, kinsata.*

   And so that's how they drew up the titles on Puka Qaqa, written with a
   chicken's feather, the three of them:

Huq kasqa kupiyun . . .

   One was a copy . . .

iskay kupiyun huqtaq mamannin.

   no, two were copies and one the mother.

CATHERINE:

Mamannin?

   The mother?

ERASMO:

Arí, chayqa ankaywan ayllupuni kananpaq ruwachikusqa warmilla papilista, papilista,

   Yes, that's how that woman did the paperwork, the paperwork, so a real *ayllu*
   could come into being.

Chayqa chay papilniyuq ayllupuni kapun PASAQ,

   And with its titles the *ayllu* exists FOREVER,

Manan ashindapaschu imapaschu.
>Not as an hacienda or anything else.

Hina chayqa chay Huallakunataq karan
>And so there were those Huallas

huq larumanta hamuq qatay chaypiqa Huallakuna karan.
>who came from somewhere to live as sons-in-law.

Chaykuna ash . . . Chay runaq qataynin kaspa hatun hatun allpayuq, karu karuta mañayta hap'iku askha,
>They had plenty—as that man's sons-in-law, they had lots and lots of land,
>got hold of a big extensive section, plenty,

askha runapaq hina aypan wawakunantin asta kunanpaq hatuchachaq allpa kashan haqaypi.
>and it was plenty for lots of people and their children all the way up 'til now;
>there's a whole lot of land there.

CATHERINE:
Riki.
>Right.

ERASMO:
Noqaykuq Huallakunaqqa.
>It's ours, the Huallas.

CATHERINE:
Arí.
>Yes.

ERASMO:
Kinsataq kayku Hualla, kinsa . . .
>And we're three, the Huallas, three . . .

CATHERINE:
Kinsa kunanchu?
>Are there three now?

ERASMO:
Kunan kashayku, ñawpa machulaykutaqyá
>Now we are three, but our own very ancient grandfather

huqlla kasqa Pidru Pari.
>was just one, that Pedro Pari.

Yuqrataq warmin.
>His wife was a Yuqra.

Ima Yuqrachá kasqapis qonqarapuni noqapis willasqallatañayá.

What Yuqra that would have been I don't know; I, too, am forgetting how to tell it.

Chayqa, KAYTAN WILLASHAYKI KUMARI,

And SO NOW I'M TELLING YOU, COMADRE,

Kumari Katalina.

Comadre Catalina.

CATHERINE:

Gracias!

Thank you!

ERASMO:

Hinan chay Huallakuna, kunanqa askhaña Huallakamallaña Sonqopiqa kayku, Sonqopi—más.

And so there were those Huallas, and now Sonqo's full of Huallas—we're the majority.

CATHERINE:

Arí, piru kunanchu, kinsa Huallakuna kan?

Yes, but are there still three?

ERASMO:

Kinsa Huallamanta kunanqa mirayku askha, kinsa t'aqamanta, piru askhaman tukupuyku, piru kinsa kayku kinsa partidu.

From three Huallas we've multiplied into many, from three branches we've become many, but we are three, three parts.

CATHERINE:

Kinsa partidu?

Three parts?

ERASMO:

Arí, kinsa runaq wawan, hawayninkunañá noqaykuqa kayku, arí.

Yes, we're children of three people, their very own grandchildren.

Aknan, Kumari, chay, chay kuntribushunta qanchi miyuta pagayta manchaykuspanku lluy runakuna t'eqesqaku:

And so, Comadre, that's how it was, all the people had run off to avoid paying their taxes of thirty-five centavos.

"Mana pagaymanchu!" nispa, chay huq kaq machulaykutaq chay Pidru Pari mana pagayta munaspa.

But, exclaiming "I don't want to pay!"—standing alone our old grandfather, that Pedro Pari, refused to pay them.

"Umayniyta wit'uspa apachun!" nispa.

"Let them chop off my head!" he said.

Chayqa: "Kaqpi tiyasaq!"

And this: "I'm staying right here!"

Alqon kasqa kinsa chunka,

He had dogs, thirty of them,

chaywan alqowan kachayusqa.

and with those dogs he chased off [the tax collectors].

"Maski imanawachunpas Gubirnu, manan noqaqa pagaymanchu," nispa.

"Whatever the Government does with me," he said, "I won't pay!"

"Umayninta apachichun wit'uspa! Kaqpi noqaqa kasaq!" nispa.

"They can take my severed head, I'm staying right here!" he said.

Wark'awan wark'akuspa.

He stoned them with his sling.

Askha tiyas—askha alqoyuq khaqpaq machula.

That—that grand old man with all those dogs.

Aknan chay.

And so that's how it was.

Chayllata yachani, Kumari, grashas.

That's all I know, Comadre, thank you.

GUIDE TO PRONUNCIATION
AND GLOSSARY

For the most part, my orthography follows Antonio Cusihuamán's *Diccionario Quechua: Cuzco-Collao* (1976a). For most place-names, I follow customary spelling. For example, I spell "Colquepata" as it appears on most maps and correspondence, although the word would be rendered more correctly as "Qolqepata."

The Quechua plural suffix *-kuna* indicates a collection of several similar things and is not strictly equivalent to English -s. When possible I use *-kuna* to indicate the plural form of a word (for example, *runakuna*, "people"). Where *-kuna* would be unsuitable, I indicate the plural with English -s (as in *kukuchis*).

Quechua is rich in consonants, including aspirated and glottalized variants that are phonemically distinct from each other. In glottalized consonants, the air is stopped briefly, giving the sound a slightly explosive character. Glottalization is indicated by an apostrophe (*ch', k', p', q', t'*). Aspiration entails letting out a little puff of air that softens the sound slightly. (Note that *ph* is closer to English *p* [as in "pin"] than to English *f*. Thus *phukuy* is pronounced *pooh-kwee*.) Aspiration is indicated by an *h* after the consonant (*chh, kh, ph, qh, th*).

A list of consonants is given below:

/ch/	as in "china"
/chh/	as in "chew"
/ch'/	no equivalent
/h/	as in "hat" but slightly more guttural
/k/	as in "cut"
/kh/	as in "can't"
/k'/	no equivalent
/l/	as in "lean"
/ll/	as in Spanish "ly"
/m/	as in "mat"
/n/	as in "not"
/ñ/	as in Spanish "ny"
/p/	as in "pat"
/ph/	as in "pin"
/p'/	no equivalent

/t/	as in "top"
/th/	as in "tin"
/t'/	as in "tsk! tsk!"
/w/	as in "went"
/y/	as in "yet"

The following consonants appear only in words derived from Spanish:

/d/	as in "dog"
/f/	as in "fine"
/g/	as in "goat"
/v/	as in "vine"

Quechua vowels are far fewer in number. They are:

/a/	as in "ah!"
/e/	as in "edible"; variant of /i/
/i/	as in "heat"
/o/	between "mop" and "mope"; variant of /u/
/u/	as in "hoop"

Y at the beginning of a word is pronounced like the *y* in *you*. *Y* at the end of a word changes the preceding vowel: *-ay* is pronounced like long *i* in *site*; *-iy* is pronounced like the *y* in *easy*; *-uy* is pronounced rather like French *oui*; *-aw* is pronounced like *-ow* in *meow*.

Normally, emphasis is placed on the next-to-the-last syllable of a word. In exceptions, emphasis is indicated with an acute accent mark, as in "Achacháw!" (AchaCHAW!).

GLOSSARY

A

Achacháw!: My goodness! Wow!

Achakaláw!: What a shame!

Achakáw!: Expression of horror or distaste.

Alaláw!: How cold! I'm freezing!

alqu: Dog.

alma: Soul or bones of the dead.

amaru: A large subterranean dragonlike serpent; may have feline characteristics.

animu: Spirit animating a living being (from Spanish *ánimo*).

Añañáw!: Oh how nice! Yummy!

apu: Lord, a term usually reserved for the most powerful sacred places.

atuq: Fox.

aycha: Meat, flesh.

ayllu: A type of community indigenous to the Andes, based on ties of kinship and a common focus on sacred places often conceived of as ancestral.

ayllu runa: An indigenous person from an *ayllu*.

C

comadre (Spanish): Godmother, or the godmother of one's children.

compadre (Spanish): Godfather, or the godfather of one's children.

condenado (Spanish): Damned soul; see *kukuchi*.

CH

chansanakuy: stylized verbal play between two parties; literally, "to joke together."

Chaymantarí?: And what then? What happened next?

chicha: Fermented corn liquor.

chinkana: A subterranean cave or tunnel.

chinkay: To disappear.

chiqaq: True or straight.

chiri: Cold.

CH'

ch'aska: Brilliant star; often refers to Venus.

ch'uño: Freeze-dried potatoes, prepared by a process of alternate freezing and thawing.

D

dispachu (Spanish): An offering composed of coca leaves and other ingredients given to the Mother Earth, Mountain Lords, and Ancestors; usually burned, sometimes buried; from Spanish *despacho* meaning "dispatch," "shipment."

E

enqa, also *enqaychu*: A small stone figure considered a repository of well-being for the animal or household it represents; see *illa*, *qunupa*.

G

guauque: Variant of huauque.

H

hakima: A small, narrow handwoven ribbon, usually used to decorate hats.

Hanaq Pacha: The Upper World; often refers to Christian heaven.

hawamanta runa: Outsider to a community (literally, "person from the outside").

hinaspas: And then.

huauque: Colonial spelling of *wawqe* (sinon *wayqe*); brother of a man. (Brother of a woman is *tura*.)

hucha: Sin; unpaid moral debt.
huq: One.

I

illa: Synonym of *enqa*.
inti: Sun.
iskay: Two.
iskaynintin: Partner; two together.

K

karahu!: Damn! (from Spanish *carajo*; however, *karahu* lacks the vulgarity
   of *carajo*—it is emphatic but not obscene).
karáy!: Variant of *karahu!*
karu: Far, distant.
kawsaqkuna: Literally, "living beings"; usually refers to the *enqa*s.
kawsay: To live.
Kay Pacha: This World, the terrestrial sphere.
kinsa: Three.
kukuchi: Cannibalistic damned soul trapped in a rotting body.
-kuna: Pluralizing suffix.
kunan: Now, at present time.
kundur: Condor.
kuraka: Wealthy authority.
kwintu: Story (from Spanish *cuento*).

KH

khuchi: Pig (from Spanish *cochino*).
khuyay: To love tenderly.
khuyaqkuna: Loving ones, protectors; usually refers to the *enqa*s.

K'

k'ancha: Bright, shiny.
k'intu: A presentation of coca leaves, often three in number, with the leaves
   carefully placed on top of one another.

L

lari (Aymara): Wife's or mother's kinsman.
layqa: Sorcerer, witch.
layqasqa: Bewitched.
león: Refers to any large feline (from Spanish *león*, "lion").
loma: High grasslands (syn. = *puna*).
lutu: Dark colored (from Spanish *luto*, "mourning").

M

machu: Old one; quasi-demonic survivor of a previous race.
machukuna: Plural of *machu*.
machula: Old grandfather.
mama: Mother.
mamacha: Female saint; image of the Virgin Mary or other female saint; literally, "little mother."
mamakucha: A little old woman.
maqt'a: Boy; youth.
masi: Comrade.
misti: Mestizo town dweller (from Spanish *mestizo*).
mistikuna: Plural of *misti*.
muyuy: To circulate, to rotate.

Ñ

Ñachu?: Ready yet?
ñak'aq: Nocturnal demon that extracts the heart or body fat from sleeping victims; literally, "slaughterer."
ñawin: Eye; principal or essential part.
ñawin puytu: A weaving motif consisting of a series of rhomboids.
ñawpa: Anterior, previous.

O

oca (*Oxalis tuberosa*): A sweetish white tuber native to the Andes.

P

Pacha: World; Earth; a moment in time; a proper name referring to the animated earth.
pachakuti: Apocalypse; literally, "world reversal."
Pachamama: Mother Earth.
Pachatira: Malevolent aspect of Pachamama (*tira* derives from Spanish *tierra*).
papa: Potato.
paqo: Diviner, ritual specialist.
Pisti Timpu: Era of the Plague.
Pizarrokuna: The Spanish invaders who conquered the Incas; literally, "the Pizarros."
puchu: Enough, plenty.
puchuela: A small ceramic bowl used in the ceremonial consumption of *chicha*.
puna: High grasslands (syn. = *loma*).

PH

phukuy: To blow; also, to ritually blow the essence of coca leaves to the Earth and sacred places.

P'

p'acha: Clothing.

p'asña: A young woman, maiden.

Q

qala: Naked.

qatay: Daughter's husband or sister's husband.

qataymasi: Those who stand together in the *qatay* relationship to the same
   people; literally, "fellow sons- or brothers-in-law."

qayqa: Malevolent atmosphere surrounding a corpse.

qero: Wooden cup or tumbler for drinking *chicha*.

qocha: Lake.

qoyllur: Star.

Qoyllur Rit'i: A range of high mountain peaks, the site of a pilgrimage during
   the week prior to Corpus Christi.

qunupa: Small stone model of a llama or alpaca thought to encapsulate the
   well-being of the owner's herd; see *enqa*.

quqawa: A bundle of food packed up to eat while traveling or working away
   from home.

qowi: Guinea pig.

QH

qhachun: Son's wife or brother's wife.

qhachunmasi: Those who stand together in the *qhachun* relationship to the
   same people; literally, "fellow daughters- or sisters-in-law."

qhari: Male, husband.

R

rimaq: An effective speaker.

rimay: To speak.

runa: Human being; person indigenous to the Andes.

runakuna: Plural of *runa*.

runa p'acha: Indigenous clothing.

S

saqra: Demon, demonic.

sut'i: Clear, true.

sut'ipi: In clarity.

suyt'u: Oblong shaped, like a dog's snout.

swigru: Father-in-law (from Spanish *suegro*).

swigra: Mother-in-law (from Spanish *suegra*).

T

tayta: Father.

taytacha: Male saint; image of Christ; literally, "little father."

taytakucha: Little old man.

tinku: Encounter, place of encounter.

tiya: Husband's sister (from Spanish *tía*, "aunt").

tiyu: Wife's brother (from Spanish *tío*, "uncle").

Tirakuna: Sacred Places.

topay: To meet up.

trago: Cane alcohol.

tukuy: To finish; to turn into something else.

U

ukuku: Bear.

uraño: A debilitating weakness caused by being frightened by a *kukuchi*; also refers to a soul who walks before death and carries off the living.

W

wayllar: A fertile bog good for growing early potatoes.

warmi: Woman, wife.

warmiqhari: Married couple; literally, "woman-and-man."

warmiqhari tiyakusqa: A married couple living together; the title of this book's master narrative.

wayruro: Bright red-and-black seed of a spiny shrub with small white flowers (*Cytharexylum Herrerae Mansf*).

willay: To tell.

willakuy: To recount, to tell a story.

Willasayki: I will tell you.

Willasaykichu?: Shall I tell you?

Y

yanantin: Helpmates; partners matched through complementary characteristics.

yuyaq: One who remembers.

yuyay: To remember.

NOTES

FRINGE

1. Johnny Payne (2000:263–271) records this story in his book of Quechua folktales as "Jesus, Yarn-Spinner."

2. This is Allen 2002a.

3. For an excellent source on Quechuan languages, see the following website: http://www.quechua.org.uk/index.htm.

4. See Mannheim 1991:9–16, 37–60.

5. Among these fellow travelers (some of whom I have never met in person), I include Denise Arnold and Juan de Dios Yapita, Andrés Chirinos, Alain Délétroz Favre, Regina Harrison, Rosaleen Howard, César Itier, Bruce Mannheim, Johnny Payne, Ricardo Valderrama and Carmen Escalante, and, of course, José María Arguedas, Efraín Morote Best, and Jorge Lira.

6. The literature on Andean textiles is immense. Among the many excellent sources are Boone 1996; Femenías, Medlin, and Meisch 1987; Frame 2007; Gisbert, Arze, and Cajías 2006; Rowe 1977, 1984; Rowe and Cohen 2002; Silverman 1994; Stone-Miller 1991.

7. See Ascher and Ascher 1988, 1997; Salomon 2004; Urton 2003; also Conklin 1982, 2002; Lechtman 1996; Locke 1923; Mackey 2002; Mackey et al. 1990; Murra 1975a; Pereyra S. 2001; Radicati di Primeglio 1979; Zuidema 1989.

8. Douglas 2007:1.

9. A pseudonym.

BEGINNING

1. See Cereceda (1987:177–184) on *wayruro* seeds as an expression of beauty.

2. Literally, "the Pizarros" (Pizarrokuna = Pizarro + plural), referring to the Spanish conquerors of the Incas.

3. On learning to weave, see Franquemont and Franquemont 1987. On the improvisational character of Andean weaving, see Franquemont 2004.

4. On the ridged fields (*wayllar*) of Paucartambo, see Zimmerer 1996:130, 143.

5. On the saints and acquisition of skill, see Allen 2002a:34.

6. In this, I follow the conventions introduced by Dennis Tedlock (1983).

CHAPTER 1

1. Itier 1999:159–163.

2. "Unay ukupiqa tiyakuqsi altuspi, utaq istanciapi huk warmi qariyuq utaq qari warmi" (Chirinos and Maque 1996:286). Unless otherwise indicated, all translations are by the author.

3. For analyses of Andean narratives in terms of highland–valley interdependence, see Itier 2007:63–77.

4. See, for example, Weismantel 1998.

5. I provide a more detailed account in Allen 2002a:129–139.

6. I provide a more complete account of this offering in my ethnography of Sonqo (Allen 2002a:59–64).

7. According to Billie Jean Isbell (1997), infants and ancestors in Ayacucho are treated as androgynous. Gender develops gradually as the child grows up, expresses itself fully in the married reproductive adult, and is finally transcended as elders approach death and ancestorhood.

8. Linguist Lawrence Carpenter and ethnographer Regina Harrison made similar observations concerning Ecuadorean Quichua speakers. Harrison comments that "self-reflection and interpretation reside in the holistic union of the two halves of the self" (1989:170). The linguistic distinctions made by Carpenter (1992) involve not a gender distinction, but a distinction between the inner and outer selves.

9. In this example from Bolivian Quechua, *qhariwarmi* is synonymous with *warmiqhari* as the word is used in the Southern Peruvian Quechua spoken in Sonqo. The comparable Aymara term is *chachawarmi*. Harris (2000:164–179) provides a fine discussion of gender complementarity among Aymara speakers.

10. Platt 1986:229.

11. Urton 1997:78.

12. The Spanish-derived *kasadu* is reserved for couples who have been married in a Catholic church ceremony; this usually takes place years after a couple establishes its union through a private ceremony between their two families.

13. This organization is discussed by Franquemont, Franquemont, and Isbell (1992).

14. According to Arnold, Jiménez, and Yapita (1992:191), in the Aymara-speaking community of Qaqachaka in Potosí, stories were told round-robin fashion during all-night spinning parties: "Y mientras trabajaban, hilando, hilando la lana, cada participante contaba los cuentos que recordaba, puntuando los versos de los cuentos con el sonido de las ruecas." (And while they worked, spinning, spinning the wool, each participant told the stories that he/she remembered, punctuating the verses of the stories with the sound of the spindles).

In Cañari (Ecuador) storytelling, tales about Fox and Rabbit can be told separately or strung together to form a longer story (Howard 1981:222).

15. A more exact analogy to a textile might be diagrammed as:

As the arrows indicate, one would read Part A from top to bottom, and Part B from bottom to top. I am grateful to Carrie Brezine for pointing this out to me.

16. Morote Best 1988:57.

CHAPTER 2

1. "Esta forma del pasado se refiere, en general, a cualquier acción, real o supuesta, que ha ocurrido sin la participación directa, o baja un estado inconsciente del hablante en cualquier tiempo anterior a la actualidad." (This form of the past refers, in general, to any action, real or supposed, that has occurred without the speaker's direct participation, or while the speaker was in a state of unconsciousness, in either time present or past [Cusihuamán 1976b:170].)

Also see Calvo Pérez 1993:108. The use of -*sqa* in Quechua narratives is discussed by Mannheim and Van Fleet (1998:318). The "proximal past" (-*shqa*-) of Huánuco Quechua discussed by Rosaleen Howard (1990:76) differs from Southern Peruvian Quechua -*sqa* in subtle and interesting ways.

2. Much has been written about Fox in Andean narrative. Efraín Morote Best (1988:55–100) provides a thorough overview in "El tema del viaje al cielo." Among others, see Chirinos and Maque 1996:286-289; Escalante and Valderrama 1997:1995–206; Itier 1997, 2007; La Riva Gonzalez 2005; Taylor 2000:143–149; Tomoeda 1982; Urton 1985a.

3. My translation is from the Quechua text, narrated by Crisólogo Torres in Sonqo, June 1978, and transcribed by Jaime Pantigoso.

> . . . chay kundurqa tapuyun, ñacha unaychaña karan,
> chaysi
> tapuyun
> "Tiyu, chiri alalanchu?"
> "MAAnan alalanchu! Hayk'aq alalanman qharita?" nispa.
> Chayqa naqa hinarayashan. Chaynaqa unaychamanta tapuyllantaq:
> "Tiyu, alalanchu?"
> "Ma-na al-la-lan-chu," nispa nin.
> Chay weno pay kundurqa puñuyllantaq,

chaymantaqa yapa tapuyun,
"Tiyula, alalanchu?"
"Alalanmi!" nispa kuntistanpis . . .
payqa tiyashan alqu hina q'esa q'esarikuspa.
Kundurqa ñas rit'ipatapi mast'aykuspa payqa labranwan tapaykuspa puñushan.
Chayqa huqtawan waharisqallantaq:
"Alalanchu?"
"AlaLAW!"
Chay ultimo urata tapullasqataq, karahu:
"Tiyu, alalanchu?"
Ch'in!
Chayqa wañurapusqa chiripi riki tiyulaqa!

Tiyulatañataq nayuspa . . . da . . . mihupusqa riki, chay dukturqa.

4. "Yaw luru sinqa! machu qallu!" Narrated by Alcides Mamani; recorded in Sonqo, July 1975.

5. See previous note.

. . . k'awchi rumipataman—PUNRUN!
pasaymusqa ch'iqipusqa! lluy . . . muntunaraq.
Chaymanta payqa merapusqa, chaynaqa Paskual atuq.

6. "De su vientre se esparcen todos los productos que había comido crudos en el cielo y que sólo ahí existían: papas, maíz, ollucos, cebada y todo los que hasta ahora existe para alimento del hombre en la tierra" (Morote Best 1988:62).

7. Escalante and Valderrama 1997:201–204.

8. "Atuqchataqsi rimapakuspa qhipan.—'Kay yarqasqa machu. Huch'uy mankachapi huq maki quinuwachata wayk'unayta munan,' nispa hatun mankata urqurqamun, yakumantaqsi yaqa arroba quinuwata churaytan. Atuqchataqsi t'inpuchiyta qallaykun. 'Kunanmi suyatasaq chiqaq p'isqi uchuwan.'—Hinaspas manka t'inpushasqanman hina wiñayta qallarin. —Buuuu! Nispa phuqchiyta qallarin, atuqchataqsi mana imata rurayta atinchu, phukchirpansi. Mankataqsi wiñarpashan phukchispa wayk'ukunan wasitas tuyturpamun q'unchakama. Wayk'ukunan wasi ña tuytuña, chayman pasarpamun patioman, patiomanta llipi corralkunaman llipi callekunaman. Hina chay pacha tayta Diospa llaqtan tuyturpasqa laguna hina p'isqi uchupi. Atuqchataqsi p'inqasqa; mana kamachin rurasqanmanta, lapt'aruytas llipinta munan, mana atipanchu. Hinas chutarayaspa puñun wiqsapis t'in. Taytachaq kutitamunankama" (Escalante and Valderrama 1997:201).

9. "Chayaqpaspataqsi phataqpan pedaso pedaso. Kay pedasokunamantas paqariqa llapa munduntinpi atuqkuna, millaymi uywamanta kawsaq runapaq, uywa michipaq" (Escalante and Valderrama 1997:204).

10. Yapita Moya 1992.

11. Salomon and Urioste 1991:56. The transcription of the original

sixteenth-century Quechua is as follows (line breaks in the original are indicated by slashes): ". . . manatac pillapas/ yachancho honcoscanta chaymi chay honcoscanca huarminpa/ pincayninmanmi camchakuptin huc muro sara callanamanta/ pahyamuspa chayaicurcan chaytam ñatac pallaspa huc ru/naman caracurca chay carascanmantam chay runa micoc/ huan hochallicoc ña tucon chaytam canan pachaca huachoc/ ta ña yupan chaymantam cay hochomanta huc machac/huay chay chica sumac huasinsaua pay(cuna)ta micoc tian huc/ ampaturi iscay umayoc maraynin hocopi tian(tac) cay(cuna)/ micucnintam (cana) manan pillapas musyancho ñispas villarcan/ chay hatoc horomanta amucta . . ." (Salomon and Urioste 1991:163).

12. According to Itier (1997:312), one should never insult foxes because they can divine what you've said about them. They do this by going to the *ichu* grass in the high *loma,* where they "turn around three times and urinate, turn around three times and urinate again, then a third time, and after that, they hear [what is being said about them]" (Itier 1997:312, quoting Aquilino Thupa; my translation).

CHAPTER 3

1. Bruce Mannheim, personal communication (May 2002).

2. See Allen 2002a:180–183.

3. Abercrombie (1998:242–243), Arnold and Yapita (1992:82), and Harris (2000:156) all report this practice in which the groom, costumed as a condor, dances with his wife's brother on his back. Abercrombie comments that this ". . . makes explicit the complementary forms of predation played out between patrilines" (1998:343).

4. Paredes Candia 1973:85. In a version told to Palmira La Riva Gonzalez (2003:20, 40) by eleven-year-old Pio Sánchez of Surimana (Canas, Cuzco), Fox and the woman are said to fornicate "like dogs."

5. "Unay ukupiqa tiyakuqsi altuspi, utaq istanciapi huk warmi qariyuq utaq qari warmi. Allqunkutaqsi kaq huk atuq. Sapa qari viajipi kaptin warmillawan rimaq atuq" (Chirinos and Maque 1996:286).

6. "Hina atuqqa niq—'Ñuqaqa mamaypa pupun patallapi puñukuyta yachani.' Warmiqa hinaspaqá: 'Hamuyyá kay pupup patallapi puñukunki!' Kusisqallaraq atuqqa pupun pataman purispa witiyta qallarisqa sapa tuta" (Chirinos and Maque 1996:286).

7. "Hinaspa atuq mancharikuymanta ullun warmip phaka chawpipi murq'ucharukusqa, mana hurquyta atisqachu. Ñataq qhariqa patiyunpiña llamakunantin kachakan . . . Warmi mana imanakuyta atispa mancharikuymanta atuqpa ullunta cuchilluwan kuchurusqa" (Chirinos and Maque 1996:287–288).

8. "Mamitáy uqallayta qupuway!" (Chirinos and Maque 1996:288).

9. "Phakanpi kachkan papitúy, phakanpi kachkan papitúy, phakanpi kachkan papitúy!" (Chirinos and Maque 1996:288).

10. "Atuqqa llaqwakuspakama kasqanta k'askachikapusqa. Chaykamataq qari

warminta sipisqaraq maqaspa. Chaymantataq chinkapusqa atuqqa, manaña runakunap allqunchu kapusqa. Aswanpis wak allqukuna chiqnirqan kunankama- pis" (Chirinos and Maque 1996:289).

11. Itier 1999:17–19.

12. "'Qhayna p'unchawmi uqayta allaysimuwarqan. Hinaspan chayta mana pagapurqanichu. Chaymantachá riki waqyakachamuwashan,' nispa nin" (Itier 1999:18).

13. "Ima khuchi uqachá!" (Itier 1999:18).

14. "Yaw, suyt'u! Ima suyt'u haykumuran? Suyt'u karahu!" (Itier 1999:18).

15. Délétroz Favre 1993:193–194.

16. Chirinos and Maque 1996:289.

17. Itier 1999:20–25.

18. See Chapter Two, note 5.

19. See Chapter Two, note 6.

20. ". . . buscando la prenda que le permitía prodigar a las gentes de su región abundantes cosechas de maíz, papas, kinua, oka y todos los productores alimen- ticios que ofrece la tierra . . . La desaparición de Wallallo fue la ruina de todos sus súbditos; las tierras se hicieron estériles; la floresta formada por keñua, linko, chachakoma que suministraba madera para leña y para las construcciones de las casas y templos, y extensos pajonales que servían de alimento para sus gana- dos—todo desapareció por la rapacidad de Wampu y que lo hizo trasladar a su propia región" (Tello and Miranda 1923:516–517).

21. Tello and Miranda 1923; the text is also reproducido en Carrión Cachot 1955:44–46.

22. Salomon and Urioste 1991:68.

23. Salomon and Urioste 1991:43.

24. In Sonqo, these stone miniatures are called *enqachu*. See Allen 2002a:41; Flores Ochoa 1977a.

CHAPTER 4

1. This retelling of the "Condor Qatay" story is quoted from a paper Nathan Garner and I published in the *American Anthropologist* (Allen and Garner 1995) about our play *Condor Qatay*, which is based on ("written around" might be more accurate) the "Condor Son-in-Law" story. Although this summary is adapted from several versions of the story that I heard in Sonqo, I have included nothing that was not told to me at least once. The entire play, along with an introduction and ethnographic commentary, is published by Waveland Press as *Condor Qatay: An- thropology in Performance* (Allen and Garner 1997). Hornberger (1999) provides two other complete versions of the story with an ethnopoetic analysis.

2. Harris (2000:156) recounts an Aymara version of this story with a signifi- cantly different ending: The girl runs home to her mother, who hides her in a pot. Condor—not disguised as a youth—lands on the roof and scratches it trying to

get at the girl, but eventually he gives up and flies away. When the mother goes to liberate her daughter from the pot, she finds only bones. Harris comments:

> One of the messages this myth contains is that for marriage to occur girls have to accept "raw meat," in other words to enter into a relationship with a wild being and give up the civilised customs of their own home, if they are not to be reduced to dry bones. (2000:156)

3. Good discussions of Andean kinship are provided by the authors in Bolton and Mayer (1977) and more recently by Arnold (1998). Also see Isbell 1986; Leinaweaver 2008; Skar 1982; Van Fleet 2008; and Chapter Three in Allen 2002a. In rural Andean communities, each household relies economically and socially on a network of reciprocal relationships; in this network, the tense bond of mutual obligation that ties *qatay* to his *swegru* (wife's father) and *tiyu* (wife's brother) provides one of the basic links. The same kind of relationship obtains between *qachun* (son's or brother's wife) and *swigra* (husband's mother) and *tía* (husband's sister). This is publically displayed during communal feasts, when the sponsor's *qatay*s act as waiters and do much of the heavy work while the *qachun*s carry the brunt of the cooking responsibilities.

4. I have included the entire bilingual text as Appendix D.

5. The Mountain Lords are an essential aspect of native Andean (*runa*) identity, for an *ayllu* (community) is created through the members' shared bond with these sacred places (see Allen 2002a:22–48, 82–88).

6. For further discussion of ethnicity in the Andean highlands, see Núñez del Prado 1973; Rasnake 1988; Van den Berghe 1977; and Weismantel 1998; as well as the edited anthologies, Larson, Tandeter, and Harris 1995; Orlove and Custred 1980; Poole 1994; and Whitten 1981.

7. "*En los Andes, el envolver un cuerpo en un textil es convertirlo en humano.*" (In the Andes, to wrap a body in textiles is to humanize it [Arnold and Yapita 1998:41].)

8. On textiles in contemporary Andean communities, see, among others, Femenías 2005 and Meisch 1997.

9. See Barstow 1981; Boas 1912; Hallowell 1926; Itier 2007. On "Juanito el Oso" in Mexico, see Taggart 1997. I published my first interpretation of the *ukuku* story in Allen 1983.

10.
Huq mistis kasqa
purimusqa uwihiruman apamusqa
baytunta apamuspa
Hinaspas sapa kutin apamun baytunta t'anta hubunta hinas apaymun.
Hinaspas uvihiruman "Hubunta qupusayki," niqtin, mana
chay uvihiru p'asñaqa chaskinchu.
um chay ma mistita manan chaskikunchu, 'Manan qowankimanchá

michishallayraqyá,' nispas manan chaskinchu.
Chaysi hinallapi kashan, hinaspas yapaqa hamullantaq, yapaqa hamullantaq,
yapaqa hamullantaq sapa kutipuni hamun.
Hinaspas chaymantaqa, pusasqañataq.
"Haku risunchis!" nispa,
uvihanta wixch'uchispa, mamanta wixch'uchispa pasapusqaku.
11.
"Maypitaq khayna unay, waway, kamunki," nispas nipun.
Hinaspis chay uviha michisqankunapi
hubunta pakasqa baytunta pakasqa,
chaykunatas maskharin.
Unay watamantañachá ripun.
Hinaspas sach'a wanu uhupi ismiapusqa.

12. Uhle 1968[1904–1905].

13. Itier (2007:63–78) interprets this story as expressing the problems inherent in exogamy, particularly between highland potato farmers and valley maize farmers.

14. Lira 1990:1–7; my translation. Due to the length of the passage (seven pages), I do not include the Quechua here.

15. Itier (2007:110) also notes this resemblance, and reports a version of "The Fox in Heaven" in which Fox meets a star who obliges him to cook quinoa.

16. "Mayninpi puñuchkanki istanciakunapi mana wakin wasikunaqa punkuyuqchu, mana kayhina llavina punkuyuqchu, kicharmaya punku . . . Sichus puñuchkanki, killapihina rikcharinki, punkuta qawarinki: atuq 'hah, hah, hah' nispa qallunta hurqukuspa qawamusunki . . . Gustanpuni chay . . . Sichus urqo hinaqa, ahinata sinqanman muskispa warmita tarin puñuchkaqta, chayqa witiyta munanpuni. Hinaqa sichus imaynapi chaykunapi kachkan . . . allqu rikurun chayqa iscapachin. Chayqa pawarikunhinaqa purichkallan ñawsahinaqa" (Chirinos and Maque 1996:196).

CHAPTER 5

1. I am grateful to Odi Gonzales for clarifying this point (personal communication, October 2002).

2. Urton 1997:13.

3. Urton 1997:52.

4. See, for example, Cobo 1964[1653], bk. 13:9–10; in English translation, Cobo 1990:37–38. Also see MacCormack 1991:269, 393.

5. See Allen 1997; Flores Ochoa 1977a.

6. This is reminiscent of Cobo's statement that ". . . any important man could have a *guauque* (brother). During his lifetime he would have a statue made or

designate a stone or an idol, made of whatever material struck his fancy, and he would take it for his *guauque*" (1990:37).

7. Robin 2005:51–52.

8. Urton 1997:58.

9. See Urbano 1981:XLVI–LIII; Zuidema 1977:256.

10. The name Paro, but not Pari, occurs in Sonqo's census records during the seventeenth and eighteenth centuries. (However, Paro for Pari is not a dialectical substitution Sonqueños are likely to make.) Possibly Pedro Pari is "Pedro the Father," as the word *pari* is a common Quechuazation of *padre*.

11. Allen 2002a:38, 76–79.

12. It is interesting that some Sonqo *runa* attribute the loss of the Yuqra family to the capture of a Yuqra woman by a rival *ayllu*. In contrast, in Erasmo's narrative, the Huallas simply absorbed the Yuqras, along with the Yuqras' ideological and legal right as *originarios* to claim the land as their own. (Something similar seems to have happened to the Pumas, as the name appears in Sonqo's roster of schoolchildren only as a maternal surname.)

13. The emphasis on marriage alliance reminds us that while the *qatay* is subordinate to his wife's family, an in-marrying outsider can nevertheless turn this lopsided relationship to his advantage. In their different ways, both Luis and Erasmo express the strongly bilateral nature of Andean kinship, acknowledging that the claims of men may be validated through women.

14. Luis was strongly aware of his Chura identity, which he came by through his mother, and he expressed resentment toward the intrusive Quispes. This antipathy, however, did not stop him from marrying Rufina Quispe, granddaughter of Pillikunka Anton Quispe. In fact, Luis built a house in Pillikunka, and spent much of his adult life there. Perhaps this in-married status fed his resentment, but, be that as it may, his children are direct descendants of Pillikunka Anton Quispe. His grown sons listened to the tape he made for me and were annoyed: "Oh, he'll say anything when he's drunk!"

In 1984, Luis asked to record another version of the Sonqo's origins. As in the first version, he began with the *machukuna* and proceded to the emergence of the Puma, Chura, and Yuqra after the first sunrise. Then the story changed. Omitting the Pisti Timpu, Luis simply pointed out that there are still Churas in Sonqo, but the Pumas and Yuqras have died out. He then mentioned the Anton Quispes, reiterating that they came afterward. Thus Luis revised history to reconcile himself with the intrusive Quispes. His second version, by omitting the Pisti Timpu, stresses the unity and continuity of the *ayllu* and the legitimate membership of both *pacariq runakuna* (dawn, or original, people) and latecomers. In it, Luis reconciles himself to his sons and their Quispe antecedents by glossing over Sonqo's painful history of decimation and repopulation, and by placing original inhabitants and in-marrying settlers in the same era rather than separating them by a *pachakuti*. When I played back the tape, Luis remarked in a satisfied voice, "Yes! Now go play that one for (my sons)!"

15. Arnold and Yapita 1998:64–66.

16. According to Urton (2003:109–112), in the Tarabuco region of Bolivia, color is classified in terms of two color "rainbows" (*k'uychi*), a red rainbow (*puka k'uychi*; also called *kamaq k'uychi*, "master rainbow") and a dark rainbow (*lutu k'uychi*, "mourning rainbow"). Also see Dransart's (2002) in-depth discussion of color in Isluga, an Aymara-speaking community in northern Chile.

17. Unlike Sonqo, marriage in Qaqachaka is virilocal, meaning that women go to live in their husband's lineage home. Male corporate lineages, conceptualized as vertical, are called "sperm lines" and are associated with particular localities and the color white. Noncorporate female ties, conceptualized as horizontal, are connected through maternal blood. Thus kin ties through and among women are spread across the landscape in a "red" network of connections (Arnold and Yapita 1998:82–83). The predominately Quechua-speaking Ayllu Kaata (Potosí, Bolivia) described by Joseph Bastien (1985) also has male and female *ayllus*, vertical through men, and horizontal through women.

CHAPTER 6

1. This compositional strategy is undoubtedly related to semantic coupling in Quechua poetics, as discussed by Mannheim (1998).

2. For the Q'ero version, see Chapter One, herein; for Coaza, see Délétroz Favre 1993:193-194; for Ambaná, see Paredes Candia 1973:85; for Arequipa, see Chirinos and Maque 1996:286–288.

3. In a version told to Palmira La Riva González by eleven-year-old Pio Sánchez of Surimana (Canas, Cuzco), the fox runs off, and the husband, on entering the house, asks his wife why she has blood running from between her legs, and she replies that she must have started menstruating. La Riva González interprets this as a narrative frame explaining the origin of menstruation.

4. Itier 1999:16–25.

5. "Hinas apamusqa wayk'ukunanpaq. Musk'apatapi saqtaqtin phakaman t'iwkarqun."

"Ima khuchi oqachá!" nispas wikch'umullantaq.

"Chaymantañas atuqqa taripusqa. Chaysi chay uqachanta uqarirqakapuspa pasapun. Hinaspas luma puntata lluqsisqa chaypi k'askaykachikushasqa atuqqa. Kuntursi altunta hamushasqa. Luma patapis laq'arqun:"

"Yaw, Lari, imatan ruwashanki?" nispa.
"Chhaynatan llant'aman mamay kachawarqan; hinaspa hachawan waqtarqukuni pichikuchayta. Chhayna mana k'askachikuyta atishanichu."
"Borriguta aparqamuy, nuqa k'askarqachisqayki," nispas nin kunturqa.
Chayqa borriguta aparquspas qurqun. Hap'irquspa kunturman mikhurqachin. Chaysi akanwan k'askarqachisqa kunturqa.

"Maytataq rishankiri, Malku?" nispas nin atuqqa.
"Nuqaqa hanaqpachatan rishani. Kunanmi kumbiru kanqa hanaqpacha-
pi. Chaymi chayman rishani, kumbiruman," nispas nin kunturqa.
"Manachu, Mallku, nuqatawan aswan pusawankiman?" nispas nin
atuqqa. (Itier 1999:18–20)

6. "Chaysi runakuna qompi ch'usita mast'aykukunanpaq qaqata sayachinku,
kiskakunata mast'anku pampaman. Chaymansi chayamusqa. Hanaqpacha Atuqpa
akanraqsi t'uqyasqa, ch'iqisqa. Chaymantas Atukuqa mirasqa. Chaylla" (Itier
1999:24).

7. Also see Van Fleet 2008:69–74. Writing of a Quechua-speaking community
in Bolivia, Van Fleet agrees that "siblings are ideally close" but nevertheless emphasizes the fragility of the sibling bonds (2008:69). Unlike Sonqo, the community she describes is basically exogamous and patrilocal. This structural difference
creates a sibling group that only marginally includes married sisters.

8. In this respect, Erasmo's narrative brings to mind Lévi-Strauss's interpretation of myth as exploring inherent contradictions in social structure (for example,
"The Myth of Asdiwal," in Leach 2004[1967]:1–48).

9. "El término aymara para este proceso de entrelazar distintos temas en un
cuento se llama k'anata, 'trenzado'" (Arnold, Jiménez, and Yapita 1992:182).

10. Huanca 1989, cited in Yapita 1992:51. According to Abercrombie
(1998:320–323), storytelling is described as a "path" (t'aki) in K'ulta, an Aymara-
speaking community in Bolivia. The Sonqueños' term karu kwintu (far-reaching
story) evokes a pathlike image, but I did not hear them make an explicit analogy
between stories and paths.

11. Yapita comments, "Uno de los aspectos más interesantes para mí es la ma-
nera en que don Enrique, como parte de su estilo, entrelaza los dos cuentos co-
munes en un cuento más amplio." (One of the most interesting aspects for me is
the manner in which Don Enrique, as part of his style, interlaces the two common
stories to make a larger story [1992:43].)

12. Escalante and Valderrama 1997:200–207.

13. It's interesting that Parrot disappears from the group and Fox rejoins it. Parrots are sometimes identified as female in the Andes, so it may be that the parrot
would not have been seeking a wife.

14. Délétroz Favre 1993:178–183.

CHAPTER 7

1. Itier 1999:170.

2. ". . . such'uyaspa astawan astawan, p'unchayman p'unchaymansa pisipay-
akapushan, tulluyaykapushan, arí. Manan imapis imananchu" (Délétroz Favre
1993:158).

3. "'Qanqa Tiáy, yachankitaq,' nispa atoqqa nin añastaqa 'tiay' nispas nin á
atoqqa: 'Qanqa, Tiáy, yachankitaq orqoriwaq á,' nispa" (Délétroz Favre 1993:159).

4. "Chay hamp'atumantaqmi kurakaq sonqonta hina, wak sonqonta qara-kunku, kurakaq sutinpi chay sonqota qarapunku á" (ibid.).

5. Délétroz Favre 1993:223–227.

6. "Pasaqtachá puñupun riki, banqueteakunchá!" (Délétroz Favre 1993:225).

7. "Hinaqa chaytaqa Taytanchischá mayninpi qhawarillawanchistaq, riki" (Délé-troz Favre 1993:227).

8. The pilgrimage to Qoyllur Rit'i is the subject of many articles as well as ethnographic films. See, especially, Sallnow's *Pilgrims of the Andes* (1987), as well as (among others), Allen 2002a:162–173; Gow 1974; Poole 1991; Ramírez 1969; Randall 1982, 1990; Sallnow 1974.

9. "'Imatas nishawaq taytay, laphara llipiq llipiq, tinua tintín tintín, pinkullu phuku phuku, warak'a q'aqraq q'aqraq, qatimushawanku, chakumushawanku. Ay! Ay!' nispa. 'Manapunichus, hina, taytáy, allinchu kasaq'" (Lira 1990:96–97).

10. "'Tarukamá kasqa' — nispa pasakapusqa chaski q'ipintin. Runamantas ta-rukaqa, chaysi mana allinchu tarukay chaykuy. Taytanchissi runaq allinninmanta ch'ikikuq runata tarukaman tukurqachisqa. Chaymantas tarukaqa miran" (Lira 1990:97).

11. Itier 1999:159. This is one episode of "The Two Gad-about Girls" story I discuss in Chapters Nine and Ten.

12. Cipriana told me a version with two sons; the three of them settle down at the end, as men-and-wife.

13. See Allen 2002a:89.

14. See, for example, Arguedas 1947; Mannheim and Van Fleet 1998; Morote Best 1988; Salomon and Urioste 1991.

15. See, for example, Allen 2002a:46–48, 2002b; Earls and Silverblatt 1976; Ortiz 1973; Ossio 1973; Salomon 1991:14–15.

16. I published my initial interpretation of the *kwintu/chiqaq* distinction in Al-len 1993–1994.

CHAPTER 8

1. See, for example, Howard 1990, 2002.

2. Payne 2000:208–212. The Quechua-to-English translation is Payne's.

3. Valderrama and Escalante 1977:37–38; also Gelles and Martínez Escobar 1996.

4. See, among others, Canessa 2000; Mannheim and Van Fleet 1998; Weism-antel 2001.

5. Ricard Lanata (2007:123–130) includes a good discussion of the *kukuchi*.

6. "Wakin nishu huchayoq wañusqakunataqsi, kay pacha tukukunankamas kukuchi hina purinaqakushanqaku. Makinpis, chakinpis tukukapushañña habi-tonpis ch'allallañan, tullupis tullullaña, manaña aychanpis kanñachu pampapi sarukunanpaq, chakinpis tukurakapushansi" (Délétroz Favre 1993:4).

7. "Hinas, anchayrayku ninku 'kukuchi chay' nispa: wakman tukupuqtin: horas runaman, horas alquman, horas caballoman. Horas ch'ukllamantas alqu phawarqashan ch'usaq ch'ukllamanta tiyanakunamantas, anchayta ninku 'kukuchi' nispa. Inti chinkaykuy horasta chayqa q'ellu inti chinkaykushan loma puntakunapi, anchay horasta lloqsimun" (Délétroz Favre 1993:3).

8. "Qonqaysi ikhurimun chay hinata, huk llanthu hinas, ikhurium á. Llanthu hina ikhurimun hinaspas, chaytas purirqantampusham, qhawa qhawata ñan ukhpi kaqtas qhawaykun arí. Ñan ukhuta qhawaykun, chaypis puñurayasharqanku hina. Millay t'oqra uyapacha, chunta ch'ulluyoq, cordinin aysayusqa pacha pasasqa" (Délétroz Favre 1993:15).

9. "Chay kukuchiqa cheqaqpuni kaq kasqa, mana chay cuentochu" (Délétroz Favre 1993:15).

10. "Hinaspa reparakuspa hawamanta nimun, 'Ay liwillay liwi,' nispa muyupayaykampushan kancha qhepakunamanta pasaqta. 'Ay liwillay liwi, ay liwillay liwi, ay liwillay liwi,' nispa waqasapa hina" (Délétroz Favre 1993:6).

11. Délétroz Favre 1993:135–138.

12. "Hinaspas qonqaysi huk kukuchiwan ñanpi tupanku uya uya pura. Huksi wichay ladomanta chay jovensi kukuchimanta p'acharqokuspa, haykusharqan, uray ladoman chay warminpaq wasinman urañapaq, huk ladomantataqsi huk kukuchi, pero kukuchipunis, lloqsiqamushasqa. Hinaspas kukuchi kukuchi pura tupanku.

"'Tolqa [syn. Qatay], maytan purishanki?' nispas nin chay kukuchipuniqa.

"Hinaspas,

"'Kay hinata, hermanitoy, warmi wak qhariwan tiyaykapusqa, hinas chay mancharichiqmi purishani," nispas nin" (Délétroz Favre 1993:136).

13. "Hinaspas lloqsirqamun hinaspas yasta qhawaykurqon wichayta urayta. Pasaqsi kukuchikuna chaypiqa kasqa. Hinaspas, 'Kunan rich'arirqonqaku hinan mikhurqowanqakupis, ima manapis kachariqanqachu,' nispas" (Délétroz Favre 1993:137).

14. "'Maymantan, joven, hamushanki?' nispas nin.

Hina chhaynata willakurqan:

— 'Chhaynata ruwarqani'; nispas willarikun chay mistimanqa" (Délétroz Favre 1993:138).

15. "Puñurirquchasqañas. Hinallaman:

— P'un! P'un! Wasi qhipata hamun.

— 'Alqu tuxu, karahu! Ayqiriy kunantawan!'

Pampanmansi chanqan 'ñachaq!' Chaymanta wasinta haykun.

— 'Karahu, sayk'urqamuni!' Nispa punkupi tiyan.

Chayqa manas runachu kasqa, kundinarus kasqa. Lluqsirqunsi kasqan chay kundinaruqa. Chay almataqa mikhunsi, qhichaq! Qhichaq!' nispa. Llik'irqapun" (Itier 1999:154).

16. "'Mana nuqa ni imatapas manchakunichu, ni pampakama sunkhayuqta, ni waqrayuqta, ni pampakama piluyuqta. Manan manchakunichu.

Luwiskurkurchallata ichaqa manchakuni. Amapuni luwiskurkurchata, karahu, amapuni,' nispa. 'Luwiskurkurchata amapuni!' nispa" (Itier 1999:156).

17. "Anchaypi librakapun. Anchaypi tukukapun" (Itier 1999:156).

18. Payne 2000:216–218. The Quechua-to-English translation is Payne's.

19. Gose 1994:123. On the journey to the afterlife, also see, among many others, Harris 2000:44–46; Valderrama and Escalante 1980; Zuidema and Quispe 1973.

20. The quotation in the text box is from Itier (1997:312): "Almas que han sido en la vida personas malvadas o pecadoras, que han sido mal ejemplo, envidiosas más que todo . . ."

CHAPTER 9

1. See Isbell and Roncalla 1977.

2. ". . . premarital sexual activity is universal, and . . . is not only considered normal, but is the essence of courtship . . . [T]he adults know perfectly well what goes on, but still 'criticize for criticism's sake' or better still, remind the young people that 'love isn't just a game.' . . . The data seem to underscore the dramatic tension, or contradiction, involved in premarital sex" (Millones and Pratt 1989:39; my translation).

3. For examples of Snake Lover and Lizard Lover, see Lira 1990:11–13 and 40–46.

4. "Manamá iskay makinchu waqyakamuchkasqa, aswanpasmari iskaynin phakakuna huk qarip rikrapatanman haytahatachikuspa. Chay qariqa witiyuchkaqa manchanataraq chay Khunkup yanataqa. Huk waka rantiq, turu rantiq, ganadiru sutiyuq" (Chirinos and Maque 1996:61).

5. Montoya, Montoya, and Montoya 1998:192; my translation.

6. This text is my summary of Itier 1999:158–163.

7. For an extended discussion of the relationship between food and Andean kinship, see Van Fleet 2008.

8. See note 6.

CHAPTER 10

1. Payne 2000:264–268. The quoted passages are Payne's English translation from the Quechua.

2. For sources on the Qoyllur Rit'i pilgrimage, see Chapter Seven, note 8.

3. Salas argues that this story is a recent tradition promulgated by the merchants of Ocongate in the 1930s (2006:255–263).

4. Payne 2000:238–249. The quoted passages are Payne's English translation from the Quechua.

5. Lira 1982:286–287.

6. Itier 1999:160.

7. See Morales 1995.

8. Payne 2000:258–261. The quoted passages are Payne's English translation from the Quechua.

CHAPTER 11

1. The Quechua quotation in Figure 11.1 is from Délétroz Favre 1993:29.

2. See Urton 1997, especially pages 191–194.

3. *Uwiha kutichisqanmanta* (Once the girl had rounded up the sheep): It is interesting that the verb *kutichiy* figures in this phrase, possibly implying a parallel between controlling the unruly sheep and rectifying moral disorder.

4. Itier 1999:158–163.

5. Gutmann (1993) would describe this reversal as a narrative zigzag.

6. "Wisq'arquspataq ninawan muyuriqmanta ruphaykachinku. Qaparkachaspas wañupun kundinaru payacha" (Itier 1999:163).

7. "Ñañanta chinkachipun, kundinaru mikhupun. Chayllan karqan" (Itier 1999:163).

8. Délétroz Favre 1993:149–157. There is a striking parallel with the death of Andrés Alencastre, a Quechua linguist and landlord, at the hands of the inhabitants of one of his haciendas. See Urbano 1991; Valencia Espinoza 2002; the event was also inspiration for a novel by Rodrigo Montoya (1997).

9. "Imapaqtaq qankuna palabrata qonakurqankichisri? Chaymi chay qatimusunki asta palabrata hunt'anaykichiskama qatisunki" (Délétroz Favre 1993:153).

10. "Palabrayta noqa hunt'ayta munani; nispas nin chay kukuchiqa" (Délétroz Favre 1993:154).

11. "'Ahora si, mamakito, viejita, kunanqa munasqayman wallusqayman simita qan qaraqonki. Kunan khayna wikch'unakunaykupaq. Kunanqa tususunmi noqawan,' nispa" (ibid.).

12. "Hinaspas kukuchiqa chaypi rupharqapun. Hinaspas q'alata ruphaykapun q'awapi mana lloqsimpuyta atimpunchu. Tukukapuqtintaqsi yuraq palomalla altoman halaripun" (Délétroz Favre 1993:156).

RETURNING

1. Itier 1999:180–183.

2. Hinaspas tapamunku:
   Kay bidachu kanki huk bidachu?
   Kay bidan kani, nispas ninku. (Itier 1999:182)

3. I first published this interpretation in Allen 2002b.

4. "Ankaymanmi unu muyun. Muyushallan Inti imayna muyu kasqanta unu muyullantaq y Inti lloqsimuy ladopi kashan huq hatun urqu y qocha unu muntanakushan y chaypi p'akchakun . . . Unu, unu, unu muyushan" (Esteban Gutiérrez Quispe, recorded July 12, 2000).

5. See, among others, Gose 1994:129.

6. Lira 1990:40–46.

7. "Chayñas p'asñaqa rimarin. Chayñas imayna rikhurisqanta q'alata willakun tayta mamanman. Chayñas yachakun lliw. Sut'ichakun q'alas. Chayqa hinapiqa alliyachipunkus wawankuta" (Lira 1990:46).

8. Délétroz Favre 1993:154. The part-for-whole (finger-woman) relationship recalls the metonymic penis-fox relationship.

9. Payne 2000:212.

10. On the Cuzco market, see Seligmann 2004.

FRINGE

1. See Zorn 2004.

2. This story is summarized from my field notes (July 1984).

APPENDIX B

1. The subject of these two lines is ambiguous. It is unclear whether it is the bear boy or the *condenado* that goes after the roast beef.

APPENDIX C

1. *P'asña kasqa.* (She was a young woman.) The translation of *p'asña* is problematic. The word normally refers to a young unmarried woman who has passed menarche. Neither "girl" nor "woman" captures the meaning; "maiden" has connotations of virginity that do not apply to *p'asña*.

BIBLIOGRAPHY

Abercrombie, Thomas. 1998. *Pathways of Memory and Power: Ethnography and History among an Andean People*. Madison: University of Wisconsin Press.

Allen, Catherine J. 1983. "Of Bear-Men and He-Men: Bear Metaphors and Male Self-Perception in a Peruvian Community." *Latin American Indian Literatures* 7(1):38–51.

———. 1993–1994. "Time, Place and Narrative in an Andean Community." *Société Suisse des Américanistes Bulletin* 57–58:89–95.

———. 1997. "When Pebbles Move Mountains: Iconicity and Symbolism in Quechua Ritual." In Howard 1997:73–84.

———. 2002a. *The Hold Life Has: Coca and Cultural Identity in an Andean Community*. 2nd ed. Washington, D.C.: Smithsonian Institution Press. Originally published in 1988.

———. 2002b. "The Incas Have Gone Inside: Pattern and Persistence in Andean Iconography." *Res: Aesthetics and Anthropology* 40:180–203.

Allen, Catherine J., and Nathan Garner. 1995. "Condor Qatay: Anthropology in Performance." *American Anthropologist* 97(1):69–82.

———. 1997. *Condor Qatay: Anthropology in Performance*. Prospect Heights, IL: Waveland Press.

Arguedas, José María. 1947. *Mitos, leyendas y cuentos peruanos*. Lima: Izquierdo Rios.

Arnold, Denise Y., ed. 1997. *Más allá del silencio: Las fronteras de género en los Andes*. La Paz: ILCA/CIASE.

———, ed. 1998. *Gente de carne y hueso: Las tramas de parentesco en los Andes*. La Paz: CIASE/ILCA.

Arnold, Denise Y., and Juan de Dios Yapita. 1992. Sallqa: *Dirigirse a las bestias silvestres en los Andes meridionales*. In Arnold, Jiménez, and Yapita 1992:175–212.

———. 1998. *Río de vellón, río de canto: Cantar a los animales, una poética andina de la creación*. La Paz: Hisbol/ILCA.

Arnold, Denise Y., Domingo Jiménez, and Juan de Dios Yapita, eds. 1992. *Hacia un orden andino de las cosas*. La Paz: Hisbol/ILCA.

Ascher, Marcia, and Robert Ascher. 1988. *Code of the Khipu Databook II*. http://instruct1.cit.cornell.edu/research/quipu-ascher/contents.htm.

———. 1997. *Code of the Khipu: A Study of Media, Mathematics and Culture.* New York: Dover Books. Originally published in 1981.

Aveni, Anthony, ed. 1989. *World Archaeoastronomy.* Cambridge: Cambridge University Press.

Barstow, Jean R. 1981. "Marriage between Human Beings and Animals: A Structuralist Discussion of Two Aymara Myths." *Anthropology* 5(1):71–88.

Bastien, Joseph. 1985. *Mountain of the Condor: Metaphor and Ritual in an Andean Ayllu.* Prospect Heights, IL: Waveland Press. Originally published in 1978 by West Publishing, St. Paul, MN.

Bauer, Brian. 1998. *The Sacred Landscape of the Inca: The Cusco Ceque System.* Austin: University of Texas Press.

Boas, Franz. 1912. "Notes on Mexican Folklore." *Journal of American Folklore* 25:204–260.

Bolton, Ralph, and Enrique Mayer, eds. 1977. *Andean Kinship and Marriage.* Washington, D.C.: American Anthropological Association Special Publication, no. 7.

Boone, Elizabeth, ed. 1996. *Andean Art at Dumbarton Oaks.* 2 vols. Washington, D.C.: Dumbarton Oaks Research Library and Collection.

Boussye-Cassagne, Thérèse, Oliva Harris, Tristan Platt, and Verónica Cereceda. 1987. *Tres reflexiones sobre el pensamiento andino.* La Paz: Hisbol.

Calvo Pérez, Julio. 1993. *Pragmática y gramática del quechua cuzqueño.* Cuzco: Centro Bartolomé de Las Casas.

Cánepa K., Gisela, and María Eugenia Ulfe. 2006. *Mirando la esfera pública desde la cultura en el Perú.* Lima: CONCYTEC.

Canessa, Andrew. 2000. "Fear and Loathing on the Kharisiri Trail: Alterity and Identity in the Andes." *Journal of the Royal Anthropological Institute* 6(4):705–720.

Carpenter, Lawrence K. 1992. "Inside/Outside, Which Side Counts? Duality-of-Self and Bipartization in Quechua." In Dover, Seibold, and McDowell, eds. 1992:115–136.

Carrión Cachot, Rebecca. 1955. *El culto al agua en el antiguo Peru: La paccha elemento cultural pan-andino.* Lima: Museo Nacional de Antropología y Arqueología.

Cereceda, Verónica. 1986. "The Semiology of Andean Textiles: The Talegas of Isluga." In Murra, Wachtel, and Revel 1986:149–73.

———. 1987. "De la belleza al *tinku.*" In Boussye-Cassagne et al. 1987:133–225.

Chirinos R., Andrés, and Alejo Maque C. 1996. *Eros andino.* Cuzco: Centro de Estudios Regionales Andinos "Bartolomé de Las Casas."

Cobo, Bernabé. 1964[1653]. *Historia del Nuevo Mundo.* Ed. F. Mateos. Madrid: Biblioteca de Autores Españoles, vols. 91–92.

———. 1990. *Inca Religion and Customs.* Trans. and ed. Roland Hamilton. Austin: University of Texas Press.

Conklin, William J. 1982. "The Information System of the Middle Horizon Quipus." *Annals of the New York Academy of Sciences* 385:261–281.

———. 2002. "A Khipu Information String Theory." In Quilter and Urton 2002: 53–86.

Connerton, Paul. 1989. *How Societies Remember*. Cambridge: Cambridge University Press.

Cusihuamán G., Antonio. 1976a. *Diccionario Quechua: Cuzco-Collao*. Lima: Ministerio de Educación and Instituto de Estudios Peruanos.

———. 1976b. *Gramática Quechua: Cuzco-Collao*. Lima: Ministerio de Educación and Instituto de Estudios Peruanos.

Délétroz Favre, Alain. 1993. *Huk kutis kaq kasqa: Relatos del distrito de Coaza (Carabaya-Puno)*. Sicuani-Cuzco: Instituto Pastoral Andino.

Douglas, Mary. 2007. *Thinking in Circles: An Essay on Ring Composition*. New Haven and London: Yale University Press.

Dover, Robert V. H., Katharine E. Seibold, and John H. McDowell, eds. 1992. *Andean Cosmologies through Time: Persistence and Emergence*. Bloomington: University of Indiana Press.

Dransart, Penny. 2002. "Coloured Knowledges: Colour Perception and the Dissemination of Knowledge in Isluga, Northern Chile." In Stobart and Howard 2002:56–78.

Earls, John, and Irene Silverblatt. 1976. "La realidad física en la cosmología andina." *Proceedings of the 42nd Congress of Americanists* (Paris) 4:299–325.

Escalante, Carmen, and Ricardo Valderrama. 1997. *La doncella sacrificada: Mitos del Valle del Colca*. Lima: Institut Français d'Etudes Andines, and Arequipa: Universidad Nacional de San Agustín.

Femenías, Blenda. 2005. *Gender and the Boundaries of Dress in Contemporary Peru*. Austin: University of Texas Press.

Femenías, Blenda, Maryann Medlin, and Lynn Meisch, eds. 1987. *Andean Aesthetics: Textiles of Peru and Bolivia*. Madison: Elvejhem Museum (University of Wisconsin-Madison).

Flores Ochoa, Jorge. 1977a. "Enqa, enqaychu, illa y khuya rumi." In Flores Ochoa 1977b:211–237.

———. 1977b. *Pastores de la Puna: Uywamichiq Punarunakuna*. Lima: Instituto de Estudios Peruanos.

Frame, Mary. 2007. "Lo que Guaman Poma nos muestra, pero no nos dice sobre Tukapu." *Revista Andina* 44:9–70.

Franquemont, Edward M. 2004. "Jazz: An Andean Sense of Symmetry." In Washburn 2004:81–94.

Franquemont, Edward M., and Christine Franquemont. 1987. "Learning to Weave in Chinchero." *The Textile Museum Journal* 27:55–78.

Franquemont, Edward M., Christine Franquemont, and Billie Jean Isbell. 1992. "*Awaq Ñawin*: El ojo del tejedor. La práctica de la cultura en el tejido." *Revista Andina* 10(1):47–80.

Gelles, Paul H., and Gabriela Martínez Escobar, eds. and trans. 1996. *Andean*

Lives: Gregorio Condori Mamani and Asunta Quispe Huamán. Austin: University of Texas Press.

Gisbert, Teresa, Silvia Arze, and Martha Cajías. 2006. *Arte textil y mundo andino.* La Paz: Museo Nacional de Etnografía y Folklore, and Embajada de Francia en Bolivia.

Godenzzi Alegre, Juan, ed. 1999. *Tradición oral andina y amazónica: Métodos de análisis e interpretación de textos.* Cuzco: Centro de Estudios Regionales Andinos "Bartolomé de Las Casas."

Gose, Peter. 1994. *Deathly Waters and Hungry Mountains: Agrarian Ritual and Class Formation in an Andean Town.* Toronto: University of Toronto Press.

Gow, David. 1974. "Taytacha Qoyllur Rit'i." *Allpanchis* (Cuzco) 7:47–100.

Gross, Daniel, ed. 1973. *Peoples and Cultures of Native South America.* New York: Natural History Press.

Gutmann, Margit. 1993. "Visión andina del mundo y conceptos religiosos en cuentos orales quechuas del Perú." In Urbano 1993:239–258.

Hallowell, A. Irving. 1926. "Bear Ceremonialism in the Northern Hemisphere." *American Anthropologist* 28(1):1–175.

Harris, Olivia. 1986. "From Asymmetry to Triangle: Symbolic Transformations in Northern Potosí." In Murra, Wachtel, and Revel 1986:260–279.

———. 2000. *To Make the Earth Bear Fruit: Ethnographic Essays on Fertility, Work and Gender in Highland Bolivia.* University of London: Institute of Latin American Studies.

Harrison, Regina. 1989. *Signs, Songs, and Memory in the Andes.* Austin: University of Texas Press.

Hornberger, Nancy H. 1999. "Función y forma poética en 'El cóndor y la pastora.'" In Godenzzi 1999:81–148.

Howard, Rosaleen. 1981. *Dioses y diablos: Tradición oral de Cañar, Ecuador.* Paris: AEA (*Amerindia* numéro spécial 1).

———. 1990. *The Speaking of History: Willapaakushayki, or Quechua Ways of Telling the Past.* University of London: Institute of Latin American Studies Research Paper 2.

———, ed. 1997. *Creating Context in Andean Cultures.* Oxford: Oxford University Press.

———. 2002. "Spinning a Yarn: Landscape, Memory, and Discourse Structure in Quechua Narratives." In Quilter and Urton 2002:27–29.

Huanca, Tomás. 1989. *El yatiri en la comunidad aymara.* La Paz: Ediciones CADA.

Isbell, Billie Jean. 1977. "Those Who Love Me: An Analysis of Andean Kinship and Reciprocity within a Ritual Context." In Bolton and Mayer 1977:81–105.

———. 1986. *To Defend Ourselves: Ecology and Ritual in an Andean Village.* Prospect Heights, IL: Waveland Press. Originally published in 1978 by University of Texas Press, Austin.

———. 1997. "De inmaduro a duro: Lo simbólico femenino y los esquemas andinos de género." In Arnold 1997:253–301.

Isbell, Billie Jean, and Fredy Roncalla. 1977. "The Ontogenesis of Metaphor: Rid-
dle Games among Quechua Speakers Seen as Cognitive Discovery Procedure."
Journal of Latin American Lore 3(1):19–49.

Itier, César. 1997. "El zorro del cielo: Un mito sobre el origen de las plantas cultivadas y los intercambios con el mundo sobrenatural." *Bulletin de l'Institut
Français d'Études Andines* 26(3):307–346. (Número Temático bajo la dirección
de César Itier: *Tradición oral y mitología andinas.*)

———. 1999. *Karu Ñankunapi: 40 cuentos en quechua y castellano de la comunidad
de Usi (Quispicanchi-Cuzco).* Cuzco: Centro de Estudios Regionales Andinos
"Bartolomé de Las Casas"; Lima: Institut Français d'Etudes Andines.

———. 2007. *El hijo del oso: La literatura oral quechua de la región del Cuzco.* Lima:
Institut Français d'Etudes Andines, Instituto de Estudios Andinos, Fondo Editorial Pontificia Universidad Católica del Perú, and Fondo Editorial Universidad Nacional Mayor de San Marcos.

La Riva González, Palmira. 2005. "El zorro mutilado, el zorro despedazado: Reflexiones sobre las representaciones de la fertilidad en los Andes meridionales
del Perú." In Molinié 2005:19–46.

Larson, Brooke, Enrique Tandeter, and Olivia Harris, eds. 1995. *Ethnicity, Markets,
and Migration in the Andes: At the Crossroads of History and Anthropology.* Durham: Duke University Press.

Leach, Edmund, ed. 2004[1967]. *The Structural Study of Myth and Totemism.* London: Routledge Press. (Reprint of 1967 edition published by Tavistock Press.)

Lechtman, Heather. 1996. "Cloth and Metal: The Culture of Technology." In
Boone 1996: 33–44.

Leinaweaver, Jessica B. 2008. *The Circulation of Children: Kinship, Adoption, and
Morality in Andean Peru.* Durham: Duke University Press.

Lévi-Strauss, Claude. 2004[1967]. "The Story of Asdiwal." In Leach 1967:1–48.

Lira, Jorge A. 1982. *Diccionario Kkechwa-Español.* Bogotá: Convenio Andrés Bello.

———. 1990. *Cuentos del Alto Urubamba.* Translated into Spanish and edited by
Jaime Pantigoso. Cuzco: Centro de Estudios Regionales Andinos "Bartolomé
de Las Casas."

Locke, L. Leland. 1923. *The Ancient Quipu or Peruvian Knot Record.* New York:
American Museum of Natural History.

MacCormack, Sabine. 1991. *Religion in the Andes: Vision and Imagination in Early
Colonial Peru.* Princeton: Princeton University Press.

Mackey Carol. 2002. "The Continuing Khipu Traditions: Principles and Practices." In Quilter and Urton 2002:320–347.

Mackey, Carol, Hugo Pereya, Carlos Radicati, Humberto Rodríguez, and Oscar
Valverde, eds. 1990. *Quipu y yupana: Colección de escritos.* Lima: Consejo Nacional de Ciencia y Tecnología.

Mannheim, Bruce. 1986a. "The Language of Reciprocity in Southern Peruvian
Quechua." *Anthropological Linguistics:* 28:267–273.

———. 1986b. "Poetic Form in Guaman Poma's *Wariqsa Arawi.*" *Amerindia*
11:41–67.

————. 1991. *The Language of the Inka since the European Invasion.* Austin: University of Texas Press.

————. 1998. "'Time, Not the Syllables, Must Be Counted': Quechua Parallelism, Word Meaning, and Cultural Analysis." *Michigan Discussions in Anthropology* 13:245–287.

Mannheim, Bruce, and Krista Van Fleet. 1998. "Dialogics of Southern Quechua Narrative." *American Anthropologist* 100(2):309–325.

Meisch, Lynn A., ed. 1997. *Traditional Textiles of the Andes: Life and Cloth in the Highlands.* New York and London: Thames and Hudson.

Millones, Luis, and Mary Pratt. 1989. *Amor brujo: Imagen y cultura del amor en los Andes.* Lima: Instituto de Estudios Peruanos.

Molinié, Antoinette, ed. 2005. *Etnografías del Cuzco.* Cuzco: Centro de Estudios Regionales Andinos "Bartolomé de Las Casas"; Lima: Institut Français d'Etudes Andines.

Montoya, Rodrigo. 1997. *El tiempo del descanso.* Lima: Editorial Sur.

Montoya, Rodrigo, Luis Montoya, and Edwin Montoya. 1998. *La sangre de los cerros.* Tomo II: *Urpischalláy/Mi palomita.* Lima: Universidad Nacional Frederico Villareal.

Morales, Edmundo. 1995. *The Guinea Pig: Healing, Food, and Ritual in the Andes.* Tucson: University of Arizona Press.

Morote Best, Efraín. 1957. "El oso raptor." *Archivos Venezolanos de Folklore* 5(5):157–178.

————. 1988. *Aldeas sumergidas: Cultura popular y sociedad en los Andes.* Cuzco: Centro de Estudios Regionales Andinos "Bartolomé de Las Casas."

Murra, John V. 1975a. "Las etno-categorías de un *khipu* estatal." In Murra 1975b: 243–254.

————. 1975b. *Formaciones económicas y políticas en el mundo andino.* Lima: Instituto de Estudios Andinos.

Murra, John V., Nathan Wachtel, and Jacques Revel, eds. 1986. *Anthropological History of Andean Polities.* Cambridge: Cambridge University Press.

Núñez del Prado, Oscar. 1973. *Kuyo Chico: Applied Anthropology in an Indian Community.* Trans. Lucy Whyte Russo and Richard Russo. Chicago: University of Chicago Press.

Orlove, Benjamin S., and Glynn Custred, eds. 1980. *Land and Power in Latin America: Agrarian Economies and Social Processes in the Andes.* Teaneck, N.J.: Holmes and Meier.

Ortiz, Alejandro. 1973. *De Adaneva a Inkarrí: Una visión indígena del Perú.* Lima: Retablo de Papel.

Ossio, Juan. 1973. *Ideología mesiánica del mundo andino.* Lima: Ignacio Prado Pastor.

Paredes Candia, Antonio. 1973. *Cuentos populares bolivianos (De la tradición oral).* La Paz: Ediciones ISLA.

Payne, Johnny. 2000. *She-Calf and Other Quechua Folk Tales.* Albuquerque: University of New Mexico Press.

Pereyra S., Hugo. 2001. "Notas sobre el descubrimiento de la clave numeral de los quipus incaicos." *Boletín del Museo Arqueología y Antropología* 4(5):115–123.

Platt, Tristan. 1986. "Mirrors and Maize: The Concept of *Yanantin* among the Macha of Bolivia." In Murra, Wachtel, and Revel 1986:229–259. Cambridge: Cambridge University Press.

Poole, Deborah. 1991. "Miracles, Memory and Time in an Andean Pilgrimage Story." *Journal of Latin American Lore* 17(1–2)131–164.

———, ed. 1994. *Unruly Order: Violence, Power and Cultural Identity in the High Provinces of Southern Peru.* Boulder: Westview Press.

Quilter, Jeffrey, and Gary Urton, eds. 2002. *Narrative Threads: Accounting and Recounting in Andean Khipu.* Austin: University of Texas Press.

Radicati di Primeglio, Carlos. 1979. *El sistema contable de los incas.* Lima: Librería Studium.

Ramírez, Juan Andrés. 1969. "La novena al Señor de Qoyllur Rit'i." *Allpanchis* (Cuzco) 1:61–88.

Ramos Mendoza, Crescencio. 1992. *Relatos quechuas: Kichwapi unay willakuykuna.* Lima: Editorial Horizonte.

Randall, Robert. 1982. "Qoyllur Rit'i, an Inca Fiesta of the Pleides." *Bulletin de l'Institut Français d'Etudes Andines* (Lima) 11(1–2):37–81.

———. 1990. "The Mythstory of Kuri Qoyllur: Sex, *Seqes,* and Sacrifice in Inka Agricultural Festivals. *Journal of Latin American Lore* 16(1):3–46.

Rasnake, Roger. 1988. *Domination and Cultural Resistance: Authority and Power among an Andean People.* Durham: Duke University Press.

Ricard Lanata, Xavier. 2007. *Ladrones de la sombra: El universo religioso de los pastores de Ausangate (Andes surperuanos).* Cuzco: Centro de Estudios Regionales Andinos "Bartolomé de Las Casas"; Lima: Institut Français d'Etudes Andines.

Robin, Valerie. 2005. "Caminos a la otra vida: Ritos funerarios en los Andes peruanos meridianales." In Molinié 2005:47–68.

Rowe, Ann Pollard. 1977. *Warp-Patterned Weaves of the Andes.* Washington, D.C.: The Textile Museum.

———, ed. 1984. *The Junius B. Bird Conference on Andean Textiles.* Washington, D.C.: The Textile Museum.

Rowe, Ann Pollard, and John Cohen. 2002. *Hidden Threads of Peru: Qéro Textiles.* London: Merrell, in association with the Textile Museum, Washington, D.C.

Salas, Guillermo. 2006. "Diferenciación social y discursos públicos sobre la peregrinación de Qulluriti." In Cánepa and Ulfe 2006:243–288.

Sallnow, Michael. 1974. "La peregrinación andina." *Allpanchis* (Cuzco) 7:101–142.

———. 1987. *Pilgrims of the Andes: Regional Cults in Cuzco.* Washington, D.C.: Smithsonian Institution Press.

Salomon, Frank. 1991. "Introductory Essay." In Salomon and Urioste 1991:1–40.

———. 2004. *The Cord Keepers: Khipus and Cultural Life in a Peruvian Village.* Durham: Duke University Press.

Salomon, Frank, and George Urioste, trans. and eds. 1991. *The Huarochirí Manuscript.* Austin: University of Texas Press.

Seligmann, Linda J. 2004. *Peruvian Street Lives: Culture, Power, and Economy among Market Women of Cuzco.* Urbana: University of Illinois Press.

Silverman, Gail. 1994. *El tejido andino: Un libro de sabiduría.* Lima: Fondo Editorial, Banco Central de Reserva del Perú.

Skar, Harald. 1982. *The Warm Valley People: Duality and Land Reform among the Quechua Indians of Highland Peru.* Oslo Studies in Social Anthropology 2. Oslo: Universitetsforlaget. (Distributed by Columbia University Press, New York.)

Stobart, Henry, and Rosaleen Howard, eds. 2002. *Knowledge and Learning in the Andes: Ethnographic Perspectives.* Liverpool: Liverpool University Press.

Stone-Miller, Rebecca. 1991. *To Weave for the Sun: Ancient Andean Textiles.* New York and London: Thames and Hudson.

Taggart, James M. 1997. *The Bear and His Sons: Masculinity in Spanish and Mexican Folktales.* Austin: University of Texas Press.

Taylor, Gerald. 2000. *Camac, Camay y Camasca y otros ensayos sobre Huarochirí y Yauyos.* Cuzco: Centro de Estudios Regionales Andinos "Bartolomé de Las Casas"; Lima: Institut Français d'Etudes Andines.

Tedlock, Dennis. 1983. *The Spoken Word and the Work of Interpretation.* Philadelphia: University of Pennsylvania Press.

Tello, Julio C., and Próspero Miranda. 1923. "Wallallo: Ceremonias gentílicas realizadas en la región cisandina del Perú central." *Inca* 1(2):475–549.

Thiercelin, Raquel, ed. 1991. *Cultures et Sociétés, Andes et Méso-Amérique: Mélanges en hommage à Pierre Duviols.* Aix-en-Provence: L'Université de Provence.

Tomoeda, H. 1982. "Folklore andino y mitología amazónica: Las plantas cultivadas y la muerte en el pensamiento andino." *Senri Ethnological Studies* (Osaka: Senri Museum of Ethnology) 10:275–306.

Uhle, Max. 1968[1904–1905]. Untitled bilingual Quechua-Spanish manuscript. Berlin: Iberoamericanischen Institut.

Urbano, Henrique. 1981. *Wiracocha y Ayar: Héroes y funciones en las sociedas andinas.* Cuzco: Centro de Estudios Regionales Andinos "Bartolomé de Las Casas."

———. 1991. *Pachamama o la madre devoradora: El sacrificio de Killku Warak'a, alias Alencastre.* In Thiercelin 1991:781–789.

———, ed. 1993. *Mito y simbolismo en los Andes: La figura y la palabra.* Cuzco: Centro de Estudios Regionales Andinos "Bartolomé de Las Casas."

Urton, Gary. 1981. *At the Crossroads of the Earth and the Sky: An Andean Cosmology.* Austin: University of Texas Press.

———. 1985a. "Animal Metaphors and the Life Cycle in an Andean Community." In Urton 1985b:251–284.

———, ed. 1985b. *Animal Myths and Metaphors in South America.* Salt Lake City: University of Utah Press.

————. 1997. *The Social Life of Numbers*. Austin: University of Texas Press.

————. 2003. *Signs of the Inka Khipu: Binary Coding in the Andean Knotted-String Records*. Austin: University of Texas Press.

Valderrama, Ricardo, and Carmen Escalante. 1977. *Gregorio Condori Mamani: Autobiografía*. Cuzco: Centro de Estudios Regionales Andinos "Bartolomé de Las Casas."

————. 1980. "Apu Qorpuna: Visión del mundo de los muertos en la comunidad de Awkimarka." *Debates en Antropología* 5:233–264. Lima.

Valencia Espinoza, Abraham. 2002. *Sacralidad y temor de los K'anaruna: Killku Warak'a*. Cuzco: Convenio Municipalidad del Cusco and Cervesur.

Van den Berghe, Pierre. 1977. *Inequality in the Peruvian Andes: Class and Ethnicity in Cuzco*. Columbia: University of Missouri Press.

Van Fleet, Krista E. 2008. *Performing Kinship: Narrative, Gender, and the Intimacies of Power in the Andes*. Austin: University of Texas Press.

Washburn, Dorothy K., ed. 2004. *Embedded Symmetries, Natural and Cultural*. Albuquerque: University of New Mexico Press.

Weismantel, Mary J. 1998. *Food, Gender and Poverty in the Ecuadorean Andes*. Prospect Heights, IL: Waveland Press. Originally published in 1988 by the University of Pennsylvania Press, Philadelphia.

————. 2001. *Cholas and Pishtacos: Stories of Race and Sex in the Andes*. Chicago: University of Chicago Press.

Whitten, Norman, ed. 1981. *Cultural Transformation and Ethnicity in Modern Ecuador*. Urbana: University of Illinois Press.

Yapita Moya, Juan de Dios. 1992. "*Kunturinti liq'uchinti*: Análisis lingüístico de un sallqa de Oruro." *Latin American Indian Literatures* 8(1):38–68.

Zimmerer, Karl S. 1996. *Changing Fortunes: Biodiversity and Peasant Livelihood in the Peruvian Andes*. Berkeley: University of California Press.

Zorn, Elayne. 2004. *Weaving a Future: Tourism, Cloth, and Culture on an Andean Island*. Iowa City: University of Iowa Press.

Zuidema, R. Tom. 1964. *The Ceque System of Cuzco: The Social Organization of the Capital of the Inca*. Leiden: E. J. Brill.

————. 1977. "The Inca Kinship System: A New Theoretical View." In Bolton and Mayer 1977:240–281.

————. 1989. "A Quipu Calendar from Ica, Peru, with a Comparison to the Ceque Calendar from Cuzco." In Aveni 1989:341–351.

Zuidema, R. Thomas, and Ulpiano Quispe. 1973[1968]. "A Visit to God." In Gross 1973.

STORY INDEX

GUIDE TO THE MASTER NARRATIVE

SUBJECT INDEX

Numbers in italics refer to illustrations.

dog/fox confusion, 23–24, 51–56, 127, 245n4, 245n5, 245n10
dove, as sign of salvation, 92, 148, 158–159, 213
duck, 44
Douglas, Mary, 5

eating: Condor eaten by parents-in-law, 64, 65–67; girls eaten by witch, 123, 124; human flesh eaten by *condenado*, 28, 139–140; old lady eats her guests, 123, 130; sexual act compared with, 23, 52, 140
emergence, as confession, 168
enqa/enqaychu, 91, 61, 236
Enrique Espejo Sepera. *See* storytellers
epidemics, 95, 96
Espejo Sepera, Enrique. *See* storytellers
Erasmo. *See* Hualla Gutiérrez, Erasmo
ethnicity, 3, 68, 76–77 80, 82, 125, 247;
even numbers, 92
Escalante, Carmen, 46, 105

falcon (*alqamari*), 46, 105–106, 111
families, and family formation.
    See kinship; marriage
Flores, Florencio. *See* storytellers
Fox: Colca Valley Fox stories, 46, 105;
    ability to overhear conversations, 48, 245n12; births of baby foxes, 25, 37, 45, 47, 59, 61, 62, 86, 98–99;
    Condor carries Fox to a banquet in Heaven, 45, 102, 250n5; as Condor's brother-in-law, 23, 56, 63; descends to earth, 45, 47, 83; disguised as boy, 23–24, 37, 41–42, 43, 48; as *lari*, 53; estrangement from human domesticity, 31–33, 35, 55–56, 101; expelled from Hanaq Pacha, 45, 83, 105; as favorite son of God, 46, 47, 105, 106; fox babies, 25, 37, 45, 47, 59, 61, 62, 86, 87, 98–99, 102; fox droppings as omens, 47, 105; gluttony of,

25, 45, 61; in *Huarochirí Manuscript*, 47; as incestuous, 23–24, 55–56, 83; *kukuchi* resembling, 128; male predator compared with, 136, 137; in the Milky Way, 47, 83; quinoa prepared by, 46, 83, 103; reproduction of, 45, 59; scorched by the sun, 46, 105, 106, 107; sexual appetite of, 23–24, 33, 48, 56–62, 83, 136–137, 141, 248n16; solitude of, 87; as trickster, 44–45, 46–48, 51–53, 59; Wallallo compared with, 61; as wife's brother, 26, 53, 56, 63, 245n3; youth in Star-Wife compared with, 82–83, 248n16
Fox's penis: birth of siblings, 103; cut off by wife, 24, 53, 55, 59; found by adolescent girl, 24, 37, 58, 85; in "The Fox and the Woman" (Coaza version), 58, 128; in "The Fox and the Woman" (Maque version), 55, 56, 101, 245n7, 245n8; in "The Fox and the Woman" (Q'ero version), 31, 101; house invaded by, 59; as oca, 55, 56, 102; as synecdoche, 59; production of baby foxes, 45, 59; reattachment of, 58, 102; as throat meat, 23, 141; Wallallo's penis, 60, 61
Fox Time (*Atuq Timpun*), 44, 45, 120
Franquemont, Christine, 241n3
frogs, 64, 123, 124, 147, 149–150, 184, 186
frost, 79, 80, 120, 124, 221

Garner, Nathan, 246n1
gender and gender identity: color, 98, 250; *dispachu* in representation of human being, 34–35, 34; female/male-like hands/feet, 34, 74; infants and ancestors as androgynous, 242n7; of listeners, 71; male-female dyad, 34, 97; marriage and, 34, 242n7; *masinitin* as same-sex siblings, 88; parrot identity as female,